# ABOUT THE AUTHOR

Ray Hammond became a professional writer three years ago. He discovered the power of computers when, as a magazine publisher, he installed computer-controlled typesetting in his publishing house in the mid-70s. Since then, he has explored the subject and has written many articles for British and American computer magazines and a book, *The Musician and the Micro*.

At 35, he is married with a six-year-old daughter who has already begun to write her own computer programs and he has appeared on television programmes on the subject.

He also writes comedy and drama for film and television. He has homes in London and Bath and travels extensively in Europe and the USA for research purposes.

# COMPUTERS AND YOUR CHILD

RAY HAMMOND

CENTURY PUBLISHING
LONDON

Book design by Jim Wire

Copyright © Ray Hammond 1983

First published in Great Britain in 1983
by Century Publishing Co. Ltd,
76 Old Compton Street, London W1V 5PA

ISBN 0 7126 0091 4 (cased)
     0 7126 0092 2 (paper)

Photoset in North Wales by
Derek Doyle & Associates, Mold, Clwyd.
Printed and bound in Great Britain by
Purnell & Sons (Book Production) Ltd.,
Paulton, Bristol
Member of BPCC plc

*To Lizzie*

# COMPUTERS AND YOUR CHILD

# CONTENTS

# ACKNOWLEDGEMENTS

Thanks are due to the many individuals, schools, organisations and companies who have willingly offered their advice in the preparation of this manuscript. In particular I would like to thank Robin Frowd of Texas Instruments, Bill Nichols of Sinclair, Cherry Watret of Apple (UK), Graham Richardson of Tandy (UK), Martin Long, Chris Reynolds, Josephine Adams, *Educational Computing, Microcomputing, Learning To Cope*, Seymour Papert, Maggie Smith and Jerry Ostrover. Special thanks are due to the many children and teachers who allowed me to watch them at work and at play with computers.

Photographs reproduced by courtesy of:
p14 courtesy of *What Micro* magazine; p21 photograph by Josephine Adams, reproduced by courtesy of *Educational Computing*; p42 courtesy of Acorn Computers; p50 courtesy of *What Micro* magazine; p57 courtesy of *Educational Computing* and the *Maidenhead Advertiser*; p58 courtesy of *Educational Computing*; p62 photograph by Jeff Tomkinson, reproduced by courtesy of Aspect Picture Library; p66 courtesy of the Institut National de la Recherche Pedagogique, Paris, and *Educational Computing*; p75 courtesy of *The Times Educational Supplement*; p92 courtesy of *Educational Computing*; p112 courtesy of *Educational Computing*; p122 courtesy of *Educational Computing*; p134 photograph by Jean Pierre Laffont, reproduced courtesy of the John Hillelson Agency Ltd; p146 courtesy of *Educational Computing*; p156 courtesy of *Educational Computing*; p157 courtesy of L.J. Electronics Ltd; p166 courtesy of Carl Byoir & Associates; p173 courtesy of Griffin and George Ltd; p175 courtesy of Tandy (UK) Ltd; p196 photograph of Sinclar ZX81 courtesy of Sinclair Research Ltd, photograph of Jupiter Ace courtesy of Jupiter Cantab; photograph of Sinclair ZX Spectrum courtesy of Sinclair Research Ltd; p202 photograph of TI-99/4A courtesy of Texas Instruments Ltd; photograph of Dragon 32 courtesy Dragon Data Ltd; photograph of Vic 20 courtesy of Commodore Business Machines; p206 photograph of Acorn Atom courtesy of Acorn Computers; photograph of Lynx courtesy of Camputers Ltd; photograph of NewBrain courtesy of Grundy Business Systems; p209 photograph of BBC Microcomputer courtesy of Acorn Computers; photograph of Atari 800 courtesy of Atari International (UK) Ltd; photograph of LINK 480Z courtesy of Research Machines Ltd; p212 photograph of Apple IIe courtesy of Apple Computers Inc.; photograph of Sharp MZ80A courtesy of Sharp Electronics Ltd; photograph of Vic 64 courtesy of Commodore Business Machines.

# INTRODUCTION

'Dad ... can we have a computer?'

If you hesitate over the answer to this question, you belong to the majority of adults. Our children are learning something which did not exist as a classroom subject until 1980, and teachers and parents are finding themselves in the embarrassing position of lagging behind the children they are supposed to lead.

The microcomputer is the biggest revolution in education since printing but, unlike the slow spread of Caxton's craft, computers are almost overnight invading the lives of all children in the developed world.

This book is intended to be a plain language guide for the generation of parents who grew up in the primitive years 'BC' (Before Computers). Children are meeting computers in a thousand different guises and, while we may still be amazed that autobanks dispense cash on street corners, our children are not and can probably tell us how the remote terminal checks the main database and issues instructions.

Computers threaten to open up a gulf far wider than the 'generation gap' that was talked about so much in the 1960s. Before long our society will be divided into the computer-literate and 'the rest'. This book is not the platform for a discussion about the effects this change will have on society. I merely record that it will happen inexorably and that parents face a choice: to understand or not.

Let's start by declaring a war on jargon! RAM, byte, firmware, alphanumeric, ROM, Peek, Poke, CPU, CP/M and a hundred thousand other words and phrases, incomprehensible to the layman, help to make up the mystique that surrounds computers. There is so much jargon there is even a microcomputer dictionary now in its second or third edition. To a large extent jargon is used unnecessarily by those who wish to exhibit their knowledge, and the outsider is left speechless, as was intended.

Meet a precocious 14-year-old or his computer-convert teacher, and their main aim may well be to impress you rather than allow you to realise they are actually talking about very mundane operations.

'We were unhappy with the firmware supplied with our CPU, so we added new boards to the bus, and we're working in an alternative language.'

Simplified, that means that the users wanted to use a different computer language for communication with the computer, and so they bought some additional electronic circuits from the manufacturer and plugged them in.

There were no computers in my school. I didn't know what they were. I'd heard and read about these great machines that governments and corporations used to speed up accounting etc., but if my graduation had depended on my description of what a computer was, I would have failed. I had never even seen one.

Around 1970 the pocket calculator arrived, and suddenly, without knowing it, we had all seen computers. As I considered myself to be 'mathophobic' or to have a 'maths block' I couldn't get these to work, and they were of no value to me. I think my first model was thrown at a wall.

Ten years later the pocket calculator had evolved into the personal home computer. In that ten years I had learned one important fact: *computers are still very stupid.*

It was this discovery which unlocked the doors to the world of computing to someone who hated mathematics. The discovery was simple but dramatic: *computers can't do true division or multiplication.*

If you provide me with a paper and pen I can add up figures and take them away. Most of us can. The point where I went wrong at school was when it came to dividing and multiplying. I could manage 'how many threes in nine' and could probably hazard an approximate guess about the number of 12s in 60; but it was when the leap into larger numbers took place that my logical mind failed to grasp the logic.

When 18,000 had to be divided by 347 or 9114.87 by 14 I was finished. In the last few centuries man has developed 'trick' techniques of working out such lengthy sums (you will recall long division). To understand what lies behind these techniques as well as simply how to do them called for an overview of maths which as a pupil I simply did not possess. Therefore when I was taught the necessary formulae to begin maths proper – logarithms, algebra, etc. – I asked 'Why?' The answer, 'This is the way we do it', did not satisfy me, and my teachers were in no position to provide me with a more forthcoming and truthful answer – it couldn't (and, often, still can't) be done inside a normal maths curriculum.

Computers can't multiply or divide in the abstract – that's the astonishing revelation! Of course they can achieve complicated division and multiplication for you in a flash, but they do it the way a mathophobic like me would do it: they add up and take away. If you ask a computer to tell you how many 14s there are in 9114.87 the computer adds up 14s until it gets more than 9114.87. When this occurs it takes one off and adds up the decimal points left. That's how I would do it, having forgotten any of the quick-method formulas that were drummed in. It would take me a long time, but because the computer's brain has only one task at a time and the human brain a million simultaneous ones, the computer will make the calculation so quickly that most people would consider the computer brain had magically carried out long division. It hasn't. (The answer is 651 and a bit, by the way.)

None of us in the developed world can have escaped the conclusion that something pretty important is occurring and that 'the computer' is at the centre of it. Governments are spending fortunes telling us about Information Technology, and cheap little gadgets such as digital watches and video games are giving us a foretaste of what life will be like in the science fiction world of tomorrow.

Our ability to provide our children with the skills they need now depends on our willingness to learn alongside them.

*Ray Hammond*

# A NEW AGE

Computers are easy to understand – at least your children will think so. But will you? The jargon which goes with the subject – bytes, bugs, RAMs, ROMs, etc – seems designed to confuse and mystify the uninitiated.

Show a computer to an adult, and his or her first question will be, 'What does it do?' or more often, 'What can it do for me?'

This is an adult approach, and if the resulting demonstration is designed to show off the computer rather than demonstrate a specific application, most adults will find computers complicated and unnecessary. It is only when a computer can assist an adult in a specific task – analysing sales figures, moving words around a screen or keeping track of thousands of stock items – that he or she will take interest. If computer assistance is of immediate benefit, most adults will take the time and trouble to learn how to use the computer, even if they remain uncaring about how the computer works.

But at the moment the computer is powerless to offer real assistance to many adults, and as a result they remain in ignorance of the real power and potential of the computer.

This situation is changing every year as computers are taught to undertake increasingly diverse tasks, but at the moment truck drivers, sculptors, bricklayers, shop assistants, chefs, actors, ballet dancers and a minority of other workers have no purposeful use for any form of computing. It is unlikely, therefore, that in the near future they will go out of their way to discover what the 'chip revolution' is all about. Despite this, the home computer boom is on us. During 1982 2.8 million microcomputers were sold in the US, 435,000 in Japan and 392,000 in western Europe.

Unlike adults, children do not have the same need to extract a 'use' from everything. If a computer can draw a pretty picture, that is an end in itself. If it can solve simple problems, like working out distances between towns, that will be more than enough to satisfy a schoolchild, and if it can also play 'PacMan', the child is hooked.

Computers are counting machines which can be taught to do different things. They are so good at counting that this ability can be

used to control things which seem to have no connection with numbers: music, designs or words for example. How a computer does this is explained in the next chapter, but it is important to understand that the ability to count at very high speed, when coupled with the ability to remember how to do specific tasks, makes a computer intelligent.

### The microprocessor

The most common form of computer we meet is the 'microprocessor'. This is the computer-on-a-chip which has attracted so much media attention. It is a collection of microscopic electronic circuits, formed on top of each other, wafer-fashion, to make a complete computer processing unit. It is the microprocessor which runs video games, controls digital watches and is at the heart of home computers. The word 'micro' describes not only the small size of these devices, but also the process of manufacture during which the tiny circuits, consisting of thousands of components, are made under microscopic conditions. For the first 30 years of the computer age computers were built by hand from thousands of separate components, and this made computers both large and expensive. But in the late 1960s we learned how to etch the outline of a complete electrical circuit on to a tiny chip of silicon, and it is this one advance which has led to the computer revolution – for you may be sure it is nothing less.

We have entered a new age, an age in which the human race is not the only trainable intelligence around. We have always shared the planet with animal intelligences, but there have been very definite limits on how their brains could be used by humans. Car manufacturers would undoubtedly have been using monkeys to assemble cars long ago if animal intelligence could have been reliably trained.

Computer intelligence is absolutely reliable – although it is still pretty dumb by human standards. Teach a computer to do a task, and it will go on doing it tirelessly until there is either a mechanical breakdown or until it is told to stop. (Thankfully it is inherent in the nature of this one-component chip-circuit that it is incredibly reliable: in fact it is perhaps the most reliable complex device mass produced to date).

But computer intelligence is still quite limited. In the next chapter I shall outline some of the advances which will occur in the next 20 years, but at the moment its most meaningful use to adults is in making sense out of highly complex tasks such as astro-navigation and birth rate statistics. But to children this intelligence has everything to offer. Once a microcomputer is taught facts it remembers them for ever and can impart them to children in a very friendly way. This is a

*Children find computers easy to use – not so many of their parents.*

15

major part of a teacher's job, and with the rapid arrival of cheap computers the teacher's job is changing beyond recognition. Children can also learn to use the microcomputer as a tool to help them learn. They can use it to discover and explore, and the difference in approach between using a computer to teach children and supplying them with computer intelligence as a tool to assist them in discovery is central to a debate occupying the thoughts of many teachers.

Whatever you think about machine intelligence, your child needs to be able to function in the computer age. He or she, even if they are destined to become brain surgeons or actors, will come up against computers at every turn in their adult life: from social security offices to airports, supermarkets and their own living rooms. These computers will be speaking, listening machines with intelligence closely matched to our own. In fact the new age will be an age of slaves, of content ever-willing tireless slaves. But for our children to get the most out of this promised Utopia, they must learn to use and control computers.

After a secure and happy home, I believe the most important gift which parents can bestow on their children is education. No matter what their own background, most parents would like to think their children will have the chances they did not. It is this instinctive desire which is one of the main driving forces behind mankind's progress.

Until the arrival of computers, most parents felt equipped to assist their children in education, especially during the crucial early years. Despite the frequent cry, 'We didn't get that in my day,' little had changed in basic curriculum structures this century.

Microcomputers have thrown the world of education into a spin. They are also throwing every other strand of our social fabric into a spin, and this is a realisation both stimulating and terrifying for academics and other professional thinkers. But it is the changes which are occurring in education that, as always, will have the most profound long-term effect.

## Computers and video games

Computers have also brought about great changes in the way children spend their leisure time.

Do you worry if your 13-year-old son hangs out in the video-game arcade? Perhaps you equate it with your own misspent youth in funfairs or pool halls, but isn't there more of an obsessional element in his fixation with 'Space Invaders', 'Galactic Wars' or 'PacMan'? Most experts agree that there is, and some governments believe that interactive video games are an evil which should be banished. In some countries (including the USA) national or regional government is imposing 'windfall' taxes on the operators of video arcades, but whether their aim is to inhibit the spread of arcades or to grab a share of the resulting profit is unclear.

A great deal of research is being done to discover if there are any ill effects directly attributable to these fascinating games. Although there would seem to be a link between adolescent misbehaviour and the video arcades – truantism, petty crime for playing money, etc. – it is hard to tell whether these computer-based games are a cause or a symptom of the problem. There is no doubt that for some children, predominantly boys, PacMan, or its equivalent, has a fascination far stronger than that which grabbed The Who's 'Deaf, Dumb and Blind Boy' all those years ago in the pre-computer days. At the same time, I have not been able to discover one medically substantiated case in which addiction to such a game has been proven.

It is, of course, fair to say that medical science, like other academic disciplines, takes a considerable while to investigate, consider and report on any new phenomenon, and as the first interactive arcade game appeared only as recently as 1979, there has not yet been time to study the response of an entire generation to this stimulus. This lack of time in which to deal with a huge change occurring simultaneously across the face of the globe is a problem which will occur again and again as successive waves of new technology arrive. This problem is doubly confounded by the fact that development is moving away from us at an ever-increasing speed. This time gap between sensing a need for change and society's ability to implement it is a subject I will return to in later chapters. Attacks of epilepsy and, less importantly, 'Space Invader Wrist', have been attributed to video games, and I discuss these problems in Chapter 6.

Computers have brought about great changes in the way children spend their leisure time.

Despite instinctive parental feelings about the undesirability of compulsive arcade games, children are spending increasing amounts of time and money on this type of electronic leisure. Atari's earnings in 1982 from the home version of PacMan exceeded the $200,000,000 gross from *Star Wars* (one of the most successful films ever made), and the total spent in the US on 'computer generated recreation' during 1982 was $5 billion!

The British market is far more 'serious' than its US counterpart, although computer sales are still 'games led'. Surprisingly, Britain has the highest number of home computers per head of any country in the world, and the forecast for 1983 UK sales exceeded 600,000 units.

## Computers and society

The principal complaint society currently lays at the door of the computer-based arcade game seems to be social, and some doom-laden pundits predict the development of an entirely passive subculture of semi-moronic unemployed game-playing teenagers. An interesting experiment which seems to remove the blame from the computers themselves can be repeated by every parent seriously worried by 'video game addiction'. Buy, borrow or rent the home version of the game. The manufacturers of the most popular games have produced home machines and programs which will play identical games on your home TV screen. Rather than encouraging an undesirable occupation, this experiment invariably reveals that it is not the game itself which is the culprit. The child usually loves the idea of having the game at home and enthusiastically plays with it for a few days or weeks. Fairly quickly he or she realises that a major part of the fun they were having was in the interaction with their friends in the arcade as well as the interaction with the machine.

This is a truth it is important to bear in mind in all discussions about computers and machine intelligence. For the normal child there is not, and cannot be, a satisfactory substitute for human contact. This apparent truism becomes more important as, in later chapters, we consider the increasingly insidious ways in which computers are going to enter our lives.

It is fair to say that computer-based games on the home TV will be more successful in holding a child's attention and interest than most of the 'seven day wonders' which make many parents despair. The child is likely to ask for other games for the home computer (for that is what a video game machine really is), and these will be of increasing complexity. The child is fascinated by having a tiny slice of intelligence at his disposal. A microcomputer is like a slice of human brain: it can carry out a few functions very well, often very much better than humans, and the gift of such a 'pet' to a child allows him

to exercise power over another whilst the rest of society exercises power over him. It is possible that within a few years many children will opt for a computer pet in preference to the live variety. (Encourage this desire: you don't have to walk a computer.)

While the teenager who wants to escape from the house and hang out with his friends will probably return to the arcade – 'You can't get "Plutonian Pirates" for home' – the child who is genuinely attracted to the intelligence embodied in such games (or 'programs' as they are more accurately described) will seek better and better games. The parents of either child must seek a bridge between the game which requires physical coordination and the game which requires mental agility. It is worth noting here that the gains in physical coordination which can be made using a game of Space Invaders or similar are often considerable and are worth considering as aids for younger children and for those with mild physical handicaps.

### Learning programs

The bridge between arcade games and programs which help children to learn has been the subject of much study in both the USA and Europe, and such connections are now being made. While teachers and academics learn to build game-playing procedures into educational computer programs, some commercial 'software houses' (companies which produce computer programs) are jumping on the bandwagon and offering programs for home computers which purportedly coax the insouciant teenager to study.

'Tired of having your kids spend all their free time and spare cash at the local video arcade? Why not let them learn at the same time?'

So runs an advertising blurb for 'Arcademic' computer programs offered by a company in Texas. These programs, and others like them, offer colourful graphics and simulate the attractions of arcade games while teaching the kid something he appears not to want to learn. It is arguable whether this is the right approach and arguable whether we should want computers to 'teach us' anything at all in this way.

Arcade video games will become very much more compulsive in the next few years. The degree of interaction between the player and the machine will increase dramatically with all-round visual simulation placing the player firmly in the cockpit of a spaceship, a submarine or a tank, all with full speech and sound facilities to back up the illusion of reality. As microcomputers are hooked up to such devices as video recorders and video disks, so the reality of the simulations will increase, and within a very few years a child (or an adult) will be able to enter a dynamic war or space situation in all aspects but the physical. While this will undoubtedly have a great effect on mental attitudes and developments, no one is in a position to predict the nature of the changes which will occur. Will children feel less and less like facing up to the real world? As they enter an adult life in which work (as we know it) plays a steadily decreasing role, will the abstract world of the computer-generated simulation fill their unoccupied minds? Will the ability fully to live out aggressions in a realistic simulation relieve mankind of its perpetual need to assert itself, personally and collectively? We can only hope that the answer to the last question will be affirmative.

The questions posed above illustrate some of the problems facing parents as they prepare children to enter the adult world of 2000 AD. It is perhaps the most complex and difficult period in history the world has yet faced, and consequently the problems facing parents are the most complex that have yet been presented. Never before have parents, or teachers, faced the need to adapt so quickly.

# UNDERSTANDING THE COMPUTER

*So little inside, yet so much power! The microprocessor and other 'chips' are shown clearly on the circuit boards of this Pet microcomputer (left) and the accompanying disk drive unit. The graphic display is from a Commodore program.*

When you first unpack your home computer you are likely to feel disappointed. Most home computers are housed in small plastic cases, and this often provokes the instinctive reaction: 'Is this all I get for my money?'

The reason that many machines are so small is that the microprocessor itself is often only $\frac{1}{4}$in (6mm) square. The plastic cases and typewriter-style keyboards are merely provided to allow clumsy humans to enter instructions with their great fat fingers.

Despite this book's opening sentence, it is not easy to understand fully how a computer works. Computers are already very complex, and within a few years they will have reached a level of sophistication

which will prevent all but a chosen few from fully understanding them and their capabilities.

For this reason I have divided this explanation of computers into two levels to allow readers to choose which level of explanation best suits their needs.

Level 1 describes the components which make up a modern microcomputer system and explains the sort of things it can do. With this level of understanding it is possible to use a microcomputer fully for educational, fun or business purposes, to write simple programs (if that is your aim) and to have an idea of where the whole science is leading.

Level 2 explains how a computer does what it does. To describe this properly it is necessary to dig into the history of computing, and some semi-technical explanations are unavoidable. Parents do not need to understand this detail to help their children use computers positively. Although this deeper explanation may prove helpful if parents are frightened or intimidated by machine intelligence, unless parents wish to write complex computer programs, or unless they have a desire to find out about the discoveries that have made this apparent miracle possible, the second part of this chapter may be skipped.

Part three of this chapter, beginning on page 45, concerns the future developments of the computer, since it is helpful to understand how this science will develop during the period in which our children will grow up.


## LEVEL 1: A working explanation

The typical home computer system consists of a home computer with a typewriter-style keyboard, a domestic TV set and a cassette recorder. The keyboard on the home computer may be either mechanical, like a typewriter, or may be a printed, pressure-sensitive membrane version of a typewriter keyboard. Both work satisfactorily, although most people prefer the 'real' touch of mechanical keys. These keyboards will have a few extra keys that would not be found on a typewriter keyboard, and individual keys may be marked with several different symbols.

The home computer plugs into the aerial socket in the back of the TV set, but it usually has to have a little box called a 'radio frequency (RF) converter' between it and the set. This box, sometimes built into the home computer and therefore seemingly absent, converts the signal which is sent by the computer from an electrical into a radio signal, similar to the radio signals which your TV aerial picks up from the skies, and sends it to the aerial socket in the back of the set. When the home computer is plugged into the aerial socket of the TV set (via the RF converter) the TV set is effectively receiving a radio frequency signal very similar to a television broadcast. The picture from the home computer is obtained by tuning one of the channels on the TV set as though you were tuning into a TV station. This process is simple, and when the set is tuned (and the computer is switched on) a message will appear on the screen from the computer. The content of this message will vary from computer to computer: it may just say, 'Ready >', it may display a colour trademark from the computer manufacturer or it might display yet another type of message. Whether the message or picture you get from your home computer is black and white or colour depends on two things: whether your home computer is capable of generating colour pictures, and whether the TV set you are using is colour or black and white.

All home computers can be made to connect to your domestic TV screen with an RF converter, but some more expensive models are available with special computer screens, which look very similar to TV screens, but which are only capable of showing messages and pictures from the computer. These screens are called monitors, and they connect directly to the home computer and do not require an RF converter. They usually offer a superior computer image to that achieved on a domestic television set.

**Programs**

Once this system is set up you won't immediately be able to do anything with your home computer unless you know how to write computer programs, although in nearly all instances the manufacturers supply ready-made computer programs which complete novices can use for a wide variety of purposes.

A home computer is useless without programs. Unless you, or your children, intend to become expert computer programmers, you will have to rely on buying programs or obtaining them from other sources such as trading them at school. Although I hammer the point home again in Chapter 10 (*Buying a Microcomputer*) I feel that the following message cannot be overstated: a home computer is only as good as the programs which are available for it. Pick one for which the programs you want are available, and ensure there is a wide range of programs easily obtainable. Programs are not interchangeable between different makes of computers! In our nonsensical world, every computer manufacturer has decided to design computers with different internal systems, and this means that even programs written in the same 'computer language' will not work on other makes of machine.

If you learn to write programs yourself, it is possible to adapt some programs – a Tandy Radio Shack TRS-80 program can be made to run on an Apple, for example – but you will have to learn a lot before this becomes possible, and you won't be able to find a shop to undertake such work on your behalf. For those with the patience, Century Publishing Company (their address is on the copyright page at the front of this book) publishes a book of 'converter tables' (*The Basic into Basic Handbook*) which allows a user to cross-reference between different dialects of Basic and thus establish a method of modifying 'foreign' programs. For most of us it is worth remembering that, no matter what technical virtues may be extolled on behalf of the latest lump of technical wizardry by an enthusiastic salesman, without an extensive range of programs any computer's use will be very limited.

Before going any further, it is worth considering what a program is.

### How a program works

A program is a set of instructions which tells a computer what task is required of it and how to do it. Home computers can carry out thousands of tasks per second, and it is this speed of operation which allows large and complex tasks to be undertaken. A computer program works by spelling out every element of a task. If you were programming a computer robot to walk across a room and open a door, you would first need to analyse the movements involved. You would have to write the procedures starting with 'lift the right foot three inches, move it forward 10 inches, put it down again, shift the body weight (with detailed instructions), lift the left foot three inches, move it forward 20 inches ...' and so on. The computer has no innate intelligence, and every single step in a procedure must be written out. A program is a list of such instructions, and only when they are entered into the computer's mechanical memory is the machine ready to undertake the task detailed in the program.

Computer programs are universally referred to as 'software'. This distinguishes programs from 'hardware' (the computers and their mechanical accessories).

Most home computers have one program embedded in their circuitry. This is not a program which tells the computer to do anything in particular, but it provides a language in which the user can communicate with the brain of the computer. As described in Level 2 of this chapter, the computer's central microprocessor operates on a language made up entirely of the numbers '0' and '1', and although professional programmers write software for computers using this laborious language, all manufacturers supply programs with their machines which offer less skilled users the ability to communicate with these machines in plain language in order to write their own programs.

Using one of these built-in 'interpreter' programs is rather like communicating with a Chinese-speaking Russian head waiter through a Chinese person who understands both English and Russian and is seated at the next table to you. It is the barman who will have to pour the vodka for you, but you give your Chinese friend your order in English, he explains your thirst to the Chinese-speaking Russian head waiter in Chinese, and the Russian head waiter issues the order to the barman in Russian. You get your vodka. It sounds complicated, but you have been spared the need to learn Chinese or Russian.

This is the principle on which computer languages operate. The language at the heart of the computer is complex and slow to use, although it is very flexible. The manufacturers provide you with an interpreter language which allows you to issue commands in a language made up of words you understand, and the built-in programs translate your instructions into the actual language, the 1s and 0s, in which the computer system runs. (Note: A vodka-pouring computer was demonstrated by the Californian company Pro-Log in 1975.)

### Loading a program

When you unpack your computer you may not be ready to start writing programs, but it is natural that you should want to make the computer do something immediately. To do this you have to 'load' a ready-made program into the computer. There are currently three methods of doing this on typical home computers. The most common requires the use of an audio cassette recorder. The instructions contained in a computer program can be stored electronically, and recording tape is an excellent medium for such storage. Audio cassettes are small and inexpensive, and their use is widespread in home computing.

Another method of storing programs is to store them in 'cartridges' which slot into the computer. Along with other manufacturers, Atari, Texas and Philips computers all use cartridges for program storage. The cartridge contains a small electronic circuit on which the program is permanently etched. It is impossible to 'wipe out' such a program as it is not stored on magnetic tape, although it is only too easy to do this using a cassette tape. Another advantage of the cartridge is that even tiny children can plug them in and 'make the computer go'. They are difficult to damage (short of sticking a screwdriver into the interior of the cartridge), and they also have the advantage of being able to transfer the program information almost instantly into the computer's brain.

There are two disadvantages with the cartridge system. One is that they are expensive to buy: a program costing $10 or £5 on cassette is likely to be $40 or £25 on cartridge. Another is that the programs can't be modified. (In overseas territories, US produced cartridges are invariably much more expensive than on their home market.) As users begin to feel familiar with computers, they like to try their hand at a bit of programming, and they may want to modify the programs they have loaded from tape. With the cassette system, the original program recording can be wiped out, and the new program (created whilst the program was in use inside the computer) can be recorded on to the tape. There is no way of doing this with cartridge-stored programs. But this book is about computers and children, and undoubtedly cartridges make the technology available years earlier than a cassette recorder will allow. At four, my daughter was happily changing cartridges unsupervised to switch programs, but most children need to be eight or nine before they can be left reliably to use a cassette recorder.

## Disk drives

There is one other program storage medium which sometimes appears in a home-computer system, and this is called a 'disk drive'. This is a device which stores programs magnetically on thin plastic disks that look like the promotional flimsy records which the record companies used to give away in promotions. The magnetic coating on these disks is used to store program information, and the principal advantages of this storage system are speed and capacity. A program which will take five minutes to load from a cassette recorder will take five seconds from disk. It is analogous to trying to find a track on a cassette version of a record album and having to wait whilst the tape winds on, or moving a record head across a record and immediately finding the track you want to hear.

Disk drives can store so much information and regurgitate it so rapidly that they allow home computers to mimic the operation of large computer systems. With a disk drive system it is possible to set up a complete filing system with many thousands of entries. With such a program, typing the name of the person or subject required causes the information to be loaded from a 'file' on the disk, and within a second the information is on the screen. Such a program is known as a 'data base management system'. The disk is by far the best method of program storage for microcomputers, but as disk systems cost several times the price of a typical home computer, it is not surprising their use is currently limited to business users and serious computer hobbyists. (At the time of writing, very much cheaper disk systems are promised for home computers in the near future.) So for most of us all program storage will be on either audio cassette or cartridge and, on some machines, a combination of both.

The leads necessary for connection to a cassette player will be supplied when you purchase a home computer (there are a few makes which are the annoying exceptions). This should enable you to load your first program. I say 'should' because invariably you will find that the plug doesn't fit, you can't find the right socket in the computer or the lead was missing from the packing. So it's back to the computer shop for expert advice. This leads us on to a basic law of home computing: *nothing works the first time*. At the present stage of development it is still an exasperating business, and it is only the discovery of the immense rewards awaiting the successful user which spurs on the millions of computer fans worldwide who put up with the inevitable snags.

### Faults, errors and snags

A snag may occur after you have connected the cassette recorder up to the computer, inserted the cassette which contains the longed-for program and followed the manual's instructions for transferring the program from tape. After all of this has been done by the book, you may well discover that the procedure has not worked.

There can be many reasons for this. The leads might be connected incorrectly, you might have misread the manual or pushed the wrong button in error, or the cassette recorder and the home computer may not match well.

It is this last fault which is the most annoying. Theoretically any cassette recorder (or indeed any tape recorder) should be able to store programs and load them into a home computer. But certain machines are very sensitive about the type of cassette recorder used: the TI-499/A, the Commodore Vic 20 and the BBC Microcomputer spring to mind (more details on these in Chapter 10). Often the only way to cure this problem on home computers with temperamental connections is to buy a cassette tape recorder specifically recommended for your brand of home computer (more expense!).

When programs are stored on cassette tape, they take the form of little bleeps which sound like radio interference, but which the computer understands as program instructions. The computer has to understand all of these bleeps in order to operate the program, and if the bleeps are distorted or too weak, or have any other problem connected with the system that transfers them from their storage medium to the computer's electrical memory, then the program will fail to load properly.

One of the main snags in home computing is that the science enters the home complete with all of the jargon which has been developed in the computer industry. Computer people would call this connection between the home computer and a cassette recorder (or a connection between anything else, including people, for that matter) an 'interface', and a certain amount of jargon of this type has to be assimilated if you are to talk on the subject with salesmen and other computer users. I have tried to avoid jargon wherever possible in this book, but some is inevitable.


## Under program control

Eventually the loading of your first program will take place. When the program is in your home computer, the next message that appears on the screen will depend strictly on the type of program you have entered. The computer is completely under the control of the program you have put in it. It is possible, for example, for a program to be written which tells the computer that all of the keys on the keyboard mean different things. Although it would be senseless, it is possible for a program to tell the computer that 'G' always means 'T' whilst 'H' always means 365. The program controls every aspect of the computer's operation including what is to appear on the screen. The program can draw graphic pictures on the screen (in different colours if your system has colour capability) and can cause sounds and music to come from the TV speaker if your home computer has the ability to generate sound (not all have).

Once the program is in the machine you can start to use it. How successful you are at using it depends on two things: how well the program itself has been written, and the clarity of the operating manual which comes with the program. A computer program consists not only of the cassette tape, cartridge, chip or disk, but also of the documentation that accompanies it and which explains to the poor ignorant user how to use the program. Documentation is the area which has been the weakest in home computing as programmers originally produced programs principally for the use of other computer enthusiasts, and a certain level of knowledge was assumed. This approach leaves the beginner in total confusion and often leads to complete disenchantment with the whole subject of home computing. As I discuss elsewhere, this is a major problem for school teachers who are trying to wrestle with the subject.

Thankfully, this situation has improved considerably over the last couple of years, and many programs are now supported by excellent instructions which are sufficiently clear for anyone to understand. Such programs are described in computer jargon as being 'user friendly'. Some programs have all the necessary instructions embedded in the program itself so that they appear on the screen, and the user has only to follow step by step instructions about which buttons to press in order to make the program operate.

### Biorhythms

A typical program for a home computer may well be a fun program like 'Biorhythms'. Most people will know of the theory which says that our moods and abilities on a particular day can be forecast if a series of cycles based on the day of our birth are calculated. In such a computer program the user will load the program from cassette into the home computer (it will take about three minutes), and the message which will appear on the screen may well be: 'Ready, press enter to begin'.

'Enter', (or 'Return' as it is labelled on some machines) will be one of the extra keys found on the home computer keyboard. This key has the function of telling the computer to carry out any task that has been typed in. A user can type a line of instructions into the machine, and the words and figures will appear on the screen, but nothing else will happen. Only when the user presses 'Enter' will the instruction be passed to the computer brain for action. This allows users to make mistakes during typing and to go back and alter their instruction before telling the machine to carry out the command. 'Enter' or 'Return' are also often used to signal to the machine that the user is ready to continue with the next stage of a program.

So in our Biorhythm program the user presses 'Enter' as instructed, the screen will clear and the instruction will be replaced with a question such as:

'Please enter the birthdate required (DD/MM/YYYY) and press Enter'. (Note: Programs of US origin will ask for dates with the month first e.g. 12/25/1983.)

Gambling games are popular on home computers.

This instruction is explicit; unless it is followed precisely the program will fail to operate and, depending on how foolproof (well written) it is, will either repeat the question again or will produce a message like 'Error' without any explanation of what should be done next. A correct answer to the above question would be '25/02/1948'. Note that the number '2' for February, the second month, was preceded by a '0' and that each segment of the date was separated by an oblique slash. If the date Entered had not been written precisely as requested, most programs would fail to continue successfully; a prompt, probably a repeat of the first request for birthdate information, would appear, and the user would have to enter the date again, precisely following the format laid down. (Computers are excellent training machines for the careless.)

After writing the date, the user presses 'Enter' as requested, and within a split second the computer will display the result of the program on the screen. This result will provide ratings for the user's intellectual ability on the day of questioning and also on the user's physical and emotional states. After listing this, the computer is likely to display a flashing message at the bottom of the screen: 'Press "1" to play Biorhythms again or "2" to end'.

The user makes his or her choice.


**Household programs**

Programs for home computers can do all sorts of things, and there are a proliferation of programs like Biorhythms which are fun, but which have limited use. Cheaper home computers aren't generally powerful enough to run business programs for tasks such as VAT returns, company accounts or word-processing (automated typing), but there are many programs available for home computers which will look after cheque book accounts, household budget accounts, address files and so on. These are often purchased and used when a family first buys a home computer, but it really is easier to make calculations on the back of cheque stubs and to keep all the bills in one drawer than to turn on a computer, load a program and update information just because the gas bill has to be paid. Such programs will be used as long as they are novelties, but will cease to be used once the procedure has become tiresome.

So of what use are home computers? There are at least four excellent answers to this question. The first is fun; I have already mentioned games. These games, Space Invaders, PacMan or similar, are great fun and usually remain popular family pursuits for some time with children asking for increasingly complex games as time goes by. Games also include such pastimes as chess and draughts (checkers), and the 'intelligence' of such games depends on the quality of the program and the power of your computer. Gambling games are popular on home computers, and a good many simulations of games such as blackjack and craps are available to work on most machines. Situation simulations are a new form of game unique to the computer. In Chapter 1 I suggested that in the future computer simulations would play an increasing role in our leisure time, but even the simulations now available are quite absorbing. I have one game which puts me in command of the Starship Enterprise; following the program's instructions, I can issue commands to Spock and Sulu that send the ship 'warping' through an enormous universe ... a universe that exists only in the computer brain. The scope of this abstract universe is vast, so big that several years of playing have yet to lead me to its outer edges. There are now many such games, and they do have a certain power to hook the player.

### Education

The second use is educational, and this is so important that it motivated the writing of this book and is prompting governments to spend millions on rushing computers into schools. All the other chapters combine to illustrate this application, but in essence it may be summed up as 'helping a child (or an adult) to become familiar with computers and to use them with confidence'. Today's average home computer can run excellent education programs. These can be of the 'drill and practice' type in which the computer questions the child as though it were a teacher (keeping score and providing marks), or of the better 'interactive' type which encourages the child to use the computer as a programmable tool. Chapter 4 is totally concerned with a discussion on this choice.

The third use might be described as 'family business'. Larger home computers can operate as simple word-processors or text editors. Loading a word-processing program allows the user to type letters or other documents on to the computer screen and to alter words and move paragraphs around with the computer rearranging the page, so that, no matter how much editing has taken place, the page appears perfect. For children this is often an end in itself, and it proves a very encouraging program when children are learning how to write constructively. Most adults would appreciate the facility to write and edit a carefully considered letter on an important topic (a letter to the Inland Revenue, for example) before printing a perfect copy. Most home computers will connect with a printer, but these cost at least the price of a home computer, and a really high quality printer can cost much more.

Financial calculations are meat and drink to computers. Annual budgets become far less tedious and can actually be enjoyable when a computer can undertake all of the slog of the calculations normally done with calculator and pencil. Programs with such capabilities are available in a wide range of complexities and can be extremely useful. Word-processing and financial 'spreadsheets', as the financial programs are called, are the two biggest selling categories of programs for microcomputers.

### Writing programs

A fourth use is computer programming itself. Loading programs from cassette (or from one of the other storage mediums) allows you to use other people's programs, but for many the challenge to write programs and thus take direct control over computer intelligence is irresistible. All home computers are supplied with a manual which provides an introduction to programming a computer – commonly using a computer language called BASIC. This language and its alternatives are discussed in other chapters, but writing simple computer programs is not difficult and is of enormous value when trying to understand how computer logic operates. Once the user of a home computer can write computer programs, no matter how small, the computer is completely 'debunked', and the power of the computers on board the Space Shuttle no longer seems so mysterious.

As with many other consumer products, optional accessories are available for the home computer. Programs are one example, but computer games often require additional hardware items. The most common of these are game 'paddles' or 'joy sticks' which connect to the home computer and are home versions of the levers that are found in arcade video games. These paddles are merely another way of controlling the computer, but they allow the user to move the characters in PacMan or Space Invaders from the armchair. These are not particularly expensive and should be considered almost a necessary extra when considering the purchase of a home computer.

Speech synthesizers are becoming common. These allow the computer to speak to the user, providing the program tells the computer how to use this facility. It will be quite a few years before computers will be able to understand more than a few words of command spoken to them. If you try saying 'I saw' and then 'eyesore' aloud, you will get a glimpse of the difficulty facing computer intelligence when it tries to extract meaning from spoken language. The subject of speech input is covered in the final part of this chapter, 'The Future'.

Within a couple of years very powerful home computers will become available at low cost. The greatest cost elements in home computers at the moment are the keyboard and the casing, and soon the power of the microprocessor itself will dramatically increase without sending the overall cost up. As more power becomes available, so the programs which control the computer can become more complex. This does not mean that they will become harder to use; it means precisely the opposite. More computer power allows programmers to make programs easier to use, with each step of a program's operation shown on the screen as a 'menu' of choices. The user selects his option, and the program continues. This additional power will make the home computer an extremely useful tool for the family. Many inexpensive home computers are already powerful enough to allow excellent easy-to-use programs to run. In a capitalist society in which we are bombarded with luxury goods competing for our cash, many families will find the home computer the most rewarding choice available.

### LEVEL 2: An explanation of computer theory

If you write '10' on a sheet of paper, you have a mental picture of ten as you do so: of ten fingers, ten sheep, ten miles, ten pounds, ten anything. If you were writing for someone who hadn't learned our system of expressing numbers, you would have to make ten single strokes on the paper, or hold up ten fingers, show ten pebbles or move ten beads along a wire – as Arabs did with the abacus 5,000 years ago. Once moved, the ten beads would stay at the end of the abacus wire as a 'memory' of the calculation.

Numbers can be expressed and remembered physically, with beads, pebbles or even with grains of sand acting as a code which represents numbers. If you understand that, you know all that is necessary to understand the modern computer.

Grains of sand are at the heart of the microcomputer. The silicon chip is a sandwich of metal and sand, and one of mankind's most fortuitous discoveries was that the best material for constructing computers was also one of the world's most plentiful: silicon, or common sand.

Although the abacus was the world's first calculator, it did not allow mankind physically to express large numbers. Building bigger and bigger abacus frames only slowed down man's ability to manipulate the beads and increased the likelihood of error creeping in. Some cultures in the world, the Roman and Chinese for example, dug themselves into a mathematical pit by inventing ways of expressing numbers which made large calculations impossible. In his excellent book *The Mighty Micro* (*The Micro Millennium* in some countries), the late Dr Christopher Evans cites the example of the Roman citizen trying to multiply CCXXXII by XLVIII. Not easy. In the Arab world the sum would have been expressed as 232 x 48, a language far easier to handle.

### Arabic logs

The language used to express numbers is the deciding factor in our ability to make calculations. Arabic numerals and the great concepts which can be expressed by using them, spatial geometry for example, have served us well, but it was the development of yet another language for counting numbers, the binary code, which opened the door to the electrical computer.

To understand today's computer it is helpful to understand the development stages of the past. The abacus was incredibly successful as a manual calculator, and its use only recently died out in Japan. All sorts of similar mechanical devices were invented to allow larger numbers to be physically calculated, but the task grew to be impossible as civilisations developed and mathematical tasks, like estimating how much would be raised for the King's exchequer by adding an extra groat per acre to tithes, took inordinate periods of time and often proved to be wrong.

The Scots mathematician John Napier came to the rescue in the sixteenth century. He discovered that big numbers could be expressed by smaller numbers which had a fixed ratio to the larger numbers. Handling these smaller numbers was easy, and to convert the answers back into their true state only required reference to a table which listed numbers and their corresponding larger or smaller ratios. This discovery was called logarithms, and up until 1975 the use of these printed aids to multiplication and division was standard in all schools. The arrival of the cheap pocket calculator ended a 400-year contribution to mankind's manipulation of Arabic numbers.

Once the system of ratio-equivalent numbers arrived, man was able to use machines which used these ratios as units to extend further his ability to express numbers physically. The slide rule, which was a linear logarithmic table, grew naturally out of Napier's discovery.

The French philosopher and mathematician Blaise Pascal invented the world's first mechanical calculator around 1600 A.D. Ironically, this metal box of cogwheels owed nothing to Napier's discovery of logarithms, but managed to solve the problem of 'carrying' numbers from one column to the next in much the same way as a car mileometer 'trips' and records tenths of miles and miles. The invention was a landmark: for the first time mathematicians could 'dial' a calculation and see the result automatically.

### The first computer

The concept of computing was developed in the 1830s. A British amateur inventor, Charles Babbage, built a huge mechanical calculator called a Difference Engine. Although stupendous in size and potential capabilities, the metal technology of the period was unable to machine parts with sufficiently fine tolerances, and the Difference Engine was unsuccessful in practical terms.

Despite the failure of this device, Babbage had demonstrated that large numbers could be calculated automatically, and complex mathematical procedures given over to machines. Babbage junked the huge pile of cogs and spindles and started considering an extension of his first idea. He reasoned (without offering mathematical proof) that if a calculator could be built to perform one kind of calculation, the structure (the 'architecture' as it would now be called) could be capable of performing any mathematical task if the various procedures of calculation could be broken down and separated.

Babbage had conceived the first programmable computer – 100 years before the technology existed to build it. His concept was for a machine which could be 'told' how to do a particular job and then would be able to be altered to do a different task. Although it was never built, Babbage's design for his Analytical Engine is remarkably similar in concept to today's electronic computer. He designed a machine in which one separate section accepted input (the numbers to be calculated), another section, the arithmetic unit, carried out the calculation and a third unit took control of the system and 'told' the system how to complete the task properly. A fourth unit was a memory store to which numbers could be shunted and remembered until they were required, and the fifth, and final, unit provided the answers to the problem – the output unit. These are also the component sections of the modern computer.

Mr Babbage's calculator.

Babbage was so far ahead of his time that he died a broken and disillusioned man, and years passed before there was any significant step forward in mechanical computing. But the increasing complexity of society repeatedly called for improvements in number handling, and an advanced calculator was developed to assist in the census of 1890 in the USA. By the early 1930s electromechanical components such as telephone relay switches became available, and work on building electromechanical calculators started simultaneously in several different parts of the world. In Germany a young engineer named Konrad Zuse hit on the idea of building an electromechanical calculator which operated not on the Arabic/decimal language for expressing numbers, but on another language called the binary code. As mentioned earlier, it was this innovation which was to allow computers to make dramatic leaps forward a few years later.

**Binary**

The binary code is a simple code in which to express numbers. Using Arabic numerals we count from 1 to 9 and then add a decimal place in front of the 0, making 10, and start again until 99 forces us to add an extra decimal place (100) and so on. This is an extremely simple and effective way to express numbers, and it is likely to remain mankind's principal method of mental counting. But the binary code is a far better language for machines. In this language there are only two symbols, 0 and 1 (try to see them not as zero and one, but as symbols), and by combining them in varying sequences it is possible to express any number. For example, although the Arabic 0 is also expressed in binary as 0 and 1 as 1, the binary expression of the Arabic 2 requires a new column (just like after 9 in Arabic numerals) and is expressed as 10. It is helpful not to see the 10 as ten, but as a down stroke followed by a circle. The Arabic 3 is 11 and 4 demands another column (as does the Arabic system when 99 is reached) and the symbol becomes 100.

It will be obvious that in the binary language more characters are needed to express a number than can be expressed with one in Arabic. By the time we reach the Arabic expression of 17, two more columns have been added, and the binary expression has become 10001. Obviously such a long string of characters for such a small number makes the language unwieldy for humans to use. But in the binary code, no matter how large a number becomes, *only two symbols are used – 0 and 1*. An eight-part combination of these two symbols, 11011000 for example, is able to express any Arabic number up to 255 (depending on the order of the symbols), and further columns of binary digits (or 'bits' in the jargon, from a combination of the two words) may be added as the number increases. The eight-bit set is referred to as a 'byte', 16-bit sets as a 'word' and 32-

bits as a 'long word'.

If it were generally agreed on, the symbols 1 and 0 could be changed to anything: for example SSTSSTTT could represent the same number as the 1s and 0s in the last paragraph. In this language the two characters may be regarded as positive and negative, or yes and no, or on and off, and it is this last method of expressing the binary code which is at the heart of all computers. George Boole, an English contemporary of Babbage, made an enormous contribution by developing a system of mathematical logic which allows problems to be solved by reducing them to a series of questions requiring only an answer of 'true' or 'false'. As will be realised, 'true' or 'false' can be expressed as 1 and 0.

**Boolean logic**

Armed with this logic, Konrad Zuse built a computer with thousands of telephone relays, each one capable of adopting two switched positions – open or closed, or if you chose you could call it on or off. But it is easy for us to see that it was an ideal expression of the binary code's 1 and 0. Thus a bank of eight relay switches, each with its own current supply, could be switched so that reading from left to right they were open, open, closed, open, open, closed, closed, closed. These positions could represent true, true, false, true, true, false, false, false, or 11011000 (the code quoted earlier), and so numbers could be expressed in an electrical machine simply by having a switch, or banks of switches, open or closed. Left in these positions the switches were a physical memory of a number, as easy to read electronically as the beads on an abacus frame and able to take the form of concrete logic.

The mechanical problems of opening and closing switches were infinitely simpler to solve than those of huge cogwheels attempting to count up to nine and then carry over into the subsequent columns of tens, hundreds, thousands, etc. In the binary code (the 'on/off' code as it should perhaps now be called) a combination of sets of eight switches, all in their various states of 'on' or 'off', is capable of expressing the largest numbers.

This 'on/off' system of machine counting led directly to the silicon chip in which electrical currents pass through minute transistors turning them 'on' and 'off' to represent either '1' or '0', and this is the counting method by which all electronic computers work.

But applying a new counting language to machines only solved the mechanical problems. The concept produced a powerful one-purpose electrical calculator. Whether it was possible to create a machine which could be programmed to do one task and then re-programmed to do another – a machine which could *learn* – remained to be mathematically proven.

## Alan Turing

In 1936 a 24-year-old mathematician from Cambridge University supplied this proof. Babbage had believed such a thing to be possible, but it took the genius of Alan Turing to provide unassailable academic proof in a brilliant logical analysis contained in a paper called 'On Computable Numbers'. This paper proved that a machine could be intelligent – could in effect be 'taught' – and the first real concept of artificial intelligence was born. His proof, which many consider as profound and influential as either Darwin's or Einstein's work, set the mathematical world alight.

Alan Turing was to the computer what Oppenheimer was to the atomic bomb – and the creative power of the computer now seems likely to dwarf even the terrible potential of nuclear fission. But, by a cruel quirk of history, Turing's contribution is still largely unknown. As recently as 1981 a major American computer journal carried a long article describing the development of the computer from its origins to the present. Turing's name did not appear even though he later followed up his mathematical proof by leading the team which was to build the world's first electronic computer. *Time* magazine, one of the world's most influential magazines, obscured his contribution when they selected the computer as their 'Machine of the Year' and made it their cover story in their 1892 end-of-year issue. They focused attention on 'the first digital computer to be built in the USA'.

The reason for these omissions is that Turing's computer was built for MI6, Britain's equivalent to the CIA, during the Second World War, and until 1975 no mention of Turing's role or of the world's first computer was allowed to appear. This omission has distorted the mythology which has grown up around the origins of the computer. Many people still believe that the world's first electronic computer was constructed in the USA in 1946. In fact the first was built four years earlier in a country house 50 miles outside London by a team led by Turing, and it was Turing's pioneering discoveries that made the building of the 1946 American machine possible.

## War and 'Enigma'

As war galvanised Germany, Konrad Zuse was contemplating using thermionic valves (vacuum tubes) to make his prototype computers electronic rather than electromechanical. He knew they would be very much faster in operation than the relays which were capable of switching on or off ten times a second, but they were expensive, unreliable and required massive amounts of electricity to power them. He suggested building such a machine to help the German war effort.

But in 1940 Adolf Hitler was sure he had won the war. His confidence is understandable, and he wound down research into weaponry, ordering that projects which would take longer than a year should be abandoned. When Zuse made his proposal to the Reich to build an electronic computer capable of cracking enemy codes, he was forced to admit that the project would take longer than a year, and he had to abandon it.

Britain did not feel so confident. In fact the British government believed they had a good chance of losing the war, and MI6 faced a particularly urgent problem.

During the 1930s, the Germans had developed a machine for coding military messages. Called 'Enigma', the machine was a mechanical collection of wheels and wires, rather like a fruit machine, which 'randomised' letters fed into it. The sender would set up a certain pattern on the machine, enter each letter of the secret message and note down the random letters that the machine provided. The message that was subsequently broadcast was gobbledegook. The recipient would also be in possession of an Enigma machine and would know the pattern in which the machine was set up. On receiving the garbled message, the recipient would set the machine up in the appropriate pattern, enter each of the letters into the machine, crank the handle and the original letters, and consequently the meaning, would appear.

It was foolproof. The patterns that could be used to set up Enigma machines were endless, and if necessary they could be changed every day. The problem this set MI6 and their cryptanalysis department was enormous. A team of the best mathematical brains in the department would take months to break the code behind one message, by which time the contents had become irrelevant. Even when MI6 managed to procure an Enigma machine they were little better off. Without knowledge of the pattern with which the machine was set up, it took months to crack each message. The Germans knew they had a code system which was totally safe, and throughout the war they entrusted messages to the airwaves on the most sensitive subjects in complete confidence that they were unreadable.

It is now known that, through the work of Turing's team in constructing the world's first electronic computer, Britain was able instantly to decipher nearly all of the German secret messages intercepted during the war. Many people believe this ability won the war for the Allies.


## Colossus

The race to build a machine capable of deciphering Enigma's codes started in 1939 when MI6 gathered many of Britain's best mathematical brains together at a house in the Buckinghamshire town of Bletchley. Turing's masterwork on computable numbers automatically placed him at the head of this team, and initially several electromechanical computers, similar to the models Zuse had built in Germany, were set to work. These proved far too slow, and the world's first computer to use valves was built. This giant machine, called the Colossus, ushered mankind into the electronic computer age.

A thermionic valve is capable of switching on or off thousands of times a second. The computer was programmed to look for language patterns in the intercepted German messages and was able to deduce the coded letters by checking how often they occurred in German language sentences: the number of times an 'e' is preceded by a 'b', the number of times an 'o' follows a 'u' and so on.

To program a computer to do this is easy. Each letter of the alphabet is given a number – a value. C might be 11000011 for example, B 01000010. These values are set into the machine as part of the program. The letters contained in the coded message were given the same values, thus when a B was entered it travelled the computer's circuitry until its corresponding 01000010 was located. In this way a computer can identify and read letters. The clever part of the program that controlled Colossus was the analysis of the German language. Analysing the frequency with which letters preceded and followed each other allowed a mathematical model of the language to be built, each mathematical value expressible in the binary code. Thus an enormous pattern was built up, and the computer constantly tried to match various arrangements of letters against this model of the German language. Colossus, and the nine other versions of Colossus which were built before the war ended, were finally able to unscramble all German secret codes in a few minutes.

To provide a measure of how secret the Bletchley computer was considered (it was appropriately codenamed ULTRA), it is said that Winston Churchill preferred to allow the Luftwaffe's infamous massed bombing raid on the city of Coventry to take place rather than alert the Germans to the possibility that Britain was deciphering codes by warning the population, strengthening air defences or arranging aerial interception of the huge bomber force.


### ENIAC

To be fair to the US effort in computing, $400,000 was made available in August 1942 for the building of an all-electronic computer following a detailed design plan put forward by John Mauchly and J. Presper Eckert of the Moore School. But no one in the USA had any experience of building a machine with such a large number of valves, and at this stage in the war America was completely ignorant of the electronic computer already at work in Bletchley. The public remained in ignorance of this fact for a further 30 years. The machine that resulted from this Pennsylvania project was finally only completed when Turing secretly went to America in 1942 to assist. It was called ENIAC and was switched on in February 1946. This computer was made up of 18,000 valves, and early computer runs were severely limited as, on average, one valve would fail every seven minutes.

Turing's contribution to computing was enormous. Tragically, his brain was lost to later generations when in 1954 he committed suicide. His homosexuality had been revealed, and society cared more about his morality than his genius. It would appear that the scandal was to override the logic of the brain that had first proved, and later developed, the existence of artificial intelligence. Turing injected an apple with cyanide and bit into it.

The progress of the computer was rapid but limited for the next ten years. The most important development was program flexibility, allowing programs to be changed in machines; but valves were expensive and unreliable, and computing tasks of any size required rooms full of machinery.

The next major breakthrough came out of Bell Laboratories when the transistor was discovered in 1947. This is now considered to be the most important physical discovery in the history of computing. Valves were used in preference to electromechanical relays because they were faster, but they carried out precisely the same on/off function. The discovery that a small piece of silicon could also carry out this function, but without generating great heat or requiring masses of power, revolutionised electronic circuits overnight. Computers were built which were as powerful as their valve predecessors, but were a hundredth of the size.

The moment John F. Kennedy promised that the USA would be the first nation to land a man on the moon, the computer scientists knew that they would have to improve their machines still further. The calculations of planetary navigation are too complex to be undertaken quickly by the human mind, and without computers such an exploration would have been impossible. When John Kennedy was assassinated, the people of the USA united to ensure his prophecy would come true and allowed the government to commit stupendous sums to the task.

### The silicon chip

Computers were miniaturised and then miniaturised still further, and out of this spectacular period of effort and investment came the 'chip'.

The chip is a minute circuit which consists of thousands of transistors linked together in a certain pattern. Until the mid 1960s, methods of constructing electronic circuits involved soldering small transistors, perhaps $\frac{1}{8}$in (3mm) long, on to a printed circuit board. But in the late 1950s scientists reasoned that the physical size of a transistor had no bearing on its ability to represent the on/off state: a piece of silicon far smaller could do the job as well.

The concept which led to the microcircuit was to take tiny slivers of silicon, to sandwich them between microscopically thin sheets of metal and, using photolithography techniques under microscopic conditions, to etch away parts of the metal leaving a pattern which formed a tiny circuit of blips of silicon connected by slivers of metal. The process is complex, but these circuits have now reached the point where they can be $\frac{1}{8}$in (3mm) square and contain thousands of small transistors. They have become so small that several different circuit designs can be layered together (like layers in a tiny sandwich) to form a microprocessor – a one-component computer with no moving parts, but containing all the necessary circuitry to form a complete computer.

Today's microprocessor usually consists of upwards of 18,000 individual transistor elements, and prototypes of 1,000,000 'bit' chips already exist. Because mass production of these chips requires only a small amount of labour (once the intensive design stage is completed),

*Today's microchip supported in its plastic case by caterpillar-like 'connector' legs. An average chip is capable of undertaking 100,000 calculations in a second.*

they are cheap to produce, and this development has led directly to today's microcomputer and will in turn lead to tomorrow's £5 or $10 all-purpose pocket computer.

The microcomputer, whether it is for the home or for business purposes, consists of five separate units linked together. These, as in the mechanical monster Babbage dreamed of, are: the input stage, the arithmetic/logic circuit which carries out the calculations, the control unit that governs which calculations are carried out in what order and also governs exchanges of information between the parts, the memory and a system for output.

Input is usually via a typewriter style keyboard. This doesn't have to be mechanical at all, as Clive Sinclair proved with his brilliantly conceived Sinclair ZX80 and Sinclair/Timex ZX81(1000), two minute computers that sold for around £50 (some US discounters were advertising a Timex/Sinclair 1000 at $79.95 at the time of writing) and gave the world a foretaste of the cheap computer power that is to come. Input can come from a variety of sources including musical keyboards, and the game paddles used to play Space Invaders are also forms of input devices.

The calculation stage is usually called the arithmetic and logic unit, and this is the unit which does all the work. Under the direction of the control unit – described next – the arithmetic unit does all the addition and subtraction that provides the required answers. All computers are limited to addition or subtraction. To divide 5467.897 by 4432.5678, the computer rapidly adds up units of 4432.5678 until 5467.897 is exceeded. It then takes off one unit of 4432.5678 and adds up what is left over to establish the decimal remainder. The computer is so rapid at doing this task that the method it uses is irrelevant. But it is comforting for humans to reflect on the great leap that will be necessary before a computer can contemplate such an abstract multiplication as 5 x 3 without having to add up the fives.

The control unit is precisely what it sounds. It is under the control of the program 'resident' at any time, and it ensures the correct sequence of events inside the computer.

## Memory

The memory is the 'location' of the ons and offs or the 1s and 0s in the circuit. Microcomputers are judged by the size of this electrical memory and this part of the circuit is usually jargonised as 'RAM' which is the acronym for Random Access Memory. As the name suggests, the control unit can fetch from or put into any part of this electrical memory on demand. The terminology for judging computers becomes complicated. The 1s and 0s of the binary code I have described are referred to as 'bits', and, as we have seen, a collection of eight of these is usually called a byte. The smallest home computer may have an internal memory capacity of about 1,000 bytes (actually 1,024) usually written with the metric/electrical symbol 'K' for a thousand, as in 1K. Average home computers have 16K or 32K. Large home/business computers have 64K, and the newer generation of business microcomputers now go up to 900K. The advantage of greater memory size is that larger and more complex programs can be run.

Memory storage on magnetic tape or disk is not the same as Random Access Memory. It is impossible for a computer to go instantly into a cassette tape or magnetic disk to find what it needs. Memories for holding programs and information which can be loaded into a computer's RAM to be subsequently used are called Read Only Memories (ROM). To provide an idea of the speed at which current microcomputers operate, individual switchings inside RAM may take place 1,000,000 times per second. Speed is everything inside a computer, and the faster it can operate, the longer programs it can process.

The output stage of a computer can take several forms. The most obvious is the screen on which the computer displays the information. But we often want written records of work done on a computer, and a wide variety of printers are available to be attached to computers. Printers are expensive, but very useful and for programmers almost indispensable. The creation of a computer program demands a logical appraisal of each step in the task to be undertaken, so that much of the work of a program will be done away from a computer, working with paper and pencil and designing the steps to be followed. Programmers draw a chart of operations called a 'flow chart', and with this graphic representation it is easy to alter and adjust a program's logic. A printer helps by allowing the programmer to take a printed copy of the program away for consideration. Most professional computer programs are written in flow chart form by senior programmers (called systems analysts), and the actual work of keying in the instructions to the computer is undertaken by a more lowly computer programmer.

## Sound

Another form of computer output is sound. A great many computers are now capable of generating speech and music, and the TV loudspeaker allows this form of output to be heard. Other forms of output can be achieved by attaching various devices to the computer. Computers can be made to control robot arms and similar mechanical objects, and signals to them must also be considered as output.

The microcomputer is a tiny slice of intelligence, operating on a number base called the binary code. Because it can be programmed it can be made to undertake any task which is within its 'mental' capacity. And capacity is one factor which is going to alter greatly in the future.


## THE FUTURE

Prophecy is generally a foolhardy exercise but, in the world of the microcomputer, there are some events that can be predicted.

The discovery that an electronic circuit could exist in one component was the breakthrough that allows us to foresee paths of development. Each year circuits are developed which have *double* the capacity and speed of the previous year's models. This explosive development pattern has continued since the first microprocessor was developed in 1971. Coupled with this unprecedented pace in technological advance is an equally new phenomenon – rapidly falling cost. In 1955, IBM's cost per data processing unit was £47.22. In 1982 it was 42p.

After the design stage, producing a microprocessor is a simple technique, and the little brains have so many applications – from controlling traffic lights to monitoring life-support systems – that the market for the products is quadrupling each year. The result is that every year we see more powerful microprocessors being offered for less and less money. It is an indicator of the depth and power of this revolution that it has the ability to turn the apparently inviolable law of rising prices on its head!

In most sciences there are constant barriers to be overcome, and usually solutions are only arrived at with great effort. In the search for a cancer cure, the very variety of cancers has proved a stumbling block. In space travel the supposed 'ultimate' barrier of the speed of light forces us to lower our sights and consider interplanetary travel rather than interstellar exploration.

But in the world of machine intelligence there are few barriers left! I am not suggesting that each advance in speed and efficiency arrives without huge investment and research, but the theoretical advance of the computer is now clear for researchers to see.

Each year microscopic charges of electricity are persuaded to move ever faster around microscopic circuits. The drive towards smaller and smaller circuits is allied to this desire for speed. For practical purposes it hardly matters whether a microprocessor is $\frac{1}{8}$ in (3mm) or $\frac{1}{16}$ in (1.5 mm) across, but when the distance a micron has to travel is halved, the speed of operation is doubled. So the descent into the sub-micro world continues – almost approaching the atomic. The obvious question is, why do we want computers capable of operating so quickly?

## Speed and intelligence

The answer is that the faster the computer, the more intelligent it becomes. A pocket calculator is far faster at doing a sum than a human brain. But while a human brain considers a sum, it is also undertaking thousands, if not millions, of other tasks. Body temperature is controlled, information from the five separate input senses is being monitored, antibody systems are operating, digestive systems, movement, breathing, healing, reproducing, and all the other functions of the human computer support system are taking place at the same time. This versatility can only be reproduced in a machine by making it operate so that in a split second a million different operations can be undertaken.

If a computer will soon be able to undertake a billion (a US billion) operations a second, part of that power can be used to solve a maths problem, part can be used to run self-diagnostic checks on the computer's own system, part can be used to monitor the supply of energy needed and so on until we build a machine capable of taking on all of the simultaneous tasks of which a human is capable.

A hint of the power to come was given by Dr Horst Nasko, Director of Research and Development for AEG-Telefunken of Germany in 1980. He is quoted in *Northern California Electronic News* as saying:

> Superchips are so small and sophisticated, it is expected, ultimately, as many as one billion components may be packed on to one wafer-thin chip no larger than a postage stamp. Even today's mass-produced chips can pack up to as many as a million components into a space no larger than a pea. They are capable of running a factory's automated assembly line, programming computers, and controlling the traffic flows of cities. After that will come the superchip. No larger than the face of any ordinary wristwatch, one superchip will (in theory) be capable of keeping the personnel records for every company in North America or Europe, watch over the world's air traffic, or keep track of every book in every library, everywhere.

If such mind-boggling ability were not enough, the reliability of such devices has already shown up how unreliable the human computer is, and the devices will become even more reliable. In *Electronic Design* Hewlett-Packard's President wrote:

> Work done in both industry and universities has been so fruitful that this area [reliability] should not be a major problem over the next decade. We have found that, by combining self-testing at the chip sub-system and system levels with high-reliability

components, remote diagnostics, and improved test equipment, we can now offer a computer system with a guaranteed up time [amount of satisfactory running time]. In a few more years, we expect down time [failure] to be measured in thousandths of a percent.

### The thinking computer

I suppose we define intellect as the ability to think and reason, and scientists have been considering the impact of the arrival of the thinking computer for many years. Whilst cinema audiences prove mankind is obsessed with celluloid glimpses of what it might be like to meet alien intelligence, we are creating the real aliens in the scientific laboratories. The shock the world will experience when one of these steps into the daylight has already been considered.

Alan Turing, a man whose enormous contribution to computing was described in Level 2 of this chapter, considered this problem (in late night discussion sessions with his mathematician colleagues at Bletchley Park). His genius enabled him to consider the implications of a machine *more intelligent than humans* long before most scientists dreamed of the possibility. Man had not yet realised that intelligence could be created from sand and so had not yet stumbled on the key to Pandora's Box.

The computer, which is cleverer than man, has to be cleverer at 'mental' operation. How do we judge when this occurs? Turing turned his brain to this in the 1940s and devised the test which is now considered to be the definitive test of machine intelligence. It is a measure of his genius that, during the crisis hours of the Second World War, he was considering how to measure something that we do not expect to be able to create before the turn of this century and, at the time of his thinking, something we had no way of building. It was a popular chant of the 1950s that 'there is not enough matter in the whole universe to construct a computer as powerful as the human brain'. Turing was not bound by such practical considerations. He lived in the world of abstract mathematics and could prove it was possible. The test he devised is internationally known as the 'Turing Test', and the participants are two intelligent educated people and a clever, thoroughly programmed computer.

The two people are put in separate windowless rooms and are each provided with a computer terminal with which they can communicate. They begin a conversation and, as anyone who has ever played the game of 'free association' will know, humans can be amazingly obtuse and tangential in conversation although their brains can still extract continuity and meaning despite determined efforts to block it.

As the conversation, perhaps deliberately obtuse and designed to test the 'humanity' of the participants, develops between the two humans, the computer 'listens' to the dialogue. At some stage, one human is disconnected from the chain, and the computer is switched in. If the computer is able to sustain the conversation, no matter where it may lead, without the human 'judge' being able to detect that he or she is talking to a computer rather than a human, the machine may be said to have passed the Turing Test and be at least as intelligent as a human and probably more so (as it is able to disguise its identity). Science has already named this breed of computers; they are called UIMs – an acronym for Ultra Intelligent Machines.

It will be obvious that the computer will have to be very thoroughly programmed in order to pass this test. It will need to have the typical knowledge and educational experiences of an intelligent adult human, it will need the sort of response speeds which allow humans to change to unrelated subjects in a split second and it will need the humour and sensitivity to examine all aspects of the human's conversation in order to extract true meaning. It will also have to have its own humour, sensitivity and ability to shock. It is estimated that the UIM will exist by 1995 (although the programs required may take a little longer).

## Super conductivity

But the microprocessor will have to be operating at very high speeds for such complex and lengthy programs to run fast enough to fool a human. Despite the ease with which we are now increasing microprocessor speed, some barriers can be predicted. The electrical resistance of metal conductors, no matter how small, is capable of slowing down the speed of the electrons as they zip round the circuit switching 1s into 0s and back again. Two discoveries have opened the way towards a speed that will make the UIM possible. The first is a matter of 'architecture', or design, in the processor itself.

Brian Josepheson, the British physicist, designed a circuit in 1962 which operated in such a way that the insulators themselves took on the properties of the silicon semiconductors. This design was made possible by the second discovery, 'superconductivity'. It was discovered that cooling a conductor such as copper to a very low temperature (close to absolute zero, -273°C) almost eliminates resistance in the conductors. In this state a new method of operation in circuits becomes possible with metal itself acting in a 1 or 0 state. Using superconductivity, the speed of the electrons begins to approach that 'ultimate barrier', the speed of light, and scientists are already considering if there is any possible way to cross this final frontier.

But the UIM will be created long before we need to reach such speeds, and the power made available by the application of the

Josepheson Junction can provoke spectacular imaginings on what may be ultimately achieved (especially when it is realised that we can pass the greatest problems on to machines cleverer than ourselves).

### The software gap

The one real problem which will face computer developers is programming. Before any machine can behave like a human, we have to analyse precisely how a human behaves. This incredibly complex task is only the beginning of the process of breaking such behaviour down into its smallest components and rebuilding it in computer logic. The task is vast and is summed up by a phrase used increasingly in the computer industry. This problem is called the 'Software Gap'. We are able to build machines with enormous capabilities, but our own abilities to develop the programs on which they will operate are not keeping pace. However, computers are now being put to the task of creating programs, and it is expected that, once properly harnessed, this aid will allow us to catch up and supply the necessary teaching to the infant computers we create.

In the meantime, smaller, less clever computers will crop up in every element of our lives. Money will disappear, crimes related to cash will be reduced and the nature of crime will change as the flow of assets and money through society comes under computer control. Governments are writing laws to prohibit the abuse of information in our new 'information society', but I believe such legislation must prove ineffective and that a lack of 'information liberty' is a price we will have to pay for a better, more ordered society. Our economies are now too complex for humans to handle. All Western politics seem to be the politics of expediency, and countries are now far too complex for any group of humans to govern properly. Governments lurch from one crisis to another and, if they momentarily relieve the worst effects of the latest catastrophe, they appeal for public approval and another term in office. The computer has arrived just in time to assist in government, a task that has become too complex for the human brain. Whether computers take over, whether they are used to enforce totalitarianism or to liberate the individual from the need to earn money is a fascinating subject which is outside the scope of this book. I can recommend you again to *The Mighty Micro* for a superb overview.

### Speaking and listening computers

As the machines get cleverer and smaller, speech input, now proving to be obstinately elusive, will finally arrive. A great deal of research has been done on trying to produce a machine which will understand

*Computers are getting
smaller all the time. The
tiny Sinclair ZX
Spectrum houses 13
microcircuits on its
single circuit board.*

spoken commands. Machines already exist which can understand a small vocabulary, perhaps several thousand words; but, before a program can be written to tell a computer how to extract meaning from sounds, we will have to learn more about how we actually communicate. Communication between humans is 75% visual, and meaning is extracted from a variety of signals other than the words used. Tone of voice, body talk and facial expressions all contribute, and humans can use words to convey the opposite of their literal meaning. To bring computer intelligence to this level requires complex programs stored in vast electronic memories. At first the application of this ability will be in such things as TV sets which turn themselves on when told to do so and in computers which can understand the spoken vocabulary of a computer language.

Speech input is one of the main goals of the much vaunted national Japanese programme to develop the 'fifth generation' of computers. Massive government funding has been provided to many laboratories in Japan with the brief that Japan's industry must get to the fifth generation before the West. The fifth generation of listening, talking and thinking computers – not necessarily UIMs – is expected to be widely available by 1995.

But even by the end of the 1980s the microcomputer will be tiny, cheap and very powerful. For our children it will be an aid to intellectual development which no educationalist could have dreamed of before 1975. How we apply this power on behalf of our children is the subject of the following chapters.

# EDUCATION'S RESPONSE TO THE COMPUTER CHALLENGE

Willingly or unwillingly, adults have the job of shaping the generation of tomorrow. How well our children handle artificial intelligence, or any other aspect of adult life, depends on how well we equip them so to do, and any false moves or vacillation on the part of the educators will have detrimental long-term effects on the children currently passing through our educational systems.

Education has, of course, always carried the terrible burden of responsibility for the future, and because this is so important, education also finds itself exposed to the prevailing political and, therefore, financial climate.

By the time our children are adults, computers will control many aspects of daily life. Few tasks will be undertaken without their assistance, and little that is worthwhile in industry, commerce, leisure and even art will be achieved by us alone. As our children grow into middle age, computers may well be providing sufficient wealth to have solved many of the world's major problems: disease, ignorance and war.

Because the impact of the computer threatens to be so far-reaching, it is impossible to predict what sort of society will develop. Some experts proclaim the dawning of a new slave-based society in which food and physical comforts are produced by cheap powerful computer-slaves. They suggest that computer laser-beam defence systems will be so advanced that the possibility of a pre-emptive nuclear strike will have become an impossibility, and thus the stalemate global peace which has existed since 1945 may continue in perpetuity. They suggest that we will spend a lifespan of 200 years or so at leisure, in the comfort of a world in which all our needs are met by machines.

Alternatively, other forecasters suggest that we will become deeply unhappy as our traditional work role is usurped by artificial intelligence. They say that the loss of productive occupations will rob many of us of any opportunity to lead fulfilled lives and they paint a landscape as culturally barren as the wilderness which might follow a holocaust. They believe this will lead first to a polarisation in society and think that the divide which will separate the classes will be between information and lack of it. They suggest that this state of affairs will lead to social anarchy and the breakdown of all order. I suppose that with a little luck we'll follow a middle path.

Whatever your view of the future, you can be sure that computers will play a central role. Our children must learn to be comfortable with computers and learn how to use them. Some children must learn everything about computers in order to carry on their development. Most children will only need to know how to apply computers, but the child who becomes an adult unable to use a computer will by the year 2000 be the equivalent of today's adult who can neither read nor write. We are in danger of producing many such adults.

### Computer literacy

Education is responding slowly to the arrival of the computer, even though governments are funding microcomputers in schools, and national TV stations are broadcasting computer literacy courses. This is partly because some teachers are slow to respond to change, partly because world recession is slowing down investment in education (i.e. in the future) and partly because many adults have not yet realised the fundamental importance of the computer revolution.

To place the computer age in the proper perspective, it is helpful to recall how few other global revolutions have occurred. The first change was agriculture which began in the Middle East about 8,000 years before the birth of Christ. For the half million years previously mankind had competed for food with the other creatures on the planet. Growing our food instead of chasing or gathering it was the first major technological revolution to affect the development of Homo sapiens. The introduction of this new technology was slow – it was 5,000 years before the wheel and the plough were invented (these devices proved quite helpful) – but by the time of Christ proper civilisations had developed, based on an agricultural economy. Nearly 10,000 years after the first seed was deliberately sown, the next revolution occurred. This time we had the means to record the event, and it is now known as the Industrial Revolution. It started in Britain about 1760 and spread across Europe between 1815 and 1890.

During the shaping of the Old World, which occurred during the Roman Empire and on into the Middle Ages, people had refined the tools with which they carried on their farming, their living and their warfare, but no significant new aspects of technology have arisen to disturb the gradual process of evolution. Even printing, the most profound development during this period, failed to set the entire world alight. It took the money generated by the Industrial Revolution to teach the masses to read, and the steam machinery, originally developed for the mills, to drive mechanised printing presses. Steam power amplified people's muscle, and by 1820 a giant steam hammer or a huge loom could be constructed which had the strength and stamina of 100 men.

This revolution completely changed society, shifting the population from the countryside to the new cities within a few years. In total the global revolution took 150 years. In that time Britain was able to snatch imperiously as much of the world as remained unclaimed and gather a store of wealth so significant that even today it remains the country's main bolster against its now rapidly declining economic and political status.

## Person plus machine plus computer

The computer age is only the third major revolution to sweep across the globe. The discovery of atomic power has the potential to wipe out all other progress, but, other than offering the dubious advantage of nuclear power stations, it has so far failed to offer other significant help to its discoverers. The revolution in which we now find ourselves has the power to change our lives significantly within our lifetime. As the Industrial Revolution reproduced and magnified muscle power enabling one man plus machine to do the job of 100, the Computer revolution has reproduced and magnified brain power, enabling one man plus machine plus computer to do the job of 1,000. Many experts consider that the computer will reverse the patterns which followed the Industrial Revolution, throwing us all back into our rural, but electronic, cottages. Already there are giant unlit unheated factories in Japan in which armies of robots tirelessly manufacture and assemble more robots, working unassisted, 24 hours a day, 365 days a year. One man turns the lights on in the giant hanger for a few minutes every day to check everything is running smoothly. (Fujitsu Fanac, a large Japanese manufacturing company, has actually agreed to pay union dues on behalf of the 200 robots installed in its totally automated plant near Mount Fuji.) And we have not yet reached the period of real acceleration in this computer revolution.

The computer revolution really got under way around 1950; and by the year 2000 machine intelligence will have surpassed human intelligence, and it will be possible to see where it is all leading. We can already guess at some of the implications for the future, although every year we are forced to revise our forecasts as the pace of computer development quickens. As one indication of the speed at which this revolution is currently running, I quote a recently published comparison which tells us that if flying had developed as rapidly as computing, we would all be able to fly around the world in 21 minutes at a cost of £7 ($12)!

So, our children are growing up and going to school in the midst of a revolution which has triggered what can only be called an educational crisis. The world-wide recession of the late 1970s and early 1980s resulted in 'cut backs' in educational spending in both the USA and the UK, although in many instances the truth is that the spending on education was not allowed to increase as fast as it had been. This is not the main cause of the crisis. The cause is the arrival of the computer in the classroom.

By the early 1960s, computers had come out of the laboratories and secret installations and were invading big business and government. These giant inefficient computers bear little resemblance to the microcomputers our children are using today, but they attracted the attention of academics and university faculties, and mathematicians were soon using the computer's incredible power over numbers to analyse statistics and build mathematical models to help them understand our world better.

## Computers in education

At the same time, many academics spotted the role computers might be able to play in teaching. A computer is very good at repetitive tasks. Once taught (programmed) how to carry out a task, the computer will carry on repeating that task tirelessly. Teaching children by our present methods does, of course, require a lot of repetition, and if it is possible to program a computer to set problems and then to mark and correct them, would this not prove extremely useful?

The original aim behind the introduction of computers to education in the USA in the late 1960s was a mixture of cost-cutting and a response to a population bulge which resulted in outsize classes. The phrase 'Computer-Aided Instruction' (CAI) was coined for the situation in which the computer takes on the role of the teacher, imparts knowledge and tests the student's ability to retain it. A second style of computer teaching was subsequently adopted in the early 1970s. This was CML (Computer-Managed Learning), and although this did not replace CAI, it offered students in higher education the opportunity to undertake study which was managed – timed, marked and prompted – by computer, essentially freeing the human teacher from administration.

Up until 1978 every school offering CAI, CML or 'Computer Studies' (a phrase that I will later suggest describes education's worst possible response to the computer challenge) had a terminal in the school which was linked to a large 'mainframe' computer in a university or in a commercial computer centre. The mainframe computer is a large powerful beast which is super-expensive to build and expensive to maintain. It is so powerful that many people can use it simultaneously, and access to it is controlled by a 'time sharing' scheme with the users often located many miles away and linked by cable.

This is the style of computing which subsisted between 1950 and

1978. Now the inexpensive microprocessor has entered the classroom, and the requirement for any link with an external 'big brother' has been significantly reduced if not eliminated.

It was quickly realised that cost-saving was the least of the advantages to be gained from applying computers to the education of a country's young. The greatest advantage was the training of young minds which could then learn to develop computing further, and so most governments initiated schemes to study the role and effect of computers within education.

### France

In France the government grasped the problem in a very determined way. In October 1970 the French National Experiment in Educational Computing was launched, initially aimed at secondary education. Unlike the educational systems of the USA, UK, Germany, Denmark, Australia, etc., France's system is rigidly controlled from a central ministry with curriculum and teaching hours specifically laid down by government. It is identical in all schools. The advantage of this system was that it allowed the government to control the introduction of computers across the country whilst embarking on an aggressive teacher education campaign. Today the scheme has developed and changed as the computers on offer have changed. One of the current schemes, labelled the '10,000 computers scheme', entails the gradual equipping of all lycées with computers and the training of volunteer teachers in their use. Before 1986 it is intended that computers will be used as a teaching tool in 1,160 lycées. The standard classroom layout will be eight computers and a printer (to type the results of the work) to each class. This will allow half of a normal-sized class to be at a computer at any one time. Seymour Papert, a world authority on the use of computers in education, has spent the last few years assisting the French government in their adventurous experiment. (More about Papert and his pioneering work with computers and children will be found in Chapter 4.) But advanced as it may seem, France's thrust into new technology has been made in an education system which in 1982 was turning out 150,000 illiterate school leavers a year.

### Britain

In Britain the government originally funded a scheme between 1973 and 1978 called the National Development Programme in Computer Assisted Learning. Only £2 million was allocated for this scheme, and because of the expensive nature of computing at the time of the scheme, the work was largely concentrated on the areas of higher

## ■■■■■■■■ EDUCATION'S RESPONSE TO THE COMPUTER CHALLENGE

education which already had access to computing facilities.

The next thrust in Britain was the 1981 announcement of a £3 million scheme to persuade every secondary school to buy a microcomputer. Although Britain had started studying the impact of computers on education early, the British government was markedly later in subsidising the introduction of microtechnology into schools than some other European countries. When it came, the government commitment was stated boldly, but was poorly capitalised. Unlike many developed countries in the world, the schools or more usually the parents were asked to pay for half of the cost of the first computer purchased for each school over and above the large amounts of personal taxation already going to support the educational system. The government stated clearly which type of microcomputer was eligible for the subsidy, and if a school wanted a different make (or more than one microcomputer) the money had to be found entirely from the parents of pupils at the school or from private funds. It is to the credit and foresight of the hard-pressed British parents that within the first year 5,500 secondary schools had taken up the 50% subsidy from the government and bought a microcomputer. This figure represents about 80% of British state-run secondary schools.

A year later the British government announced a similar scheme to encourage primary schools to purchase microcomputers. This scheme, estimated to cost £9 million, covered Britain's 27,000 primary schools.

*Lowbrook Primary School, in the county of Berkshire, England, is now recognised as being one of the first schools in the world to apply microcomputers in education for the under-11s. Under head teacher Graham Sullivan, the school has integrated the microcomputer into the curriculum and offers even the youngest children access to computer power. Here, two pupils experiment with an attractive Pet-based program assisted by Ajmal Sohal of the British organisation, Micro Scope.*

These schemes offered similar terms to both state-run and private schools.

### Europe

In the rest of continental Europe the countries most involved in bringing microtechnology into the classroom are Denmark, Sweden, West Germany, Switzerland, Holland and, most recently, Eire. In Germany and Switzerland the problem is one of fragmentation. Both countries contain highly autonomous regional education authorities which vary in their views about computing. Progress has been more substantial in Germany where the constitution allowed the local regions, or Länder, to work hand in hand with central government on the planning of education. Responsibility for the introduction of computer-based learning has rested with individual area authorities, and some areas are significantly more advanced than others. Until recently the method of experimentation adopted was to develop 'model' schools and then to monitor development. Despite the difficulties of regional autonomy, there is a strong thrust in both countries to introduce classroom computers, the funding for which now comes entirely from the public purse.

Denmark has adopted something of a radical position on the

*In Sweden, computer studies continue even while the students are travelling. In a reserved compartment of a train travelling between Stockholm and Uppsala, students of the University of Uppsala use a Sinclair ZX80 microcomputer to continue their education. The course is run twice weekly during the university term.*

subject. The country's experts have thought long and hard about the best approach, and the government scheme now provides a Danish-built computer and a specially developed computer programming language, COMAL 80, which is claimed to be more suitable for school use than BASIC, the main American-developed language in use in Britain and West Germany. Following her long-standing tradition of independence, France also developed her own language for computer programming.

The Republic of Ireland has recently started introducing microcomputers into the classroom, and following the Danish lead, is basing its approach on an Irish-built version of the Danish microcomputer which operates on the Danish computer language. Since 1 May 1981, the Irish government has offered an 80% subsidy to the 834 secondary schools in the country.

Surprisingly, the USSR is currently using American-built microcomputers with American languages which are adapted with Cyrillic characters, but, unsurprisingly, computer penetration into classrooms is rigidly controlled by regional authorities entrusted with the task of ensuring such power is integrated with regional planning.

## Australia and New Zealand

In Australia the situation mirrors that prevailing in the USA, West Germany and Switzerland, although some states are also seeking additional public funding for computers. Highly autonomous states are free to direct the introduction of microcomputing at their own speed with minimal interference from central government. One problem which is unique to Australia are the large open spaces between communities. In Western Australia, for example, the Education Department is actively promoting computer education, and 95% of major secondary schools now have some form of computing power; but smaller schools in outlying areas have to share a pool of five systems which are transported from school to school. In-service courses have been organised for teachers in the state, and at the time of writing the introduction of computers into primary schools was under consideration, and guidelines had been laid down. A dollar for dollar (up to $1,000) subsidy is offered to primary schools, providing the approved make of computer is purchased, and the state's Education Department also makes interesting points about the integration of computers in primary curricula (a subject which is discussed in Chapter 5). In the 11 education regions of New South Wales, consultants have been appointed to advise schools on the introduction of microcomputers. Apple II microcomputers are the most common machine in use although a new arrival, the home-produced MicroBee computer, is gaining acceptance. At the time of writing, two thirds of secondary schools had at least one microcomputer, and primary schools were only just starting to equip.

New Zealand has been late in providing micros in schools. The country's universities and technical institutes have been supplied with computing power for some time, but at the time of writing the New Zealand government is still in the process of checking which machines meet education department specifications, claiming that the recession has forced economic restrictions on the government which prevents them from offering funding for computers. Frustrated by this delay, many of the country's 389 secondary schools have jumped the gun and purchased microcomputers out of funds raised independently. This lack of direction from the government has led to a price war between manufacturers, with Apple slashing the price of their machines by 75% to beat off competition by the home-grown Poly microcomputer. The Government has responded by slapping a $NZ880 (£390) duty on the Apples. The price war has, however, resulted in 554 computers appearing in the secondary schools.

Even in quite small territories such as Singapore, the computer's potential contribution has been recognised. A 'computer appreciation programme' was started for Singapore secondary schools in 1975, and teachers attended courses conducted by Japanese advisers. By 1981 each secondary school had its own microcomputer, and across the state the 128 school-organised computer appreciation clubs have a membership of 6,000.


## USA

In the USA the situation is also fragmented, and many politicians feel that the government has failed in its duty to prepare the youth of America for the computer age. Despite Britain's uncertain entry into computer-aided education, in 1981 the example of the British initiative was held up by a member of the House of Representatives in order to shame the US administration into agreeing to his bill for a $4 million National Centre for Personal Computers in Education. But the size of the country militates against concerted efforts, and the sheer size of a top-heavy educational system makes it slow to respond to change. One quarter of the USA's working population is either attending, or employed in, the educational system!

There are 83,334 public (state-run) schools, 21,749 private schools and 3,453 colleges in the USA, and it is estimated that the number of microcomputers in use in American schools is over 100,000 compared with 52,000 only 18 months ago. This level of resource places one computer at the disposal of a national average of every 400 pupils. Given the complexity of the country's educational system, it is understandable that there has been no directive from central government, and education boards have equipped classrooms with microcomputers as public demand and cash allowed. Unfortunately the arrival of microcomputers has coincided with a funding crisis for many of the school boards, and in the USA a great deal of attention is still being given to the cost-saving potential of computers.

Some states perform significantly better than others at equipping schools with microcomputers, and in Minnesota there is one computer for every 50 children (the local education board also has a home-produced software library of over 700 programs). In another state only 50% of schools have any microcomputer at all. One of the main concerns of the American teaching fraternity are the cut-backs in salaries and staff levels that have occurred in the last few years. Since the late 1970s, teachers' salaries have been declining between three and seven per cent, and in Massachusetts, for example, 25 per cent of the teaching population have been forced to move to other states or leave the profession.

The mid term Congressional elections which took place at the end of 1982 have gone some way in modifying the hawkish attitude of the Reagan administration. The Democratic Party gains seemed likely to lend support for bills calling for assistance in education at all levels. In particular, the Computer Equipment Bill, promoted by Apple Computer Inc., would provide tax advantages for companies supplying computers to primary and secondary schools. (A 25% tax write-off is available for equipment supplied to colleges.) The sugar on the Apple pill is the company's offer of one free microcomputer for every state school in the country – an offer worth $200 million at retail prices! Congress had not approved the idea at the time of writing, but California has agreed to a similar deal.

But in the generally affluent USA children find more home support than in many other countries. More money is spent annually on games and home educational equipment for children than is spent directly on institutionalised education, and this is certainly a foretaste of things to come in the rest of the developed world. Because the USA still leads the field in the development of microtechnology, it is likely that American schoolchildren will be the first to feel the benefit of the second wave of the microcomputer revolution which is about to hit us. This involves networked computers communicating inexpensively via satellites and optical fibre telephone lines – a system which will link the thousands of separate computers in a giant computing force with central cohesion.

## Japan

As many Westerners have come to realise, Japan is laying claim to the computing crown currently worn by the USA. Computing is a hobby of obsessional proportions for a large minority of Japanese children, and in Tokyo and Osaka there are chains of shops which specialise in selling computer components: the fun pastime for Japanese 13-year-olds is building their own computer-controlled radar systems. Children from eight upwards head for the 'electronic city' district of Akihabara in Tokyo as soon as school finishes, and their spending per head on electronic components and computer-generated leisure outstrips that of every youthful population in the world.

The school system in Japan is four-tiered, but compulsory education only continues until children are 15, and most pre-school kindergartens are privately operated. There are 14,893 kindergartens which children attend until they are five. From five to 12, they attend one of the 24,945 elementary schools, and this is followed up by a three-year period at the 10,780 lower secondary schools. A further three years of education is available for all at upper secondary schools, and 90% of the population choose to continue their school education until they are 18. Private schooling follows the Western trend and is provided for about 7% of the population.

Because of Japan's obsession with the scientific side of computing, the accent in Japanese schools is on programming and electronic design with a very high level of microcomputing equipment provided throughout the school system. As in France, all Japan's state-run schools conform to a national curriculum, and in theory all students

*Electronics is more than a casual occupation for many Japanese teenagers. For many, 'build it yourself' is the only acceptable approach. This is an electronic superstore providing every sort of electronic component for DIY enthusiasts.*

receive identical schooling. Although many observers might consider Japan's programming and computer-design education to be way ahead of anything available in the West, other experts point to the system's narrow applicational considerations (efficiency being the most important goal) as being indicative of impoverished logical and philosophical thinking. (Some obvious differences in computer technology between US and Japanese computer companies would seem to bear out this critical view: the Japanese seem amazingly expert at applications, but stunningly unimaginative when contemplating the pure leaps in logic that are necessary to see beyond the improvement of a particular development stage. The 'fifth generation' project that the Japanese government is now pursuing is designed to push Japanese thinkers away from their semi-traditional role as improver-imitators and towards an originating force in artificial intelligence.)

As an example of the nation's technical achievements, the following news item, written by Barbara Casassus and quoted in full from Britain's *Times Educational Supplement*, provides food for thought:

> Tokyo: A new electronic method of 'cramming' secondary school pupils at home will be introduced by a tutorial school in Kyoto this autumn [1982].
>
> The system, known as 'Faxstudy', consists of a small facsimile unit installed in each child's home, through which the school transmits information and questions, the child responds, and corrections and explanations follow. Any problems arising can be solved by telephone contact between teachers and pupils.
>
> Initially, 120 facsimile units will be leased from a manufacturer for use by lower secondary pupils, who will be offered two hours of English and two hours of maths evening tuition a week.
>
> The monthly fees of 18,000 yen (about £42) for the course are estimated to be higher than the usual rates for attending a tutorial course, but lower than those for coaching at home. It is expected the system will also be operated from teachers' homes in the future.
>
> Professor Yukihiko Motoyama of Kyoto University's Education Department was quoted as saying: 'It is handy for the children to be able to stay home and study by using facsimile communication, but it is also important to foster human relations between children and their instructors.'

## Canada

Canada has taken the arrival of the microcomputer in education very seriously. A high level of equipment already exists in most metropolitan areas, and the funding has so far come entirely from education budgets. In the city of North York area of Ontario, for example, the education board has been selling surplus building sites to finance the rapid introduction of microtechnology in elementary, middle and secondary education, and much emphasis has been laid on the integration of computers into the curricula of all state schools. Memos from the Superintendent of Schools prove the board's awareness by quoting from Seymour Papert's *Mindstorms* (see next chapter), and although computer-aided instruction still plays a role in North York schools the microcomputer seems to be applied creatively. Teachers in North York are urged to introduce computers from the first kindergarten grade right through to Grade 13, and provision for additional computer exposure is being made both for children with learning disabilities and for those who show a particular aptitude to the computer itself. Teachers are even urged to ensure that both male and female role models of adult involvement in technology are made clear to students (a very important consideration which is discussed in later chapters).

The city's declared aim is to ensure that by 1987 every elementary school has at least six microcomputer systems with associated peripherals. It is also intended that every middle and junior high school shall have a minimum of 12 microcomputer systems and peripherals, and every secondary school will have a computer laboratory equipped with a minimum of 36 microcomputers plus back-up peripherals. Over and above this ambitious equipment scheme, each school, from kindergarten up, will be equipped with separate terminals which will allow the school to connect to a central external computer. This computer will contain a large number of approved educational programs which (together) are described as 'courseware' – programs designed to operate together and in sequence. The terminals will also allow the schools to 'plug in' to other data bases, and the amount of information at the command of each school promises to be formidable.

This ability to link to central computers and between schools is central to Ontario's educational philosophy. An information network of regional minicomputers (several times more powerful than microcomputers) called the Educational Computing Network of Ontario (ECNO) has been set up, and with every school connected by telephone or cable this system will facilitate the rapid distribution of approved programs. (France has successfully pioneered the use of a similar system.) The North York school board (and many other Canadian school boards) is committed to Commodore and Apple microcomputers, but although it wants to see compatibility between the computing systems in the area's schools, it makes it quite clear that adherence to board guidelines on purchases should not restrict a school from buying a microcomputer of its choice for a specific application – music is one example mentioned in internal education board memos. At the time of writing every elementary school in North

York had at least one microcomputer system, middle and junior high schools had at least three and secondary schools had at least eight.

Despite this shining example, most countries are in internal disarray over the introduction of this rapidly moving aspect of technology, and it is hardly surprising that the few feeble attempts which have been made at international coordination have been less than successful. Under UNESCO's wing the International Federation for Information Processing has established an annual World Conference on Computers in Education; but this event tends to sink to a 'lowest common denominator' approach; and as each country is currently proving unable to move quickly enough to catch up with technology there is little useful advice available which is capable of being translated across cultures.

Despite the confusion, the developed world is unanimously acknowledging that computer power is desirable and necessary in education. For some countries the computer offers opportunities to save money, to others it offers the chance of improved teaching, whilst a growing group of educationalists argue that the arrival of cheap artificial intelligence demands that we completely rethink our approach to education.

### Teachers and computers

As governments approve and encourage the use of computers in education, manufacturers are motivated to produce machines and programs tailored to educational requirements, and in their turn parents respond to media pressure and expect to see computers in the classroom. At the bottom of this enormous pressure pyramid is the teacher. And he or she does not appear to be responding well.

The reason this book has been published is that many parents do not understand computers, although many are coming to the conclusion that they at least ought to understand the impact of new technology in order to help and advise their children properly. In many cases teachers are equally ignorant.

For the first time teachers are learning a new subject alongside the children they are teaching, and usually the children show themselves more able to learn.

In many primary schools computers arrive and remain in their packing while the bemused staff wonder what to do with them. If a nine-year-old is allowed to read the manual, it is likely that he or she can get the system connected and running before the teacher. (Commodore, a major microcomputer manufacturer, report that half of the offers of programs and program ideas it receives come from schoolchildren.) But once the system is running, the teachers' problems really begin.

In France the government insisted that at least two teachers from every school attended a year-long in-service training course to learn computer programming. In theory this is excellent, but do teachers have to learn to program computers in order to be able to use them? What about the percentage of teachers who disliked programming and therefore took their phobia back to the classroom? This is currently the subject of a great debate in which one faction argues that teachers and children must be taught to program computers, while another argues that this is an unnecessary waste of time and that all that is required is for teachers and children to learn how to apply computing power. Indeed, they argue that unnecessary education in the programming of computers can be a dangerous and off-putting process.

*The French educational computing programme has been nationally organised. Microcomputers are provided for many schools, but many also use a network system of minicomputers. France has also developed its own educational computer language, LSE (Language Symbolique d'Enseignement).*

In Britain the government scheme for subsidised computers demands that teachers attend a two-day familiarisation course organised by regional educational authorities, while in America teacher training is carried out by both commercial and educational organisations. In the city of New York, the board of education has appointed a coordinator and equipped him with his own classroom network of computers. He calls teachers in from the 1,000 state-run schools in the city and trains them in the basics of microcomputer operation and programming during a course of ten two-hour lessons. Recently sub-coordinators for each school district have been appointed, have received training and are now going into schools to train teachers on the spot. In a parallel move, the Tandy Corporation, makers of Radio Shack computers, undertake to give teachers a two-day course in their own teacher-education centres, if a school decides to equip with Radio Shack products. These centres are located in all major cities (and are now rapidly spreading around the world). Other manufacturers also offer assistance and training to teachers.

### Alienated by technology

But many fine teachers are instinctively alienated by all forms of technology. The many mechanical teaching aids of the 1950s and 1960s which are now consigned to dusty cupboards bear silent witness to this fact. Even when a teacher is 'gadget-oriented', it may be impossible to persuade him or her to adapt ingrained teaching methods to the arrival of a new intelligence. A study recently concluded that it is almost impossible to persuade an experienced teacher to change his or her teaching methods for more than a few weeks or a few months. Therefore, the authorities and computer manufacturers are attempting to introduce computers in a way which is compatible with the existing formats of teaching, an approach which may offer the worst of all worlds.

With a little understanding of the power which microcomputers have to offer, it is easy to become over enthusiastic about the role they will play in future education. The reality is sketched in a grim report which in 1981 looked at current practices in state-run secondary education in a large British city.

British law demands that all children between five and 16 must

Some teachers are alienated by all forms of technology.

attend school. For a minority of children, and their parents, this requirement is seen as a prison sentence. Even for the majority of pupils this period is turbulent and difficult as puberty interacts against the authority represented by teachers and schools. As a result, the first requirement for any secondary school teacher is to maintain order in the classroom. It is only when the jump to voluntary education is achieved, at 15 or 16 in most Western countries, that the emphasis on order decreases. As a result of this requirement, classroom activities are based on this 'survival imperative', and a custodial element enters a teacher's duties. It is certainly a regrettable fact that in private secondary schools this role is diminished for teachers. Parents choosing to pay twice over for their child's education separate their child from those who come from families which collectively reject education, and the fact that a disruptive pupil can be unceremoniously ejected from a private school, an operation now fraught with difficulties in the state sector, refines the private school pupil population still further.

The study, conducted over an eight-year period, discovered that many teachers maintain classroom order by assigning large amounts of 'seat work', making sure that children stay in their places whilst copying from a blackboard or carrying out written work. In this style of teaching, misbehaviour is easily spotted. The study also noted that many teachers abused this practice and chained pupils to their seats with lengthy written work, to allow the teachers time to prepare for forthcoming lessons or to mark work previously submitted. Preparation undertaken by teachers for lessons averages about 12 minutes per lesson and, if done outside of classroom hours, would mean an extra two hours' work each day for secondary teachers.

Equally depressing statistics revealed that 5% of classrooms did not have enough tables or desks, and 25% did not have any form of storage facilities for materials. The average interaction between teacher and pupils occupied less than 10% of teaching time, and few of the teachers 'roamed' the class during seat work to offer assistance. Under these conditions children's attention spans ranged from two to 30 minutes.

**Financial gloom**

The financial background to this scenario only casts more gloom. The amount of money available to be spent on equipment and materials for British pupils in state-run schools ranged (at the time of the study) from £64 to £23 per pupil per year, with an average figure of £31.80. Basing calculations on the likelihood that secondary school pupils take eight subjects, this level of funding offered £4 per subject per year or approximately 2 pence (5 cents) per lesson per pupil. With these figures it is not surprising that central government has had to subsidise the introduction of microcomputers to schools outside of normal educational budgets, even though education is the largest single item of government expenditure after social security benefits. It is important to realise that most other developed countries do not offer significantly more money for educational materials, and some offer less.

In this tightly constrained situation, the study observed the impact of the introduction of one microcomputer per school. Each use of the computer involved moving it from classroom to classroom or from a secure storage area, setting up the equipment and getting it working. The attention-catching quality of the equipment and the requirement for pupil attendance at the keyboard was observed to be in direct conflict with some teachers' seat-bound discipline techniques, and in these situations the introduction of the technology made little headway.

The setting up of the equipment and running of programs required the teacher's full concentration and thus reduced his ability to maintain order in unruly classes. Whilst programs were run he had to intervene regularly, and as a result the continuity of work away from the computer was disturbed.

### 'Computer studies'

An average of two hours per week was allocated to 'computer studies' in the schools examined during the survey. Allowing 30 minutes of this time for setting up and for activities not associated with the computer, the time available to each pupil at the machine was three minutes per week. As the vast majority of secondary schoolchildren cannot type, their slow keyboard skills limited them to an average of 45 keyboard strokes per week. This then is the reality of 'computer studies' in many British state-run secondary schools. Some other national school systems have made an even worse response to the arrival of the microcomputer.

Anyone who has worked with microcomputers knows the value they have to offer to the pupil. The ideal is that each pupil should have at his or her disposal a microcomputer which will assist in all subjects, but even with the rapidly decreasing cost of computing power, such funding will have to come from outside the existing educational budgets. A precedent has already been established by the fact that many schoolchildren are now supplied with pocket calculators by their parents. Thankfully, microcomputers will become almost as cheap within the next ten years.

Britain's private secondary schools have taken the arrival of the microprocessor very seriously. An organisation called ISMEC (the

Independent Schools' Micro-Electronics Centre) has been formed to act as an information exchange between member schools. Private schools usually have fewer bureaucratic and financial constraints on their purchase of resources, and as a result many are taking a lead in curricula with fully integrated computer assistance.

But what of the children now in state secondary education? Even affluent parents can't supply their sons or daughters with microcomputer systems to take to school. Even if certain children are privileged to own a £50 Sinclair or similar, they will require access to a TV screen or monitor to use it fully and that causes disruption to the smooth running which is the first aim of most secondary schools.

There has to be a fundamental change in schooling to reflect the fact that the teacher has now been joined by another teaching intelligence in the classroom. The extent of this change will be considerable, and it is required at a speed outside of any normal conception of curriculum revision. Research has revealed that gradual curriculum reform takes about 20 years to be effective and planned; engineered reform cannot take place in under five. But change must be put in hand, and methods and ideas are discussed in later chapters.

In the meantime, the results of the British study quoted above (and I am sure of other similar studies around the world) is that computer introduction programs are being shaped to fit the existing educational format. 'Computer studies' is being retained as a separate subject, and the computer wheeled into classrooms like some sort of carnival novelty twice a week. The subject of computing is 'taught' with 80% of the work being paper-based at the pupil's desk. Not surprisingly, the only pupils currently benefiting from such a system are those who are

In the future even the dullest lessons will become interesting.

bright enough to see the potential of the computer. These pupils join the after-hours' computer clubs and quickly develop into the 'star' pupils who are trotted out whenever a school is required to justify its response to the challenge of microtechnology. In practice these children tend to be allocated more time on the computer than is their fair share, thus making a bad situation even worse.

In the USA the resources situation is generally easier, although the standard of teacher-training in microcomputing is very low. Most teachers in middle and senior schools receive only 15 minutes training before they begin to use microcomputers in the classroom and, as a result, they tend to use the machine for CAI, supporting and reinforcing their present teaching approach.

In order to balance this pessimistic view of the short-term educational response to computing, it is worth examining one educationalist's view of future education in US high schools. Imagine a class of 50 pupils in an English lesson, the class staffed by one teacher and one assistant. Eight microcomputers are provided, and whilst one half of the class works on the computers in small group projects, the other half watches an interactive movie on a video tape which is under microcomputer control. This group supplies plot development decisions and governs the development of the story. This futuristic scene suggests that the technology has somehow converted reluctant and often downright hostile adolescents into interested students at the flick of a button. In the company of many experts, I believe this to be possible, and the present negative impact of a large number of mediocre teachers will be offset by the vital interaction between human and artificial intelligence in the new computer age.

**Data banks**

We can be certain that the imminent partnership between telecommunications and microcomputing will remove some of the idiosyncracies from computer use in individual schools. For the past couple of years data banks such as the USD's CompuServe have offered a large amount of information and many programs over the telephone lines. A subscriber to the service can connect his or her computer to the telephone line and gather news and information about entertainment, sport, travel, financial dealings, etc., but he or she can also use the service for more serious applications such as collecting programs from the central data base. There are now 1,450 data bases in the USA available for access by telephone.

A similar, but less ambitious system is being developed by Prestel, British Telecom's data base. Prestel is experimenting with holding a library of educational programs which will be made available to all Prestel subscribers. This system allows a user to dial into the Prestel computer and then 'down-load' (transfer) programs from the central data base into his or her own computer.

Also in Britain an even more exciting development is under way. Called Telesoftware, the system (undergoing trials at the time of writing) broadcasts computer programs through the air which are received by an 'intelligent' Teletext television. Britain has, of course, led the world with its Prestel, Ceefax and Oracle television/telephone data base connections, and if the trials of Telesoftware continue as well as they have started, a unique system will have been set up.

By the autumn of 1983 the system will be broadcasting programs alongside conventional schools' television broadcasts, and the need for a television with a built-in computer will have disappeared: schools will be able to hook up their own computers to the television set. This will allow schools to view an educational television programme, to down-load the computer program which was transmitted over the air and then pursue the projects started during the television programme using the computer programs. With the addition of video, it will be possible for schools to record both television programme and computer program for reuse at any time. It is anticipated that many home computer owners will tune into this system and gain 'free' software from the air, but this is understood by the organisers (the BBC and Brighton Polytechnic among them). More importantly schools will be able to pluck their library of educational software out of the air.

# LOGO–A LANGUAGE CHILDREN AND COMPUTERS CAN UNDERSTAND

Logo is a computer language specifically developed to allow children 'natural' access to artificial intelligence, and it is principally the work of a man called Seymour Papert.

Papert is an American Professor of Mathematics and a researcher into the subject of how children learn and, more specifically, how they learn when they are assisted and stimulated by computer intelligence. During the 1960s he worked in Switzerland with Jean Piaget, the Swiss psychologist and educator who developed so much of our current thinking about a child's learning process. This is not the place to discuss the theory of 'Piagetian learning', but the two principal arguments which developed from his work were that a child will learn automatically from his experiences provided he is supplied with the right materials with which to build and that a child's ability to learn develops in clearly defined steps linked to age chronology. Piaget says that up to two years old a child develops strictly from sensory input. From two to seven children can think beyond their immediate situation but are only able to handle concrete concepts. After seven children begin to make the leap into the abstract when, for example, counting is done mentally and not on the fingers. At about 11 Piaget suggests children begin to think in fully abstract terms, as adults, becoming capable of considering problems totally unrelated to their physical or mental environment. The majority of educators have accepted Piaget's theories.

In the late 1960s Seymour Papert returned to America and went to work in the Artificial Intelligence Laboratory of the Massachusetts Institute of Technology. This institute is hallowed ground in the field of educational research, and Papert began to probe the potential use of computers in early education. When Papert started work, the only computers available were the large university mainframes, and the concept of small powerful machines had not arrived.

## Programmers aged 4

Working with a small team, Papert developed Logo to allow children – even children as young as 4 – to program computers. The main thrust of Papert's argument is that children must be put in command of this new technology: they must not be commanded by it. In Papert's own words 'the child programs the computer instead of the computer programming the child'.

These words are taken from *Mindstorms*, an influential book published by Papert in 1980 which explained his theories (and offered some practical evidence to back them up) and which provoked considerable re-evaluation of teaching techniques as a whole throughout the world's educational community.

It may seem an obvious imperative that a child should be taught to control a computer, but a glance into many elementary school classrooms in which a computer has been installed will reveal that the reverse is happening only too often.

Most of the work that has been done on providing programs for classroom use has been based on the expectations of traditionalist teachers who ask for programs which reinforce old methods. Only rarely have attempts been made to re-evaluate these methods in the light of such a significant arrival as artificial intelligence. Many of these reinforcement programs which have been developed are quite sophisticated, and their main aim is to drill and test children. My six-year-old daughter happily answers the computer when it asks her whether Boston is a noun, and the spoken praise and little tune it plays when she provides the right answer is quite encouraging. Equally, the sad 'try again' and the low note that is emitted when she gets the answer wrong clearly indicate that she must try again.

This type of computer application is currently the most widespread and stretches around the world throughout the education systems. It is not hard to program a computer to ask questions, monitor the answers and provide scores. Some programs almost completely replace the teacher's role in this respect. In geography, for example an advanced program may introduce the student to the River Nile with an attractive graphic map on the screen in full colour. The computer may slowly 'scroll' along the length of the river providing a written or spoken commentary as it does so. Every so often this panorama may be halted as the computer asks the child for input: 'How many countries does the Nile flow through?' The child's response may be correct, may require correction or may provoke an additional comment from the machine; but no matter how complex and sophisticated this type of program, the computer is drilling, i.e. programming the student.

### The child in control

Papert argues that this system should be turned on its head. He wants the child to grasp the computer and create a program to answer the questions the child wants to ask about the River Nile. (Clearly a child will need assistance to discover which are the right questions to ask.) In justification of his plea, Papert returns to his Piagetian source and points out that children learn far better by doing than by being told. Although he refrains from quoting it in his book, I do not hesitate to requote the old Chinese proverb: 'I am told, I forget. I am shown, I remember. I do, and I understand.' I consider this sums up part of his thinking.

Papert actually goes on to disagree with some tenets of Piagetian law. He suggests that computers can break down the barriers which stop a child grasping abstract concepts before a certain age and, as proof, advances case histories from junior schools in which he has tested his theories. It is this digression from approved theories which provokes the majority of criticism about his 'strategy' for learning. Although many educators have cautiously penned critical questions about Papert's work, the results of the increasingly widespread application of his methods around the world seem to bear out much of

*Seymour Papert.*    his argument. Today even the most ardent critic suggests only that

more information is needed before the Papertian approach to computer-based learning can be finally assessed.

The present versions of Logo (there are several) were initially developed over a ten-year period, and the structure of the language has proved good enough to please expert programmers as well as teachers who apply it in kindergartens. As a measure of the importance of Papert's work, and of the acceptance of Logo as a vital tool in introducing the young to computers, it is worth noting that implementations of the language have been made, at huge expense, by computer manufacturers including Texas Instruments, Apple, Atari, Sinclair, RML, Tandy (Radio Shack) and Acorn (makers of the BBC Microcomputer) with another five versions currently being prepared for other manufacturers' machines. A significant number of American schools have started to use Logo, and in Britain the Artificial Intelligence Laboratory at Edinburgh University has spent years investigating the language. Seymour Papert has spent the last two years advising the French government on the introduction of computers into elementary education.

## BASIC

The majority of educational computer programming carried out in the United States, Britain, Germany, Canada, Australia and the USSR is currently done in a computer language called 'BASIC'. This language was developed at Dartmouth College in America in the 1960s, and the name is an acronym of Beginners All-purpose Symbolic Instruction Code. This language is relatively easy to use for simple programming by children of 11 upwards, but once a program takes on any complexity, the language becomes convoluted and hard to use and encourages shortcuts which computer experts describe as 'sloppy' programming. Until now it has been thought that the right approach is to start children on BASIC programming and switch them to another language as they develop, but already considerable argument has developed in Europe with a strong case being presented for a switch to a beginner's language called COMAL, which is a distant descendant of the now quite antiquated BASIC. It is arguable whether children should be taught formally to program computers at all, but in this context I use the phrase programming to mean 'controlling' computers. The complexities of full computer programming are, quite properly, a completely separate science.

BASIC was built into small microcomputers in the mid 1970s because it did not require the availability of a great amount of memory power – indeed the little Timex/Sinclair computers run the language happily on minute memories. At first BASIC appears remarkably easy to use. For example, entering the command:

# ▇ LOGO – A LANGUAGE CHILDREN AND COMPUTERS CAN UNDERSTAND

10 PRINT "HELLO"

commands the computer to display 'HELLO' on the screen, although nothing will happen until a second command is added. (The number '10' at the beginning of the line of command is called a line number and exists to inform the computer of the sequence of instructions. Although the command could have been numbered as line '1', numbering instructions in tens – 10, 20, 30, etc. – allows instructions to be inserted later between previously written lines.) The second command necessary to make this word, 'HELLO', appear as intended is 'RUN'. The word 'HELLO' will then appear once on the screen. Enlarging the program by adding a second line:

20 GOTO 10

instructs the computer to go back and repeat the command that was first given. Thus, on 'RUN', the computer executes line 10, seeks the next command, finds line 20 which tells it to 'GOTO' (go back to) line 10. It does this, carries out the order in line 10, looks for the next command, and so the 'loop' program continues, displaying 'HELLO' repetitively until stopped. This is not difficult for an 11-year-old to grasp, nor indeed for a seven-year-old. But once BASIC programs set about trying to find the solution to problems, or start trying to draw on screens, the programs require the knowledge of formulae and a considerable amount of program entry before anything happens. This leap into the abstract lies the other side of the 11-year-old barrier Piaget identified, and even Seymour Papert considers that younger children will not easily be able to use BASIC.

Computer languages can be accurately compared to spoken languages. In his book Papert considers the differences between American school children learning French in American classrooms and the same children learning French while in France. Papert and his team have developed Logo as a language which can be learned as though the student were in 'Mathland' – an imaginary computer country which provides the programming equivalent of a French-language student visiting France.

A computer language is a form of communication which is understood by both the programmer and the computer. It follows that if the language is close to the programmer's native language (for many, English), it will be easier to learn than a language more removed. Papert took this as his touchstone and developed Logo so that English-language commands would cause a computer to do something. This is vital if young children are to accept that they can control machine intelligence.

# ■ LOGO – A LANGUAGE CHILDREN AND COMPUTERS CAN UNDERSTAND

### The turtle

*The floor turtle. This robot is at the heart of the Logo computer language for children. This version is 'The Edinburgh Turtle', made by Jessop Acoustics of London, which evolved out of the research into Logo undertaken by the Artificial Intelligence Department at Edinburgh University, Scotland.*

At the heart of the Logo approach to computer programming is a turtle. This 'creature' exists in both physical and abstract form and provides a blissfully easy introduction to the idea of getting a computer to do something.

For the youngest children, three and upwards, the turtle takes the form of a robot – a transparent plastic dome 9in (23cm) across, which houses an electric motor and a pen and which runs about the floor on wheels. This plastic, clearly mechanical turtle is attached to a computer by a long cable. The computer sends commands to the turtle. Children are introduced to this beast and told that the turtle will do their bidding if they talk to it in 'turtle talk'.

It is anticipated and intended that children will treat the turtle like a toy and will want to 'make it go'. The turtle is placed on a large sheet of paper in the middle of the floor, and the teacher or parent introducing the child to the turtle discusses which way the child wants the turtle to move. 'Forward' is a likely suggestion and the teacher, with the child's help, types 'FORWARD' into the computer. One other decision remains to be made by the child. 'How far forward?' asks the teacher. 'How many steps?' The child considers, and in some instances will walk forward a few steps as he or she thinks. A confident child will provide a suggestion, another child may need a little coaxing. The teacher adds a number to the command: 'FORWARD 10', for example. The moment the teacher 'Enters' the command to the computer – telling the computer to implement the command – the turtle runs forward a short distance, drawing a line behind it on the paper – a kind of 'turtle trail'.

Such an action is a huge novelty to a young child and quickly he or she is asking for the experiment to be repeated, or for the turtle to do other things. Very soon the edge of the paper, or the child's imagination, will prompt a request for the turtle to turn. The teacher asks the child how the turtle should turn and most children respond by turning around themselves. 'So you stay in the same spot, but turn either right or left?' The child must agree with this logic, and the teacher asks the child to choose a direction, assisting in the naming of right or left where necessary. The teacher types 'RIGHT' into the computer, and then asks the child, 'How far right shall we make it turn?' With the teacher's guidance the child considers by turning his or her own body. A suggestion, '10', is added to the instruction 'RIGHT', the command Entered and the turtle moves slightly to the right. It is still not facing the way the child would like, and the amount of turn can then be explored. The adult reader will guess that '90 steps' ensures a right-angle turn and 180 a complete about-turn. But this is something a child must explore.

79

### 'Heuristic' methods

In this procedure the child relates the movement of the turtle to his or her own physical movement, and expresses commands – through his teacher – which cause physical effect. Of course, the child has begun to learn geometry, and the pen inside the turtle, which can be raised or lowered on command, provides the physical proof on the paper. Papert argues that lessons learned in this way, through relating computer-controlled movement to physical knowledge (which the child has already learned as he or she learned to walk and move), are far better learned than by attempting to explain them in abstract. Papert suggests that geometry, the mathematical expression of our physical world, can be learned many years earlier than conventional methods allow and that this advantage is also available when computer technology is correctly applied to help children teach themselves by 'heuristic' (experimental) methods. It is right to point out that many primary school teachers are already encouraging young children to explore basic geometry by helping the child to explore movement with his own body, but Papert's turtle, leaving its vital turtle trail, builds a bridge between the physical and abstract notions of distance and angle.

The above scene suggests how a three- or four-year-old might be introduced to the turtle at the time of writing. But by the time this book is published it is likely that the teacher's interpretative role between the child and the turtle will be reduced. Several educators working with Logo have developed systems by which nursery children can control the turtle by pressing just one key on a computer keyboard. Indeed, the existing Logo languages allow the commands to be abbreviated as 'FD 50' for 'FORWARD 50', 'RT 90' for 'RIGHT 90', 'BK 10' for 'BACK 10' and so on. An abbreviated version of Logo that is concerned only with the turtle and not with other aspects of this wide-ranging language, is available in Britain with a floor turtle originally designed by Edinburgh University. In this version of Logo, single key commands control the movement of the turtle.

Once the concept that the turtle will move under the control of the computer is grasped, the teacher can introduce the next, *and most important*, concept: the computer/turtle can be taught to remember how to do things. The turtle can draw a square on a piece of paper, and the computer told to remember the sequence. After that, the child or teacher has only to tell the turtle to 'SQUARE', or 'SQ', for the turtle to execute the square. This 'program', or procedure, as Papert prefers to call it, can be joined to other procedures remembered by the computer, and complex geometric drawing can take place. The next step is to help the child discover that the procedure may be adapted, the size of the square altered, for instance, just by altering a 'variable'. So the concepts of programming are learned.

### A leap into the abstract

Once a child reaches six or seven, the whole situation can take a small leap into the abstract. Although the use of a physical floor turtle is of tremendous help, the concept can be introduced on the computer screen where a small triangle of light, called a turtle, sits in the middle of the screen awaiting identical commands to its floor-bound ancestor.

There are many other aspects to the Logo language which I describe in Chapter 9, all designed to be building blocks from which the child can construct 'models' and problem-solving techniques. The language is powerful enough to sustain development from the nursery through to the secondary school, although in the versions currently available its facilities for tackling abstract numerical tasks are limited, and the child who wishes to develop into programming proper will have to switch to another language. It is likely, however, that Logo itself will be significantly extended, and the fuller versions of the language, at present only available on large computers, will also be found on microcomputers.

Papert considers that an important aspect of computer learning, and of learning as a whole, is 'the bug'. In computer jargon a 'bug' is a fault in a computer program. Such a fault invariably occurs because the human creating the problem has overlooked a logical step or has failed to give the computer appropriate commands; for example when writing a procedure to tell the turtle to draw a square, the programmer may have forgotten to tell the turtle to make a right turn at the last corner. Thus the computer fails to execute the program properly, and the programmer must go back to his program to investigate his error. The majority of computer programs do not work properly the first time they are tried. The ultra-flexible nature of the computer immediately allows the programmer to go back, find and correct the error and try again. The program may still not work properly, and the programmer may again have to examine his logic or execution of a program to discover and finally iron out any fault. Papert suggests that the concept of the persistent bug is one that we can usefully transfer to all learning patterns.

Imagine a class of 11-year-olds asked to write an essay on that evergreen subject, 'What I Did on My Holidays'. The traditional educational approach is to mark each child's composition against the following parameters:

1   handwriting
2   use of language
3   spelling and grammar
4   general presentation
5   imagination.

The priority given to individual aspects will vary from teacher to teacher and culture to culture, the better teachers putting imagination nearer the top, others preferring to award marks for spelling and grammatical construction. But Papert upturns these conventions by suggesting that the child should write the compositions on a word-processor.

## Word-processing

A word-processor is a computer which is operating a program to allow text to be edited on the screen. The program allows the user to type words, delete them, move them around and generally correct text, with the computer making all the necessary adjustments to the 'page' to ensure that the finished text looks like a perfectly typed sheet. Many word-processing programs incorporate dictionaries which compare words typed by the user with a list of words held in computer memory, highlighting any that are not recognised. In this way, typing and spelling mistakes are reduced with the aid of the computer. With this sort of computing power, the essay writer may begin his or her story about a holiday by the sea, and as it develops paragraphs may be moved about to improve the flow of the story, change the chronology of events or insert items that were forgotten on the first draft. He or she may even consider each word in each sentence, savouring it for its

In essay writing a computer can encourage the development of the critical faculty

style and use of language.

In the paper-based classroom today's 11-year-old gets little opportunity to approach writing in this way. The 'rough books' provided to encourage trial workings are invariably used for other purposes. The effort of writing and rewriting an essay is too much for most adults, let alone children. The pupil's first thought must be to the presentation of his essay, and a page which contains moved paragraphs, deleted and inserted words and similar major revisions would indicate to many conventional teachers an inability to be decisive in narrative and a thoroughly sloppy approach. Poor marks would be given. Papert, and many others, argue that our present system concentrates on developing precisely the opposite qualities to those which are desirable.

The concept of the 'bug', so firmly embedded in computer consciousness, is in fact the concept of critical appraisal. Allowing children to read and reread their essays before completion in the knowledge that they may alter and adapt it to their heart's content without having to rewrite it (while still being able to supply a perfectly clean and clear printed sheet to their teacher) encourages them to consider fully all the decisions they have taken in working on the story. This encourages the development of the critical faculty – an ability which usually does not start developing in Western school children until they are much older. Then it has to be fostered by teachers as pupils begin to consider their logic and writing techniques when they prepare for examinations before college or university. The computer allows the techniques to develop as soon as the child starts to write. But teachers will have to adapt to such a situation in order that advantage may be taken of this power.

### Logic and handwriting

Many traditionalists would question such approaches, pointing to the inevitable deterioration in handwriting skills and lamenting that children will not have to think an essay through before committing themselves to paper. But although handwriting must still be taught, the opportunity and requirement for its use in the computer-served future will be quite limited. Logical consideration of the form of the essay is a vital point, but the foreknowledge that change can be effected at any point during the composition must surely develop the sort of logical thought which currently seems all too rare. If examinations continue to test a candidate's ability to express him or herself first time, the experience of creating a composition in a flexible environment will have familiarised the student with the concept of 'thought rearrangement', and he or she will be more able to undertake this process before committing himself to paper.

The 'critical appraisal and reappraisal' approach made possible by the computer in essay writing is also available in other disciplines such as mathematics, art and music. Computer contributions in these areas will be discussed in later chapters, but the importance of a child growing up with the concept that every creation must be worked on to be perfected – the 'bug' concept – is one that must not be overlooked.

Texas Instruments in Dallas were the first company to implement a version of the Logo language for a microcomputer in 1978. This was the TI 99/4A Home Computer, now superseded by the 99/4A. For this tiny, but advanced, machine, Seymour Papert developed a truncated version of the language he had previously used on huge university computers and tested in schools in Massachusetts. Not surprisingly, one of the first schools to start using the TI version of Logo was a school close to the Texas headquarters, the Lamplighter School. The founder of Texas Instruments is described as a 'long-term friend and underwriter' of the school.

The Lamplighter School is of the type most teachers and parents would describe as 'progressive'. This epithet has almost become a sneer, and it is surely a symptom of the ultra-conservative thinking that surrounds education that the adjective of the noun progress should have become a sneer when used in the context of education! Perhaps this has developed because so much change has been attempted merely for the sake of change, but with the arrival of the microcomputer, some change is now imperative. The Lamplighter School is a private school consisting of 450 pupils and running under a regime which 'provides no report cards, rings no period bells and allows children to work at their own pace in non-competitive situations'. This description is quoted from a report on Lamplighter's experience with Logo which was submitted by the school's teachers to the American magazine *Microcomputing*.

**Integrated computers**

Whatever you may think of a school that bends over backwards to break many rules considered sacrosanct in other institutions, its Logo experiences make interesting reading. Computers are integrated into the curriculum at Lamplighter, and the staff are aware that they are learning alongside their pupils. Children work with the computer every day, and the level of equipment is sufficiently high to allow small groups to work with computers for long periods, children often being able to work with Logo on a one-to-one basis. Pre-school pupils are introduced to Logo via four procedures written by a Lamplighter teacher which enable the children to experiment with concepts of shape, colour, direction and speed using just one-key commands to the computer. In primary grades Logo graphics are introduced and children are often instructed using their own body to 'play turtle'.

The staff report that careful questioning can reveal insights into the children's concepts of movement, direction and distance, and once the child progresses to the computer keyboard he is able to experiment with shapes, discovering, as the teacher reports, 'that a square has four equal sides and that it took four equal turtle turns to make the corners'. Another child might discover a triangle and a rectangle, and the two children might work together to draw a house.

Of course, the children at the Lamplighter School, and in the other schools which are adopting Logo as an introduction to computers, are encouraged to translate the physical discoveries they make into formal learning, absorbing the concepts as they go.

### Small group activity

Group activity is something which a computer seems to encourage rather than discourage, providing the group is only two or three in size. Many critics of computers in education cite as a major problem the isolation which might occur when a child interacts in solitary communion with a machine. (Indeed, they cite the isolation that will occur in society generally as computers reduce the need to travel.) But the experience at Lamplighter, and at almost every school which has introduced computers whether on a computer-aided instruction or computer-aided learning basis, is that there is much to be gained when small groups work with computers.

Group discussion around the computer has proved to be an extremely powerful force as two or three children discuss what is wrong with a program and offer suggestions for improving it. Computers are now being cited as the cause of pupil interaction rather than as the destroyer of it. Because Logo has now been in use over several years in American schools, a few research teams have had time to deliver preliminary findings. A research group from the Bank Street College of Education, New York – a teacher-training college – has discovered that much more cooperation and collaboration goes on around the computer than in other classroom activities and that children are much more likely to call on their peers for help with computer programming than with other tasks. The group noted that, although teachers start out ahead in their knowledge and usage of Logo, children rapidly catch up and often overtake.

Another part of the study asked children which of their peers they would consult for help on a variety of problems, maths, spelling and other skills as well as computer use. The purpose of this test was to see whether the class's acknowledged experts retained their position as leaders during computer use. What emerged was that, while there was no class consensus about the best pupils at other subjects, two or three pupils were regarded by the class as outright leaders in computer use. This emergence of particularly gifted children during computer-assisted learning is a subject I will return to in a later chapter, but it is interesting to note that very often these computer stars are often also-rans in all other academic stakes.

A disturbing comment contained in the Bank Street interim report, and one that has been echoed and repeated elsewhere, is that girls are far less keen to use computer technology than boys. This is another subject which receives fuller attention in later chapters, but it seems that even Seymour Papert's alternative approach to CAL fails to redress this imbalance.

Logo was designed as a language in which children could communicate easily with computers, but its simplicity is also proving of great use in other educational areas.

Elsewhere in this book I have painted a rather gloomy picture about the state of contemporary conventional education. I am anxious not to detract from the outstanding work which millions of gifted and dedicated teachers are doing year after year, but it is again necessary to refer to the poor standard of student teachers in order to describe a particularly useful application of Logo.

## Mathphobia

Although I have so far avoided the subject, one of the central themes of Papert's book is that in the past many children (now adults) have developed mathphobia – a maths block – during education. Papert considers that such blocks usually develop through poor teaching and lack of suitable models during childhood and states that for the vast majority of sufferers help may be available from Logo. Work undertaken by the Artificial Intelligence Department of Edinburgh University seems to bear out this claim. Studies have found that a depressingly large proportion of students entering teacher-training colleges are innumerate. This is a major problem. College students are usually unhappy to admit to total incompetence in mathematical concepts at such a late stage in their education and are likely to have managed to learn sufficient maths techniques to mask their inabilities until they are confronted with the need to explain their procedures to others. Using computers and Logo, the Department has worked with groups of innumerate student teachers and found that the language allows them to visualise and express concepts which have previously eluded them. In this way many have been able to grasp mathematical principles for the first time in their lives.

Educationalists demand a pedagogical explanation of an educational procedure, and the Edinburgh team sum up the Logo approach as follows: 'The rationale behind this Logo-based approach is, first, that the activity is fun and intriguing and should break down the student's negative attitude to the subject. Second, writing a computer program about a mathematical topic forces the student to confront that topic and her understanding of it. Third, use of the computer's graphic capability provides a visual, and possibly dynamic, illustration of a topic the student might otherwise find hard to visualise. For example, a student who has trouble visualising multiplication of fractions can run a program that illustrates this idea in a series of diagrams, seeing how that program behaves with fractions of her own choice.' (That extract is taken from 'Re-learning Mathematics Through Logo', a paper by Benedict du Boulay and Jim How published in *Microcomputers in Secondary Education*, London 1981).

That particular explanation of how Logo works might apply as well to an eight-year-old as to an eighteen-year-old. The child, however, is unlikely to start with any of the negative attitudes developed by the student.

During my limited experience of introducing Logo to children I have come across a few children who become impatient with the turtle and other introductory aspects of the language and press for the sort of applied problem-solving results associated with languages such as BASIC and COMAL. These children seem to approach computers in a way similar to the adult approach mentioned at the beginning of Chapter 1 – demanding computer help for specific problems. This is very much a minority reaction to Logo, and these children probably have an instinctively healthy attitude to computing – one that would please Seymour Papert. His aim, and the adopted aim of an increasing band of educators, is that children should harness the potential of the computer and feel confident to use it to help solve the problems they will meet in life.

# COMPUTERS FOR THE UNDER-11s

There are really two separate groups of children in the under-11 category: the under-8s and the 8- to 11-year-olds. In many countries, schooling is split into three groups with children attending an elementary school (including a kindergarten), a middle or junior high school and a secondary or high school.

Children can benefit from contact with computers as soon as they enter the kindergarten, and some basic skills, such as reading and arithmetic, can be taught with computer aid to ensure a solid foundation in the subject. But, apart from anything else, young children find computers to be enormous FUN!

Despite this, some parents are offended by the idea of their five-year-old child spending hours staring at a screen. Some consider it simply as a screen-based activity and prefer to encourage other activities such as play, outdoor pursuits and 'creative' occupations such as painting, reading and model-making. Many teachers report that some parents resist the idea of any screen-based occupations entering a child's life before the child is 11 or so. Although there is no medical evidence that damage can be caused to child or adult from moderate close-up use of TV or computer screens,* trades unions and medical researchers are concerned about long-period exposure for adult workers. Symptoms attributed to such exposure include headaches and eye-strain, and for any adult undertaking long sessions of close-up screen work doctors advise that short rests away from the screen every hour are better than longer rests between longer working periods. There is, however, no evidence that normal use of a TV or computer screen causes any problems for children. Young children are usually too active to undertake the long concentrated screen sessions which seem to be causing problems for some adult screen workers.

But there is a phobia about screens. Some parents even go so far as to ban television from the home. Many of these parents are

---

* Colour televisions made before 1970 may be unsuitable. Recent US research has revealed that sets from this period are capable of emitting a low level of radiation. This has no effect when a TV is used normally, but it is possible that the 'close-up' use necessary for computer work could cause some problems.

themselves resistant to computers and 'gadget technology' and wish to encourage their children in their own preferences and prejudices. This is their privilege, of course, but it is for this reason that elementary schools have a vital role to play in demonstrating to young children that artificial intelligence is a friendly tool which can be used by everybody and is not something which belongs to scientists, maths wizards or academic achievers.

In Chapter 4 I mentioned that Seymour Papert has identified the 'maths block' as being the root cause of much adult suspicion about computers: adults who feel threatened by (or uneasy with) computer technology are unlikely to purchase a microcomputer for their young children and often adopt a superior stance to justify their exclusion. The problem is that these parents inevitably pass on their phobias to their children and make it very much more difficult for them to use computers later in their school career.

Even rational parents worry about the amount of television their children watch. In Britain children are currently watching an average of 19 hours of television a week, while in the USA the figure is nearer 30 hours. Few worthwhile studies have been done on the effect of prolonged television viewing on children, but what is certain is that television is an entirely passive occupation. It is sometimes educational, often entertaining, but it is never interactive. Some cable TV stations are pioneering the development of interactive TV in which viewers participate in shows, but even when this two-way facility is fully developed it is unlikely to be used for more than vote gathering or 'armchair shopping'. At its best television is stimulating, challenging and informative; but quality is rare, and most TV programming is mediocre and opiate both in stance and content. Most parents instinctively feel it is right to steer their children away from such passive pursuits.

The computer is the most mentally active pursuit it is possible to find, *providing the computer is used in the right way*. Once a child has learned that a computer can assist in the discovery of the world it will be hard to prise him or her away from it. In the chapter on Logo, I described the sort of approach currently being used to demonstrate computer-power to the very young – the fours and fives – but most children will not meet microcomputers until they go to school and, even then, often not until they are seven or older. One exception is a Montessori nursery school in Wynnewood, Pennsylvania. Here children work with an Apple computer from the age of two playing 'games' in which the computer responds to curious key-prods by displaying the corresponding letter on the screen in colour and playing a short tune. The computer (with programs) was introduced to the school by computer-programmer parents, and many other pre-school nurseries have begun experiments with similar 'reactional' programs.

It is in primary education that we have the greatest chance to use computers effectively. Children over 11 are having a difficult time at school. They are being forced to meet computers in a role outside their usual school curriculum at the same time as having to prepare either to leave school or to take examinations which will allow them to go on to further education. Because it is so urgent that these children leave school with *some* idea of how computers can be used, governments and school authorities have naturally concentrated on providing computer education for this age group first. This education is at the moment patchy and unsatisfactory, and because the syllabus of the secondary and high school is so well defined and tailored to examination requirements, computers may stay outside the main curriculum for some years to come.

Computers should be integrated into everyday class work for the under-11s. The concept of a 'computer room' or of 'computer studies' indicates that the school considers computers to be outside their normal curriculum, and pupils are led to believe that computing is a subject as separate and individual as geography and physical education.

## Computers and the humanities

Computers can help in the music room, the history lesson, the French class and the hiking school. Nearly all school activities will benefit from computer back-up. Ten-year-olds working in a British classroom have recently been discovering the secrets of the *Mary Rose* (the recently salvaged Tudor warship) using a program which includes 20 working drawings of the stretch of water in which the wreck was discovered, a booklet and comprehensive teachers' notes. In the first part of the program, the user moves over the seabed trying to spot an anomaly between the charts and the screen information. Accidental finds may include an old boot, a tin can or even a Russian submarine! As well as the *Mary Rose* project, other excellent primary school programs include such simulations as the exploration of an Egyptian tomb and an interplanetary space trip. Historical investigation is spurred on by the ability to search through data bases for maximum information on events, people or places which will foster interest in the period without bogging young minds down in laborious library searches. In English the word-processor frees the young author from the restraints of pen and paper, and in mathematics the child is able to build a model of the world around him from which to learn.

Computers must be used as tools capable of doing all these things. The element which prohibits this approach in many schools (especially secondary schools) is the reluctance or inability of the geography or English teacher to learn how to use the computer. When the British Open University recently produced a 'teacher awareness pack' for uninitiated teachers, they felt it necessary to include brightly coloured sticky labels which the teacher is instructed to paste on to connecting plugs and sockets for easy identification. Such desperate measures reflect desperate problems.

Another severely limiting factor is the shortage of computing resources. If a primary school has only one microcomputer, how can it be used simultaneously by the class doing nature studies and the class learning about American Indians? Security is another problem which places restrictions on free computer movement within a school. If microcomputers are left in ordinary classrooms they may be stolen.

Because of these problems, computers are often kept in 'resource centres' or 'computer rooms', and the one or two staff members who are 'computer mad' take over the role of custodian/enthusiast. As a result computers become separate from the main thrust of a school's curriculum, a role which is the opposite of the one they will play in a child's later life.

'I loathe computer studies.' I heard this sentiment expressed by many adolescents during my research for this book, and I can sympathise with them. For many it means that computer studies consist of 80% paper-based seat work (see Chapter 3), followed by three minutes weekly work at the computer keyboard. In this time the non-typist pupil may hesitantly be able to enter 45 keystrokes. If computers are presented in this way, we can be sure we are turning out children as unfitted for the information age as they would be for the Stone Age.

**Computers in primary schools**

The teaching style described by these unfortunates also appears in primary schools, but in a less clearly defined way. Because the academic pressure *should* be less in the primary school, the opportunity exists for children to explore their environment in a less pressured way. In this atmosphere computers should be introduced gently into ordinary classrooms where children can with a little prompting discover computer power for themselves. Whether this happens or not depends on two things: the willingness of class teachers to learn about computers, and the availability of computers in education.

Working on the assumption that teachers will invest the time and energy to discover how a microcomputer works (and discover how to match coloured labels in order to push the right plugs into the right sockets), it is still necessary for primary teachers to rethink their approach to their job. Most teachers work from habit. Over the years they develop tried and tested methods of imparting information, and the great temptation for them must be to use the computer to back-up or to duplicate their existing teaching methods. In one case a British study (quoted in Chapter 3) actually went so far as to plan a method of microcomputer introduction which was designed to slot directly into existing methods of teaching. This approach makes nonsense of the benefit computers have to offer and merely provides some additional *instruction* for the children.

While schools attempt to adapt to the computer age (with differing degrees of success), parents lucky enough to be able to afford to buy a microcomputer are well advised to compensate at home for educational shortcomings. But choosing the right computer for your child requires careful consideration.

Computers exist in many forms. There is a flood of electronic games which are meant principally for entertainment, but there are some computer-based toys which, as well as being fun, have a very serious application.

If your boy or girl is attracted to toy cars *and* gadgets, it is hard to beat the 'Bigtrak,' or a similar programmable toy, as an introduction to the concept of programming. This large plastic 'Tonka Truck' type toy has a built-in microprocessor which allows the child to program the path the truck will follow. Using the program buttons, the child can work out how the truck will travel in a circle or a square, and by entering the appropriate commands – and making mistakes and correcting them – he or she will discover the concept of teaching

*The Bigtrak: is it a toy, or a learning tool? Toys such as this are crossing the traditional boundaries and, while a child can have enormous fun with such a machine, the programming steps necessary to make this 'tank' follow the desired route, provide a vivid demonstration of computer-control.*

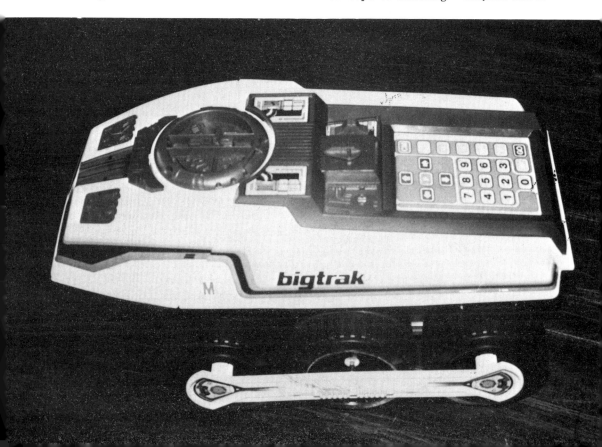

machines what to do. The problem with the Bigtrak (and other similar programmable toys) is that it only does one thing. However interesting it is to program, most children will tire of it after a while.

## Sexual discrimination

Some fathers reading about the programmable truck may regard it as a boy's toy. In traditional terms, there is no doubt that is how a toy truck would be considered. This raises an important and worrying point about how children are learning about computers. There seems to be great sexual discrimination against females in computing.

It is highly unlikely that many teachers or parents are deliberately introducing boys to computers while excluding girls, but it appears that some element in the way we are currently presenting microtechnology to our children is discriminatory. It is in the under-8 age group that such trends can be nipped in the bud most easily and, conversely, the group in which such prejudices are most easily laid down.

In the British 11–18 age group 'microchip inequality' has taken a firm hold. Two out of three candidates for computing examinations in 1982 were male – even though the overall number of candidates rose by 40% in 1981 and 50% in 1982. The situation is so serious that an area education committee in Britain has requested a large grant from the Equal Opportunities Commission specifically to help introduce more primary and middle school girls to computers. At the time, the Chief Education Officer for the area was quoted as saying, 'the project was designed to help combat the general feeling that computers are essentially a matter for boys.'

*Personal Computer World*, the UK's leading monthly computer magazine, estimates that female readers account for only 0.4% of its readership.

Complaints have been laid at the door of some computer manufacturers, and some are guilty of running advertisements in which a father and son are depicted at work on the microcomputer while being admiringly watched by mother and daughter. But the problem seems deeper than this, and it may well be that the deep-seated inequality which still exists in our society is being shown up in high-relief under the glare of the spotlight on microcomputing. University entrance in Britain is still split 9.3 boys for every 6.8 girls.

Even when computers and computer training are provided specifically for girls, there is a danger that if the girls are over 11 they will be taught applications designed to fit their sex role, such as word-processing, which are intended to prepare them for the clearly defined functions society has earmarked for them.

Some may argue that gadgets appeal less to the female than the male mind, but it is vital that the power within the computer's tangle of wires and buttons is released to benefit everybody. Thankfully, computers are getting less and less gadget-like each year, and within a very short space of time will operate without tedious connections, temperamental breakdowns and bug-riddled software, problems which were the hallmark of the first generation of home computers.

Perhaps the fact that in most countries around 80% of primary school teachers are female has a bearing on this problem. (In Japan female teachers in elementary schools make up 56.6% of the teaching staff.) If the majority of those women teachers suffered sexual pigeonholing during their own childhoods, they are ill-placed to deal with any subject such as computers which, by them, would be seen as a 'male' subject. Evidence for this theory is supplied by Britain's National Union of Teachers. At a recent annual conference on microcomputers in education, organised by the NUT, only 13% of delegates were women, and even this tiny percentage was achieved only *after* positive attempts to include equal numbers of men and women at the conference. The problem, therefore, is deeper than just the problem of sexual discrimination in school computing. If the vast majority of female teachers, who make up 80% of all primary school teachers, can't relate to computing, how are our children going to receive the necessary familiarity with computer aid? It is a serious problem.

A British government survey, conducted in 1982, probed the maths abilities of boys and girls in over 200 secondary schools. The report seems to indicate that boys are actually cleverer than girls at maths. At the age of 11 boys lead the girls in applied maths by an ability factor of five per cent, and by the time the group reaches the age of 15 the boys' lead has jumped to eight per cent. But such seemingly concrete evidence is hedged with uncertainty: the report offers this finding with the proviso that the reason behind this apparent lack of ability may be that girls see maths as a boys' subject and simply stop trying.

### Handheld games

For children between eight and 11 computers often first arrive in the home in the form of electronic games. Sometimes handheld and battery powered, these little versions of the arcade games have been the no. 1 Christmas present for several years. Only a few of them have any educational application, and this is usually clearly defined. Texas Instruments, for example, produced 'Speak and Spell' in 1978, a game using their speech synthesis chip to test children's spelling. Other similar educational 'games' followed including 'The Little Professor'.

These gadgets are fun and great novelties, but like so many computer programs they are drilling the child. An adult could as easily sit down with a child and say words which the child has to spell. It is merely the mechanised version which provides the temporary attraction.

Whether or not your children have any of the ubiquitous electronic games, it is worthwhile considering the purchase of a proper microcomputer, even for a child as young as four or five. Technical information about choosing a microcomputer and programs appears in later chapters, but there are some fundamental points worthy of mention when considering equipment for the very young.

If the concept of using Logo appeals to you, you will be limited to a choice between computers which offer Logo as an available program. Currently these include Tandy (Radio Shack), Apple, Acorn (the BBC Computer), the Texas TI-99/4A home computer, the Sinclair Spectrum and the Research Machines 380Z microcomputer. New versions of Logo for additional machines are appearing regularly, and if you are considering the purchase of a microcomputer not mentioned in this list it would be worthwhile enquiring about the availability of Logo. Don't believe a salesman who tells you he has something just as good.

The turtle mentioned in the Logo chapter is available as a separate physical object (a robot) in both Britain and in the USA. In Britain the turtle is marketed by a London company called Jessop Microelectronics and called the 'Edinburgh Turtle'. This is because the Artificial Intelligence Department at Edinburgh University has undertaken all the research work with Logo in the UK, and the turtle has been used experimentally in many primary schools in the Edinburgh area. The Edinburgh Turtle is large, and its transparent plastic dome clearly reveals the motors, pen and wheels. At the time of writing, the Edinburgh Turtle was available with software which could run on a Research Machine 380Z, a BBC Computer and the Apple computer. Jessop anticipate that software will become available for use with other machines. The program supplied with the Turtle is a truncated version of Logo which allows children to experiment with the Turtle and program it, both in its physical and screen-based form, but the software does not continue into the important second stage of Logo learning, the 'Sprites' (see Chapter 9). The software is, however, very simple to use, and commands have been simplfied to single keystrokes such as 'B' for 'BACK' and 'F' for 'FORWARD'. This allows even the youngest children to control the Turtle and use the alphanumeric keyboard.

Buying an Edinburgh Turtle for use by one or two children is something only the affluent could contemplate, but for schools the Turtle makes an excellent investment and allows even nursery school children the chance to 'play turtle' and understand that machines can be taught lessons by humans.

Even if you are unsure about the Logo approach, or wish to use some other types of educational programs for young children, there are some important points to consider.

### Hardware for under-sevens

Under seven, children need help and supervision in turning on a computer and TV set and loading a program. If the program is good enough, they may then be left to use it, although this depends on their reading skill and ability to provide answers to the program's questions. Hardware requirements are pretty simple. A microcomputer has to be robust: children *do* hit the keyboard with clenched fists, they pull at the electrical connections and they constantly touch and prod the screen. If a system is flimsy, poorly connected or hard to use, it will fail to interest a young child.

Some experts consider that a computer keyboard for a very young child must have large, clearly defined keys: this seems a sensible requirement for computers to be used by the youngest children – say under six – but as children's motor movements become fully developed (usually by seven), they are capable of dealing with 'fiddly' keyboards which would seem difficult even to adults. The touch-sensitive keyboards found on the cheapest Sinclair microcomputers are not really suitable for children under nine or ten, although the larger versions of the printed keyboard, such as used on the Philips Videopac 7000, are suitable for four-year-olds. It is a question of size and ease of use.

Do try to provide the computer with a permanent home. Moving a computer from room to room with consequential disconnection and reconnection won't do a computer any harm (unless you drop it), but it makes the procedure tedious and likely to be skipped by the child in favour of something instant – like television.

In an ideal world, the child's computer should be set up in his or her bedroom complete with its own TV screen. If you are serious about your children developing a positive attitude to computers, consider setting up a work-station in one of their bedrooms and supplying a secondhand TV exclusively for their use. (Put the computer centre in the oldest child's bedroom: he or she may want to use it after the others have gone to bed.) Old black and white TVs can be purchased very cheaply and, providing there is a provision for channel tuning, they are perfectly capable of displaying computer information. There is a great deal of argument about the value of colour in computing for young children; some experts say it is vital, others consider it a bonus, but unnecessary. It seems obvious to me that if the choice is between a permanent connection to a black and white TV set in a bedroom, or the temporary connection to the family's colour TV, the permanent set-up is infinitely more desirable. (Also, many programs are written in black and white.)

### The computer work/play centre

If you are able to set up a permanent or semi-permanent computer work/play centre in one of the children's bedrooms, it is a good idea to arrange things so that the computer can be removed without disturbing the set-up. When organising the computer table or bench, tape down all the leads and connections so that the children won't accidentally pull one out. (Ensure that all mains connectors are safely protected and taped down in such a way that they cannot become unsafe, and don't supply an aerial connection to the TV, otherwise repeats of *Bonanza* may 'accidentally' appear on the screen at bedtime.) It is important that the microcomputer is stable and doesn't bounce around. Timex/Sinclair can supply a tray which holds their very light Spectrum computer steady, and if your children are boisterous you might consider building some 'clamp' or other means of holding the microcomputer down.

Of course, the computer you buy for your children will also be of use to the whole family. You may wish to use the machine for the analysis of stocks and shares, for connection with one of the TV teletext information services, for playing 'PacMan' or chess or for any of a thousand other purposes. If you decide to set up a computer centre especially for your children, it is worthwhile buying duplicate leads and (where necessary) a second mains supply pack for the computer. These are relatively inexpensive, and they will allow you to say a firm good night to your kids, unplug the computer and cassette recorder (or disk drive) from their bedroom centre (leaving all leads taped in place) and scuttle downstairs to plug them into your own TV using your duplicate leads. If a computer has to be set up and taken down in the living room whenever your children wish to use it, the fuss of lead connections and the possible disputes with members of the family who would prefer to watch an early evening soap opera may, unless carefully controlled, kill the idea of computing as a leisure activity for children even before it begins.

After the age of five, most children resent going to bed early. Some indulgent parents allow children to sprawl on the living room floor on the justification that 'they'll sleep as much as they need to', but I am a firm believer in parents' rights and feel that young children should observe a fixed bedtime, even if they are allowed to remain active in their rooms.

With my six-year-old I have found that the computer becomes her bedtime friend. Often she sneaks an extra hour of awake time 'playing turtle' or answering one of her favourite 'drill and practice' type

*Don't supply an aerial connection to the TV, otherwise repeats of Bonanza will appear on the screen at bed time.*

of programs before we have to switch everything off and insist she really can sleep if she tries. Although we encourage this behaviour, the activity is of her own choosing. We merely provide the materials. The computer is switched on only if she asks for it to be so, and she is left to select her own software (in cartridge form), changing at will between a dozen programs. If we are disturbed during the blissful hour after the story-telling and the first good night has been said, it is likely to be squeals of delight because an elusive problem in a program has been solved. She will then descend and drag one of us to her room to prove that she has found a way to 'do the game'.

### Cartridge software

The subject of software and young children is touched on elsewhere in this book, but it deserves some comment here. Jane has only been able to use computers independently without our help because the software comes in cartridge form. She has been using the TI-99/4A home computer for some time, and in this system even the Logo program is supplied in the form of a solid-state cartridge which encapsulates and protects a solid-state ROM (read only memory) chip in which the program is electronically stored. Jane (and her friends) can bang the cartridges in and out of the computer slot, even throw them about, and their behaviour is unlikely to cause damage to the computer or the programs. If it was necessary to load all programs from a cassette recorder, Jane would not be able to use the computer unsupervised. No matter how loving and dedicated they may be, most parents are not prepared to supervise all their children's leisure activities, and the constant demand for parents to 'Do something, it's all gone funny' is another irritation which could ensure that computing is a short-lived occupation for the children.

Another trouble-free system of loading programs is based on special ROM chips which are installed inside the microcomputer after purchase and which become integral parts of the computer's circuit. This system provides the best of all worlds for users (as against programmers), but it is only just becoming available. These chips, similar to the programmed chips inside solid-state cartridges, are inserted inside the microcomputer (usually plugged in) and the program stored on the chip is loaded into the computer by pressing one or two buttons on the computer keyboard after the system is switched on. The program is always available. With this integrated program system, there is no possibility of damage or loss, although most computers are limited to the number of chips which can be installed inside the computer at any one time. The BBC Microcomputer has been constructed to facilitate the fitting of ROM chips, and several programs are now available for it in this form. Most important among them are Logo and word-processing chips.

At six Jane is able to handle floppy disks more easily than she can handle cassette machines, and she is able to start up my business microcomputer and get a program running more easily than she can load a cassette-based program into her TI machine. Disks are expensive storage systems, however, and are unlikely to find their way into many homes unless the home is also a place of work.

Cassettes are fiddly and slow. They often don't record and replay properly, but they have one enormous advantage over ROM programs: they can be used for storage of 'work in hand'.

When a program is loaded from a computer-installed ROM chip or a solid-state cartridge, the program can be used and manipulated; but, if the user has developed a program or procedure that he or she wishes to keep, solid-state ROM provides no storage facilities. At this stage the user must 'dump' the work on to some magnetic storage system such as a cassette tape or floppy disk. This is not so important for very young users of computers who are unlikely to want to store programs for later work, but older children, perhaps eight or nine upwards, will require this facility.

Once children can handle a cassette recorder with ease, ensuring that all connections are right and that data has been stored safely, then the full power of the micro is available to them. At this point the parent has to consider the choice of both computer system and software. One overriding consideration is the type of computer the child is using at school. If your son or daughter gets any worthwhile exposure to computers at school, then it makes good sense to purchase a similar model to the school's. All schools will be glad to allow you to copy some of the programs they use in their curriculum, and this integrates the home and school computers. (You may also get the chance to introduce some of your chosen programs into the school's curriculum). Perhaps the only time when the purchase of a different machine is worthwhile is when the child is at a school in which the computer is misused, or in a situation where the school model will not run a particular program (such as Logo) which you consider important for your child's development.

Misuse of computers in education is widespread and ranges from the over-reliance on drill and practice techniques to the over-liberal attitudes which allow children constantly to play computer games.

When parents consider buying a home computer as a present for their son or daughter, it is unreasonable of them to expect that the machine will not be used for game playing. Do buy some 'Space Invader' type programs to go with it and encourage the idea that computers can be fun as well as being helpful.

You will undoubtedly consider carefully which educational programs are worthwhile purchasing, and this is a decision fraught with dangers. A visit to any computer store will reveal that there are a plethora of educational programs available, although scanning the columns of the educational press will suggest that many teachers are complaining about a drastic lack of good educational programs. What most teachers mean when they make this complaint is that there are not enough programs that teach in the way *they* teach.

## Teachers as programmers

Many teachers are now writing their own programs, but this can create its own problems. The first, and most important, is that very few teachers are skilled programmers. It is not difficult to write a program which asks a child questions and provides the answers when the program is intended to be used solely during a class conducted by the teacher who has written the program. Most teachers could learn to write such a program in a few days. It is a very different matter if the program has to be used by children outside the teacher's class and if the program has to be at all 'user-friendly'.

Making a program easy for a novice to use is the key to writing a successful computer program. The hard work is not in writing the program lines which present the questions, evaluate the answers and provide the score. The hard work is in anticipating all of the things that can go wrong when a novice first uses a program, and in providing *clear documentation* to support the program and explain its intricacies. Many so-called educational programs are available for £5 or $10 and arrive on a cassette with an inlay card announcing its title. That card may often be all the documentation provided. From this the user has to work out how to load the program from cassette tape and how to check if it has been loaded properly, to understand the first questions that appear on the screen and then to discover how to correct things if he or she accidentally hits a key which sends the program haywire or produces an 'error' message.

Writing user-friendly programs is a complex job. After creating the basic question and answer part, the program has to be made foolproof. The programmer has to anticipate every sort of wrong response from a user and protect the program against crashing. This demands a 'search through negatives' by the programmer and is far more demanding than the consideration of the 'positive' side of program writing (working out what a user ought to do). Having created a program which will run well on the screen and present all questions in a clear form with the suggested mode of answer clearly displayed (and which will not go wrong if the rules are ignored), the programmer has to turn his or her attention to the documentation that will accompany the program. This is vital and should be considered as part of the program itself.

Most young users and their parents will be novice computer users. This means that they require the maximum explanation, and it is here that the busy programmer often falls down.

'But of course you have to type "load" to load the program in,' a teacher might respond if challenged about the omission of such an instruction from program documentation.

'Well, if you get an error, just press "reset" and start again. It's obvious.' It might be obvious to a programmer, but it is not obvious to a novice user. Programs from the major companies, Texas, Tandy (Radio Shack), etc. are very much more expensive than many programs advertised by mail order and on sale in computer stores. The reason is simple: the negatives have been thought through, and the documentation is written very clearly. The extra money is well spent.

### Educational rules

But conversely, writing a program professionally and making it user-friendly is not the same thing as writing a program which is based on sound educational theory. Teachers are exasperated by commercially produced programs which break fundamental educational rules. Primary school teachers recently rejected a whole series of handwriting programs from a major manufacturer because the words on the screen were not formed in the way that children are taught to form them in class. Primary teachers also reject programs when the screen words are written in capital letters. Teachers spend their days trying to rid the children of the confusion between capital and lower-case letters.

Clearly teachers and programmers have to work together. The teacher must supply the pedagogical information, and the programmers must ensure the programs meet all the novice's requirements. Some companies are already doing this, and some excellent software has been the result.

But, however well written, programs also have to be flexible enough to suit the differing temperaments of children. Sometimes simple programs are more appealing than elaborate creations. My daughter spent some months happily working with a simple drill and practice maths program produced for the Philips Videopac 7000 computer. The program would display random sums on the screen, and a flashing question mark waited for her answer – endlessly if need be. If she got the sum right, a point was added to her score. If she got it wrong, a low note sounded, and the sum was repeated. After three wrong answers the program supplied the right answer, held it on the screen for a few seconds and moved on to the next problem.

Jane then moved on to a program called 'Addition and Subtraction 1' by Scott, Forseman & Company on the TI home computer. This software seemed very much more advanced than the Philips, with full colour graphics, music, sound and speech. The program gives examples of simple counting, with attractive colour graphics and speech synthesis to reinforce the lesson. When Jane selected to be given problems rather than watch problems explained, she was presented with a problem, and a severe voice announced, 'Your turn'. A flashing question mark indicated that her answer was awaited. In her fashion, Jane hesitated, pondering the problem. Very quickly the voice reminded her it was 'her turn'. Jane began to get flustered. The program then confounded the situation by going into 'remediation' and suddenly reverting to an explanation of the topic, even as Jane was working out the answer. The concept was explained over again, and then the problem was returned to the screen with the (by now) impatient-sounding 'your turn' announcement. Jane was flustered, tried an answer and got it wrong. This happened several times before she pulled the software cartridge from the slot and said she 'didn't like that one'.

I didn't blame her. The problems were well within her reach and aimed at her age group. But overelaborate programming had not allowed for children responding at different speeds. The authors had tried to ensure that remediation was automatically available for those who had not understood the concept, but in Jane's case this facility proved to be a drawback. This reaction was produced by software generally considered to be among the best 'drill and practice' software produced in the USA. In the accompanying manual the notes explain that great care has been taken 'to make the response to incorrect answers low-key and non-intimidating', but in practice I discovered the program to have the opposite results when tested with several other children. To be fair it must be said that adult supervision would have solved the problems. But, once familiar with computers and simple programs, children, in my experience, are very anxious to work on their own, and it is against this desire that I consider the program should be assessed. It is difficult to find the right drill and practice software for children, and it seems that overelaborate program writing can be just as harmful as poorly thought-out programs.

### Typing skill

The most important ability for any presentday computer user, child or adult, is the ability to type. This is likely to remain a requirement for at least ten years, after which speed recognition systems will probably become universal.

It is not necessary to know how to type properly if you are just going to use the computer to play PacMan or Turtle, but any serious usage, whether for programming or for using programs, will be difficult without some familiarity with the typewriter keyboard.

It is worth teaching children to type properly. Although it is possible to type with two or three fingers, speed and accuracy can never develop properly, and accuracy is vital when communicating in computer languages.

*The Maltron Keyboard is designed so that the most commonly used letters are placed together. The makers claim that the layout affords a 20-40% increase in typing speed.*

One of the main drawbacks we face is the present typewriter keyboard layout. The present internationally adopted configuration is known as 'QWERTY', after the first six letters ranged along the top left of the keyboard. This keyboard was designed over 100 years ago to slow typists down! Early typewriter technology was poor, and during rapid use the keys constantly stuck together. To solve this problem, engineers devised a keyboard in which the most commonly used letters were placed as far apart as possible, making it difficult for skilled typists to exceed a certain typing speed. This solved the problem of poorly machined typewriter keys, but it left us with a legacy of obstructive design which is a continuing burden.

Even mechanical typewriters have long been capable of working at higher speeds than the qwerty keyboard allows, but the problem remains of retraining the world's typists. Many valiant attempts have been made to introduce new keyboard designs in which the keys are laid out ergonomically and positioned for maximum speed. The advent of the microcomputer has renewed an alternative and several models are now in commercial production. One example, available internationally, is the 'Maltron' keyboard, which is shaped to the palm and which arranges letters in two groups under each hand. The most commonly used letters are grouped together and the makers claim that the keyboard allows a 20%-40% increase in working speed and a reduction in typist fatigue. This unit, and its ergonomic competitors, can be made to connect to most home computers, but the problems caused by introducing either yourself or your children to a non-standard typing system are considerable.

It is also worth pointing out, that because of the development of speech recognition our children will not have to use the keyboard as a general input method later in their lives (unless they have a speech handicap), and the value of weaning them on an ergonomic (but uncommon) keyboard and making them swim against the tide seems debatable.

For the foreseeable future we will all go on using a keyboard designed to slow us down, and we must discover how best to use it. Many typing tutor programs are available for microcomputers, and several have been produced especially for children. The first task is to get children familiar with the keyboard and with the position of the letters.

**Learning keyboard layout**

The British 'Micros In Primary Schools' association has an excellent 'Cat and Mouse' program which uses an animated graphic of a mouse being chased by a cat. A flashing letter appears in the middle of the screen and the child is encouraged to find and press that letter on the keyboard in order to save the mouse. There are several levels of speed at which the program can run, and when the child finds the right letter on the keyboard the mouse escapes, and the cat has to start its chase all over again, with a new letter flashing for the child's attention.

Once a child is old enough and is familiar with the layout of the keyboard, it is worthwhile seeking out a proper typing program. Most schools are not currently taking this step, but are allowing children to operate computers 'one finger' style. This may be acceptable for the simple programs children first encounter on computers, but any serious use, such as writing essays with word-processing programs, will be made much easier if they can type properly. Because of the inherent text-editing potential of the computer, the typing-training programs on microcomputers allow students to gain the skill much more easily than conventional electromechanical typing courses.

Motivation is the key to any successful endeavour, and providing children with the motivation to use the computer keyboard has been the aim of several program authors. Games like 'Space Invaders' motivate children to use the game paddles and 'fire' buttons – so much so that significant motor movement improvement and coordination is sometimes noticed – but there is usually insufficient motivation for the child to learn to type properly.

Heinemann, the British publisher, produces 'Looking at Letters', a motivating program which is designed to help very young children learn the alphabet on computers. If alphabet learning takes place on computers, then the child naturally assimilates the keyboard layout. Interactive fiction is another method of involving children and motivating them. This is a new type of program, which tells a story with accompanying computer graphics and then asks the child for a decision about the story plot. The child types in his or her decision, and the story develops according to the choice that has been made. This type of program (examples are now available from Atari and Tandy Radio Shack) teaches much more than typing – the logic of computer decision making, for example – but it is this type of program that will pull children in to the computer and get them using the keyboard.

Word games are also very useful in promoting keyboard familiarity, language development and logic. Versions of 'Hangman' or 'Scrabble' are available for nearly all computers, and the game itself is sufficient motivation to make the child want to find the letter on the keyboard quickly. In the computer version of Hangman, the computer chooses a word and offers a number of blank positions on the screen. The child tries a letter and is told whether or not the letter appears in the word. The child has eight tries to guess the word. More advanced versions of word games ask the user to find a phrase, to guess an animal or to do a simple crossword.

## Word-processing for children

Once a child can read and write competently (and can type reasonably well), there is a strong case for encouraging him or her to use the computer as a word-processor for composition purposes. There is a vociferous lobby against what is seen as a Godless activity, and the plaintiffs' main argument seems to revolve around the potential loss of handwriting skill. I suppose your view of this depends on whether you care more about what you write or about the physical appearance of the writing itself. Certainly all children need to develop readable handwriting, but its role is rapidly decreasing, in the way that human arithmetic calculation has given way to the pocket calculator.

Until now word-processing has been an expensive program available only on the most powerful microcomputers. Today word-processing is available for small (32K) home computers for little additional cost. The one significant item necessary to allow full use of word-processing is a printer. Although the cost of microelectronics is spiralling downwards, the cost of electromechanical printers is unlikely to follow the same path. The least expensive of these is likely to cost the same as the microcomputer itself and, depending on the print quality required, can cost several times the price.

If a child composes an essay on the screen, corrects and edits it, it is natural that he or she should want a printed version. If the essay has been composed for educational purposes, it is vital that the child can hand in a perfect copy for marking. Nearly all schools have some printing facility attached to their microcomputers, but it is an expensive purchase for the home computer centre.

In the last chapter I reproduced some of Seymour Papert's comments on the power of word-processing as a creative tool. The subject is worth a little more exploration. Word-processing is a program which instructs the computer to manipulate letters and words on the screen. Because the screen is always 'live', the arrangement of words or letters can be changed at any time. A child may make a typing error in an opening sentence of an essay: moving the 'cursor' (the flashing position-indicator on the screen) back to the mistake, the child can retype the mistyped or misspelled word straight over the error. The error disappears, and the correction appears in its place. If the correction takes up more or less room in the sentence than the original, the other words can be rearranged around the correction to provide a perfectly spaced sentence.

If a child writes a page before realising that he or she has left an important event out of the story, he or she may go back to the first paragraph, press an 'Insert' button, and insert as much text as he or she chooses with the following text moving down automatically to accommodate the insertion. When the child has finished, the text can

106

be reformed to present a perfect page once again. Only when a page (or a number of pages) appears perfect on the screen does the child press the button and produce a printed version on paper. Even then the child can go back to the screen, alter the work again and produce a second, updated, print-out. This procedure can be repeated endlessly. In a nutshell, the program breaks the task of writing down into its separate components: deciding what to say, choice of words with which to say it, editing, correction and finally printing. Such a facility allows attention to be given to individual parts of the process of writing.

This power has an impact far more fundamental than mere ease of use. We are all conditioned in our style of writing by the methods at our command. Using paper, whether with pencil or typewriter, allows us a 'once only' chance to get it right. In some people, this produces a 'writing block'. For most it necessitates first, second and sometimes third drafts with all the laborious rewriting involved whenever any important document is written. Imagine the freedom of being able to go back over every word and consider the alternatives in every sentence and wonder whether there is a better way of expressing the meaning. This is possible with word-processing because, even after a short exposure, the writer realises that the constraints which have so long hampered creativity no longer apply. For a child this facility produces the concept of critical analysis much earlier than our present methods of writing. Even quite young children are prepared to go back and revise their compositions – if they know that the final product they produce will be both as well written as they can make it and appear pristine without involving the labour of a rewrite.

If you decide that word-processing would be a valuable tool for your child and you decide to invest in a program and a printer, you may find some resistance from school teachers to the idea of the program being used for school work. This is likely to be on one or both of two counts: the child's handwriting will not develop properly, and/or the child will not realise the requirement for a considered approach before work is started.

## Handwriting versus creative writing

If my child were stuck with a teacher worried more about handwriting than creative writing, I think I would encourage the child to create the essay on a word-processor and then copy it out in longhand, submitting both for marking. The time saved during the composition on the computer would still allow both tasks to be completed within a reasonable time.

The second objection deserves more consideration. Some schools provide children with 'rough books' in which they are supposed to work out their thoughts before committing themselves to paper. All present examinations demand the child to complete a paper without the assistance of word-processing facilities, and it must be asked whether or not reliance on word-processing at an early development stage will rob the child of the ability to write a composition manually. I do not know the answer to this and, despite all their protestations, I do not believe that educationalists yet know the answer either. Until word-processors have been freely available in schools for some years, it will be impossible to carry out a study which will provide the answers. I value the development of the critical faculty above the ability to create a presentable first draft, but perhaps in the interim a middle course, in which a child writes in both the electronic and physical medium, is called for.

All word-processing programs are complex and relatively expensive. A few are designed especially for children and educational use. One shining example is the 'Wordwise' word-processing program for Britain's BBC Microcomputer. This program is supplied as an inexpensive ROM chip which is plugged into the computer's circuit board.

The best thing about this program is that the upper- and lower-case letters appear in a large form on the screen. This allows the program to be displayed satisfactorily on ordinary TV sets and helps young children use the program. At the touch of a button the text can be reduced in size, allowing users to view the layout as it would appear on the printed page. The program requires no loading from external storage before use (it is summoned from ROM into live memory by a single key stroke) and cannot be accidentally erased or damaged. (Another word-processing ROM chip, called 'View', is produced by Acorn, the manufacturers of the BBC micro.)

Some word-processing programs are described as 'text editors', but this should sound a note of caution. Some programs are not very powerful and consequently demand a complex operating procedure before paragraphs can be moved or major alterations take place. Try the program out in the computer store (don't buy a word-processing program by mail order) and if you can delete sentences and move paragraphs with ease, it is likely to be a powerful program.

Many children under 11 will be meeting computers for the first time in their classrooms. Most will enjoy the experience, and the pioneering work carried out by a few schools has provided clues about the best way of introducing children to computers.

## Robotics

Robots have been a popular childhood fantasy for decades, and several types of robots are now available to demonstrate the power of the micro to young children. The word 'robot' is no longer a description of a tin-man who speaks with a metallic voice (it now seems unlikely that such an absurd creation will ever be built for practical use), but robots have arrived as remotely controlled arms or tools. The addition of a physical control unit such as a robot arm fascinates most children, and the desire to make the arm do a particular task provides sufficient motivation for many to learn how to create the necessary programs. It is not yet feasible to introduce robotics into the average home, but their use in schools gives computing a physical dimension in much the same way that the turtle robot does for very young children. The power of the computer is instinctively grasped from the robot's actions.

Attempts are being made all over the world to teach the under-11s how to program in the BASIC computer language. As discussed in the chapter on Logo, BASIC takes a quick leap into the abstract that leaves many younger children floundering. Many booklets aimed at younger children have appeared which try to give the subject some humanity, provide drawings of computers with legs, or give friendly names to the various parts of the system; but in all cases the attempts to explain abstract concepts to under-11s are only partly successful. Thankfully, some teachers and schools are now reconsidering this approach.

Although your consideration of adding a computer to the home environment is of vital importance, the selection of a good computer-oriented elementary or middle school is even more important. To a large extent, choice of school is dependent on where you live. Even within the same country there are considerable differences in regional response to microcomputers in education. Only in a few, nationally controlled education systems (such as those of France and Japan) will a single policy persist in all schools.

### Rejection or over-reliance

There are two extreme stances on the subject of microcomputers in schools. The first is the total rejection of such aids as 'gimmicks', while the second is an over-reliance on artificial intelligence with a resulting loss of traditional educational values. There are far more schools in the first group than in the second. Many schools still adopt a stance of rejecting microcomputers until children are in their teens and then offer 'computer studies' for those who want to enter science, engineering or mathematics. (This attitude often persists in schools despite the official approval and encouragement of microcomputing by both local education authorities and central government.)

In selecting a school for a child under 11, it is important to find one in which the computer is not a feared object. A common head teacher's response on being asked about computers in the school is: 'Ah, that's our Mr Smith. The things he does with computers are

When selecting a school it is important to find one in which the computer is not a feared object.

marvellous. Come and see!' (He or she usually wants to pass the buck!)

In this type of school the visit to the classroom in which the computer is installed is likely to be followed by a boy being called out to demonstrate his prowess on the machine. This type of approach indicates that the computer has remained the province of one teacher who is particularly interested in the subject and, in turn, is used by a few pupils who have shown themselves particularly bright at programming. It is likely that computing is seen as a subject outside the main curriculum by most of the staff and pupils.

School philosophies follow the lead set by the head teacher, and only if he or she fully understands the contribution microcomputers can make to education can the school begin to build a curriculum which makes full use of these powerful learning aids.

In the ideal school the response to your question about computers would be less easy for the head teacher to answer. 'Which subject shall we start with?' might be an appropriate response. In this school you should expect to see several microcomputers installed in different classrooms. The microcomputer should be *integrated into the school's curriculum*. All teachers should be able to use the computer, and all the children should understand how to use the system to help them with their lessons. If one obviously capable pupil is called forward to demonstrate, ask to see how a less able pupil gets on with the computer. If the teacher has to intervene constantly to help the child set-up, load and use the program, you can be sure that the child does not get casual access to the system.

### The school software library

The acid test of how well a school uses its computer is an examination of its software. Ask to see the school's software library. A school may have one central library or each classroom may keep a separate stock. The method adopted is unimportant. When you see the range of software, ask about Logo. If the teacher doesn't know what you are talking about cross the school off your list. It is permissible for a teacher to have examined and rejected Papert's approach, but it is inadmissible for a teacher (or a school) to have remained unaware of such important work. Ask about programs for geography and history. There are many good programs which can help the under 11s in such subjects. You will certainly be shown programs for maths and reading instruction, but a school which has integrated its computers in general studies will also have programs for French classes, music lessons and nature studies. A narrow range of software is a clear indication that the computer is used in a narrow and restrictive way.

Most elementary and primary schools are free enough to be able to select the way in which they choose to work, but when examinations come into view the curriculum changes to match the syllabus requirements. In most Western countries, the attempt to stream children by examination at 11 has been abandoned in the knowledge that the system was unfair and produced irreversible injustice for many. But a few educational anachronisms exist which force 11- or 13-year-olds to meet examination requirements. One such system is the British 'public school' common entrance examination. In keeping with this anachronistic status, 'public school' in Britain means that the public are not admitted. Children must pass a stiff entrance examination, based on traditional subject syllabuses, and if they are successful their parents must pay a considerable sum of money each year to keep their child at the school. (Interestingly, some of the British 'public schools' are clear leaders in the use of microcomputers as integrated teaching aids, but the syllabus for the common entrance examination still excludes the use of computers.) If the primary school you are inspecting is particularly geared to pushing children through the common entrance exam, it is unlikely that computers will play a major role in the curriculum. Almost certainly, some lip service will be paid to the subject, but the real application of the micro as a learning tool for the children will have been put aside.

One final test for a school is to ask the class teachers about their experience in using the computer in the classroom. Ask them whether in general the children work better with the computer individually, in pairs or in larger groups. Most of the available research points to pairs being the most successful method of allowing children to use the computer, and this should be echoed in the teacher's reply. In a group

111

of two, the children are forced to explain what is happening to each other, and a particularly useful combination is when an able child is paired with a less able child. The tuition the more advanced child passes on helps both of them. Other recent research has also revealed that this combination also helps slow learners. If an older child who is slow at learning is asked to demonstrate a computer or program to a far younger child, both benefit greatly. The slow learner (providing he or she does have an understanding of the system) explains more carefully and slowly and in the process grasps the concepts more thoroughly for him or herself. Groups of three around a microcomputer have been found to be unsatisfactory; one child is inevitably left out, and his or her attention drifts away. Larger groups can only work successfully with a microcomputer if the group is under the direct instruction of the teacher at all times.

Choosing the right school for your child is an immensely difficult task. Factors other than computer use may come higher on your list of priorities – quality of teaching often being the most important. You may not be able to find a school which has been able to integrate microcomputers and which also offers a happy atmosphere and good teaching. If you have to choose a school with able dedicated teachers, but which is still in the Dark Ages as far as computing is concerned, perhaps you can use your home computer to demonstrate some of the benefits they are missing.

*'No, it's my turn!' Perhaps not the ideal way for children to use a microcomputer, but enthusiasm is evident.*

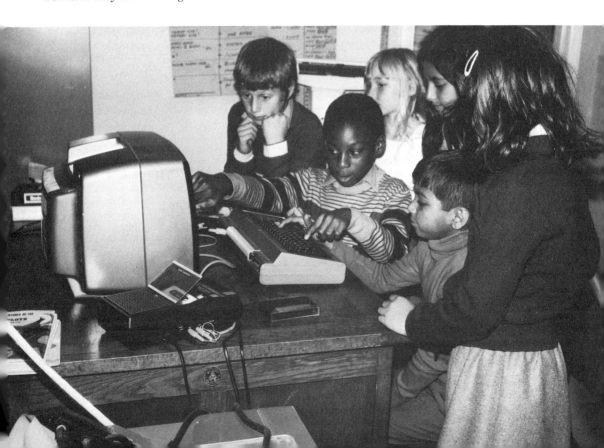

# COMPUTERS AND THE 11-18s

Teenagers in many parts of the world are being educated in systems which are in a state of chaos. The mass arrival of computers, coupled with the increasing likelihood of post-school unemployment, has denuded most educational systems of any coherent policy. Since 1980 there has been a mad scramble to provide teenagers with some computer literacy before they leave school, and as recession has spread around the world the threat of unemployment has lent a sense of urgency to the programme. Most parents feel that their child needs to 'understand computers', but no two people seem able to agree on how best to impart this understanding, or of what the understanding should consist.

Unemployment is particularly severe among school leavers: in Britain a quarter of school leavers become unemployed. In an attempt to give adolescents a better chance of finding employment, most secondary schools are now offering some form of education in computing. The most common approach is to attempt to teach the children programming in a 'computer studies' course. The most commonly taught programming language is BASIC, but many teachers are now considering alternative computer languages such as COMAL and Algol.

Children under 12 are not really able to deal with any of these abstract algorithmic languages, and in many secondary schools computer education does not begin before the child is in his or her third year (eighth or ninth grade).

There is now a strong suggestion that the attempt to teach teenagers about computers by teaching them programming is wrong. The procedure has been compared with teaching someone to fly a plane by teaching them how to build one. By compartmentalising computing into a separate study and requiring the student to attend the resource centre or computer room (often in the maths department), schools segregate computing from other 'ordinary' subjects and underline the subject's base as being in either maths or science. This situation often persists because it was a maths or science teacher who first introduced computing to the school, and he or she is anxious to retain personal power over their own 'territory'.

# COMPUTERS AND YOUR CHILD ■■■■■■■■■■■■■■■■■■■■■■■■■■■■■■■■

In some schools, computing subjects have made little headway in the mainstream curriculum, and the subject is still taught as a branch of science. One interesting theory for this (put forward in *School Subjects and Curriculum Change* by Ivor Goodson, London 1982), suggests that computing science, along with other subjects such as environmental studies and physical education, is pushed out of curricula as ambitious teachers turn their attention to subject areas which bring them more money and more power within the set-up of their institutions. The present curricula in secondary schools are 'examination led', and both students' and teachers' performances are monitored only by examination successes or failures. The kudos, promotion and money go to the teachers who teach theoretical academic studies which can most easily be assessed in the examination format. There seems to be much evidence to support this theory, and as a direct result of these and other pressures in many secondary schools the computer remains locked up in the science or maths room.

## Computing as a male preserve

There is a second grave consequence arising from this pigeonholing of computers. In the 11–18 age group computers and computing are seen as a predominantly 'male' subject. This is partly because of the way the subject is presented – the computer is often kept in the 'male' preserve of the science or maths department and the promotion given to computers is still very male-dominated – and partly because of the way the computer is used in the curriculum.

Differences in mental development between the sexes has long been the subject of research and controversy, and as mentioned in the previous chapter there is some superficial evidence to suggest that boys are better at maths than girls during the teenage years – although once again such findings must be considered with the rider that such a situation might in the first place be caused by the way in which maths is presented to girls. The influential British government study *Social Trends*, published annually, shows that girls do better overall at school than boys, with 32% of girl school leavers going on to further education compared with 22% of boys. But in the very brightest groups – those with two or more A-level passes – boys slightly outnumber girls, by one percentage point.

What is clear, however, is that computers are for the boys – at least for the moment. The demands of teenage boys (many space-game-crazy) motivate many families into becoming computer owners. The manufacturers are aware of this enormous market force and trade on it, reinforcing the trends already existing. In children's early teenage years the sex roles are polarised, and as boys and girls begin to discover their sexuality they retreat to their respective corners to consider the situation. In this market place the ads and displays for home computers are principally based on the many games now available, and these invariably feature illustrations of savage space wars and deeds of heroism, all male in approach. Manufacturers dare not present the image of the computer as 'cissy' to teenage boys – a group not old enough to have recognised and controlled their fiercely separatist chauvinism. The result is that the computer falls into the category of the go-kart and football, and girls who are not fortunate enough to discover computers on their own terms classify the whole subject accordingly,

Home computers are *the* big buy for the teenage boy market. Two decades ago it was the electric guitar, and, just as parents in the 1960s were hoping their child would go on to play a 'proper' instrument, so today's parents are hopeful that Space Invaders will give way to more constructive computer use. They are more likely to have their hopes fulfilled than were their parents.

Arcade-type games are a wonderful attraction for boys (although many girls do enjoy them), and with the right encouragement boys and girls will progress to more creative computer occupations. Some children do seem to become very attached to 'PacMan' or its equivalent, but although the word 'addicted' is often used there is no evidence that any condition follows which could be described so seriously. (Once they are into proper computing programming, there is a separate worry. This is discussed later in this chapter.)

Home computers are the big buy for the teenage market.

# COMPUTERS AND YOUR CHILD ■■■■■■■■■■■■■■■■■■■■■■■■■■■■■■■■■

## Rewards of arcade games

There has been considerable research into the motivation that drives teenagers to spend large sums of money and leisure time on arcade games. In 'PacMan' for example, every dot devoured is an achievement – there is instant success, and the opposition – the machine – is in no position to sneer if performance is not up to the mark. The games do provide players with a chance to exhibit status among peer groups, and highly skilled players can gain an 'arcade reputation'. To look further into the attraction of the arcade computer/video game, it is necessary to consider its intrinsic rewards. It is obvious that players become totally immersed in the activity – a feeling which they might find hard to achieve in many other pursuits. This absorption has been described as a mental 'flow state', and two researchers (Csikzentmihalyi and Larson, *Intrinsic Rewards in School Crime*, 1980) describe this state of true interaction found at the controls of a computer game:

> Flow is described as a condition in which one concentrates on the task at hand to the exclusion of other internal or external stimuli. Action and awareness merge, so that one simply does what is to be done without a critical, dualistic perspective on one's actions. Goals tend to be clear, means are coordinated to the goals, and feedback to one's performance is immediate and unambiguous. In such a situation, a person has a strong feeling of control – or personal causation – yet, paradoxically, ego involvement is low or non-existent, so that one experiences a sense of transcendence of self, sometimes a feeling of union with the environment. The passage of time appears to be distorted: some events seem to take a disproportionately long time, but, in general, hours seem to pass by in minutes.

The above explanation, although wordy, seems a likely explanation, and the nearest real-life comparison to the arcade game experience is probably fighting or committing an outstanding act of bravery. The mind and body are fused in a single 'glorious' purpose, oblivious of everything else. The exhilaration experienced is common to both simulated and real actions. The endless drilling and training of soldiers is directed towards achieving this 'fusing of consciousness' when the soldier is faced with the enemy. Whether these outlets substitute for the average teenage male's need for violent action has not yet been established.

One ill that can be laid at 'PacMan's' door is the ability to provoke attacks of epilepsy – although to be fair attacks of photosensitive epilepsy and TV epilepsy can be induced by every other screen-based game and TV set. Some years ago researchers discovered that a screen flickering in the 10,000 to 25,000 Hz waveband could induce attacks in those persons subject to epilepsy, and as the craze for video-games has spread a growing number of young people stare intently into screens no more than a couple of feet away from them. As a result, there has been some increase in epileptic attacks, even among those who have no other personal or familial history of the complaint. Consideration given to this problem in Australia suggests that US users may be less subject to this problem than either their European or Australasian counterparts because the US electrical supply system operates on 60 Hz instead of 50 Hz. The 50 Hz system causes a flicker at 25 Hz whilst the 60 Hz supply produces a flicker at the less sensitive rate of 30 Hz. Manufacturers of video games are now struggling to find systems that help to cancel out the flicker and thus avoid adding to the inherent problem.

It is not only video games and TV broadcasts which can cause epilepsy. Users of home computers are also at risk. One case reported in *The Lancet*, cites a 15-year-old boy who was playing with a Sinclair ZX-81 microcomputer in a shop. The boy programmed the computer to display a rapidly repeating pattern. He immediately began to feel dizzy and lost consciousness. It must be stressed that no game, TV or microcomputer is more, or less, likely to cause epileptic attacks than another; if the susceptibility exists, any flickering image can induce an attack. (Parents may well recall the spate of attacks which were reported during the stroboscopic days of the psychedlic era.) The prevalence of photosensitivity has been estimated to be one in 10,000, and these odds should not cause any parent special concern unless there is a family history of epilepsy.

Another ill which has been identified in both the USA and UK is called 'Space Invader Wrist'. Although this was originally the subject of a medical student's tongue-in-cheek letter to *The New England Journal of Medicine* a couple of years ago, other researchers have announced that it is an identifiable malady that has occurred around the world. The symptom is pain and stiffness in the wrist concerned, the cause is minor ligamentous strain and although not important it must be considered in a category which includes hula-hoop dislocations, jogger's itch and skateboard ankle. The cure is a few weeks' rest.

While most primary schools are using microcomputers for CAI (computer-aided instruction), the majority of secondary schools are teaching children how to program them. As mentioned in the example of the pilot and the plane, it now seems that this approach may be a blind alley. Until now, there have been only two ways of using a computer. The first is to use it without ready prepared software (CAI); the other is to program the computer to do something specific by writing our own computer programs.

# COMPUTERS AND YOUR CHILD ■■■■■■■■■■■■■■■■■■■■■■■■■■■■■■■■■■

## Computing as a hobby

Since its arrival in 1975 home computing (and much school microcomputing) could have been fairly likened to the crystal set that many schoolboys (but very few girls!) constructed in previous generations. It has been a hobby in which the difficulties of construction have been an intrinsic part of the attraction. But computer languages have become better as computers themselves have improved, and it now seems likely that in the very near future we will *not* need to understand a computer language in order to be able to program computers – just as we do not now need to be able to tune a crystal in order to pick up radio stations. In a few years computer languages such as BASIC, Algol, FORTRAN and COBOL will all be defunct for normal programming purposes and of academic interest only. As computer capacity and software intelligence increase, detailed programming will become less and less necessary. Already there are programs such as 'The Last One' which write the programs for the user and promise that he or she will never have to write another computer program. Although this promise is at the moment a little optimistic, it is clear that the days of 'Peeking' and 'Poking' are over. (I consider these two jargon words sum up all that is worst in microcomputing. They describe programming procedures which were considered technologically primitive even in the 1950s, but they remain operations of intense interest to today's 'crystal set' brigade.) What will be necessary, however, is a thorough understanding of how computer logic works. Without this, programs such as The Last One, which merely automates program writing, cannot be used.

Despite the imminent arrival of programs which write programs, schools continue to teach programming, separating the computer from the mainstream curriculum. All pupils must be taught how computer logic works, but the notion of sweating over any particular computer language is outdated and should soon be disregarded. Only a tiny percentage of children will go on from school to become professional computer programmers, and once they enter university or vocational training they will throw away any fluency in BASIC or other high level languages, and begin studying how to talk directly to the microprocessor using machine code or assembler languages. A thorough grounding in computer logic will be of more use to these pupils than the teaching of a particular high level language.

Privately educated children may fare much better in computer-related studies than their less privileged counterparts in state schools. Independent schools often have a far higher equipment level than state schools, and as a result the computer is more closely integrated into the general curriculum. Private schools are already demonstrating computer power over such diverse subjects as stage lighting, ecology, the electronic timing of athletic events and musicmaking. One British boarding school even chains a Pet computer to the banisters on the last day of term to allow pupils to check the timetables of buses, trains and planes which will whisk them back to the bosom of their families for the 'vac'. But only 7% of children attend private school (the average figure in the developed world). What of the other 93%? In the absence of a fully integrated computer-assisted curriculum, learning to program a computer is the only way of picking up a superficial understanding of the way artificial intelligence works. It is better than nothing.

### 'Code junkies'

For some children, particularly the more intelligent, computer programming can become almost addictive, far more even than the arcade games which may have attracted them to computers in the first place. Dr Chris Reynolds, a reader in computer studies at London's Brunel University, has identified this group as 'code junkies'. Often socially inadequate, these children form attachments with computer intelligence and, under the encouragement of their misguided parents who consider their clever child is headed for technological stardom, retreat from the real world into a bedroom world filled with the subroutines of clumsy old-fashioned computer languages. This situation becomes masturbatory as the child is producing programs entirely for self-gratification. The private world of the bedroom provides a sanctuary in which the child is king, and the computer provides both him or her and the parents with justification for totally irrational and harmful behaviour patterns.

The appalling ignorance of teachers about computing often conspires to produce a situation in which these children are genuinely, but mistakenly, considered stars. The teachers are left behind as the child delves deeper into the possibilities of artificial intelligence and are completely unable to judge the real value of the child's achievements. Often gross programming malpractices develop, and the child is unable or unwilling to get any practical advice on his or her programming development. For a while the child impresses peers, parents and teachers alike with complex programs with flashing screens and sound effects. But in reality the child is escaping from the world and is forming bad programming habits in a complete academic vacuum.

Assuming these pupils remain sufficiently conformist to gain the entrance requirements, universities usually have to retrain them (reprogram might be a better phrase) before they can move on to their study of computer science.

Dr Reynolds considers that providing a home computer for

adolescents can sometimes have an *adverse* effect on student studies and even on employment prospects. He argues that providing a computer for adolescents at a vulnerable period in their lives in the hope that foundations may be laid for an exciting career may actually be counterproductive. He points out that to work properly in computers, programmers have to think in the language they are using, just as fluency in French or German demands thought in those languages. Most languages currently available for home computers are fussy and old-fashioned, and if a young person develops a deep understanding of these, his or her ability to learn a new language is impaired.

One possible answer is to broaden our approach to computers. Children must be taught what they can do, rather than how to program them. In the home this means that parents should ensure that computer use covers many fields, and in the school computer power should be spread right across the curriculum – it should come out of the male science department and offer assistance with all subjects. It must become a tool that is naturally used alongside atlases and video recorders.

Teachers of computer studies seldom have any real knowledge of the subject they are teaching. This was publicly recognised by the board which sets London's GCE 'A-level' computer studies examination when they revised the A-level syllabus for 1983. The main course elements for this particular exam now are: applications, information systems, computer science and programming skills as well as a particular project. The board found that recent examinations have revealed an astonishing lack of understanding among entrants of how to go about testing programs and how to provide security against failure of hardware.

**Computer studies and industry**

A British study sought to establish how relevant the exam subject of 'computer studies' turned out to be when students went on to university or entered industry. The researchers canvassed opinions from both areas and discovered that further education establishments preferred to take pupils with a sound background in mathematics and physics rather than computer studies as the students with this latter background were likely to have picked up bad habits. Industry saw little relevance in the computer studies qualification, and the survey produced a report which concluded that the subject of computing is changing so rapidly that the time delay between producing an examination syllabus and the years of study required to achieve a pass ensure that the knowledge gathered is out of date before the successful student steps up to receive his or her diploma.

Our children are beset by compounded problems: if we accept that teaching them how to program computers is the wrong approach, how do we re-educate our educators to provide a broader, more general computer-based education in which the machine is a means rather than an end. As humans get older their imagination decreases in inverse proportion to their experience, and the 'old dogs and new tricks' syndrome frustrates any hope of rapid change. But if we shrug and decide to make the best of a bad job by accepting the 'computer studies' approach, we are faced with a situation in which the teachers do not understand enough about the subject to be able to teach it successfully. How are we to help our children?

Once again, the answer has to be provided in the home. The parents who are aware of the dangers of teenage isolation can do their best to ensure that their child does not turn into a code junkie. They can also seek to broaden their child's attitude to computing by providing examples of computer application outside the school curriculum. In this they may face a difficult task. Programming has become a snob subject in many schools, and senior sixth form boys who are preparing for university entrance, with computing science high on their list of academic achievements refer to computer use (as against computer programming) as 'Noddy' computing. This type of slur is insidious and difficult to deal with; yet the student who is happy to use 'Noddy' computing to further his or her studies may well be better placed to develop a real appreciation of the role artificial intelligence will play later in life.

Computer camps are one alternative which many parents consider. Sending a teenage child away to summer camp is a tradition in many countries, and it is tempting to consider combining this visit with a crash course in computing if the child in question is not at a computer-oriented school or if he or she seems to be either particularly enthusiastic or particularly unreceptive towards computers. But there are some problems attached to the idea.

The camps range in quality from the excellent to the bogus, and not many parents are experienced enough to spot the difference. Most are situated in country houses or large schools and typically stress that 'this is the ideal way to introduce your child to tomorrow's world of computing.'

What your child will find when he or she arrives varies from camp to camp and country to country, but nearly all camp organisers equate computing with programming and the drive is directed towards this end.

The better camps offer a wide range of facilities other than computing and also have enough computers to ensure that each child is allocated an individual machine during his or her stay. It seems that, as well as attracting a percentage of children with no computing experience, these camps are also becoming an annual meeting place

121

for the code junkies, or those well on their way to becoming computing addicts.

Some of the camps teach applications as well as programming, and these are the sort to look for. Camps which suggest that suitable attendees are maths oriented and then list the computer languages they offer are primarily concerned with programming; but a few camps talk about word-processing, robot control and musicmaking, and obviously these have a broader approach. Many camp leaders report that it is difficult to stop the children using the computers at the end of the day. These statements are usually made boastfully in the colourful prospectuses sent out each year, although they usually serve only to indicate the limitations of the organiser's vision. One particular British camp brochure happily informs parents that the principals have to do the rounds of the computer rooms at midnight throwing out the absorbed children!

Computing can be absorbing, but such absorption in adolescents requires very careful control, and a computer camp may be the worst possible situation for them. Here the child will meet a group of other children also fixated with artificial intelligence and usually the many alternative pursuits – canoeing, swimming, basketball, etc. – find few takers.

*A typical scene at a computer camp (note the complete absence of girls). Computer camp organisers often boast that they have to pull the adolescent boys away from the computers at midnight, but some experts argue that such obsessional programming can be harmful. Better camps offer robotics and examples of broader computer applications – such as music and art – as well as providing outdoor pursuits for the campers.*

122

### 'Young Computer Brains'

Having said all this about the dangers of teaching children to program computers, it must also be said that a teenager's imagination and power to learn can, if harnessed properly, turn out some quite brilliant programmers who are capable of earning huge sums of money before they leave school. Most countries now have some sort of 'Young Computer Brain of the Year' contest, and in these the really clever children get a chance to show what they can do. The winners of such competitions have invariably addressed themselves to a particular application of computing and win their prizes because they have developed a program to help handicapped people, to assist in the detection of criminals or some other cause which is of direct benefit to society or commerce. Some children prove themselves so adept at writing programs (usually games) which appeal to other children that the microcomputer manufacturers are buying their programs for large initial sums as well as paying royalties on sales. Numerous cases have been reported of 15-year-old computer entrepreneurs who are making large sums of money in their spare time.

But these gifted children have managed to become 'balanced' programers, with an ability to see the need for a specific type of program within society, and this ability is as great as, if not greater than, their pure ability to write computer programs. These children may be absorbed in programming, but they are unlikely to be using the activity as a psychological prop or as a defence against the outside world.

Many boys and girls with a healthy approach to programming finish school on a Friday and, instead of taking up Saturday jobs in a local store as their parents did, head for the local software company (or their bedroom) to continue development of a particular commercial project. It must be emphasised that these children are a tiny minority and usually fall into the 'gifted child' category; but it is their ability to discover a computer application which will either find a market or assist society in some way that is at the root of their success. Their ability to create the programs is less important, and as their career progresses they are unlikely to do much physical programming themselves; they are likely to work in three stages:

1  Identifying a specific problem which needs solving
2  Analysing the problem, and
3  Designing a program which will provide a solution.

The actual detailed work of developing the program will be left to other, less creative programmers.

For the majority of children, therefore, computing ought to be an integral part of their education at the end of which turning to a computer for assistance with history research or musical composition will mean as little as going to a library and taking a book from a shelf. They should be familiar with how computers work, what the machines can and cannot do and the best way to use a variety of types of hardware. This may be an ideal state, and it is one that will be realised slowly. The problem occurs only if your child is likely to be leaving school in the next two or three years.

Many schools keep the micro locked up in maths and science. In a smaller number it will be found entering the domain of English classes. Still fewer allow it into French, geography, or history classes, and in very few does it reach the art room or music department. There are two main reasons: lack of money and lack of teaching expertise. But, as the price of microcomputers falls, lack of expertise will prove the hardest problem to beat. Even if you give a 50-year-old piano teacher a computer which will allow his or her students the chance to compose, and then edit and alter that composition before finishing the work, it is a big gamble whether the teacher will approve or be able to work the thing or understand its resounding implications for the future of music. But not to provide your musically talented son or daughter with an early appreciation of the changes occurring in music is to put them at a considerable disadvantage to those who have been lucky enough to appreciate the changes taking place.

**Computers in science teaching**

In science the use of computers is obvious. Examining the life cycle of the inhabitants of a lake is a subject easily fitted on to a computer program. The *Odell Lake* program, developed by the staff of the Minnesota Educational Computing Consortium (MECC, one of the most advanced educational computing organisations in the world), allows students to build a model of a lake and study the food chain which develops. An animated display of a mackinaw trout's jaws snapping as it consumes whitefish is the sort of attractive programming that can lift computer-aided instruction from the repetitive to the exciting. The program is part of a suite of programs called *Understanding Food Chains*, and the user is able to plan his or her lake and introduce various life forms into it. The program is capable of recognising instantly which life forms are incompatible – e.g. trout and whitefish – and will advise the pupil accordingly. In trying to create a balanced pond the pupil will have to accept some losses in the whitefish stock and consider ways of controlling the more powerful predators.

With this sort of interactive program, the pupil is stimulated to ask for more and more information about the roles of various life forms in a water environment and, depending on how powerful the program is, should be able to receive a great deal of information directly from the computer. This type of program has proved powerful at capturing and holding the pupil's attention and virtually dispenses with the services of a human teacher whilst the pupil plays God and creates an aquatic world. At the end of the project, the pupil will have created a more or less balanced lake, and a paper print-out should show a drawing of the lake itself and offer all relevant information about size, volume, plant life, fish life, animal life, etc. This type of program often throws up thought-provoking stock combinations, and the variety of successful lakes that are created is always surprising.

Programs such as *Quake*, also from MECC, allow the pupil to play the role of seismologist and help him or her plot the epicentre of the earthquake as secondary wave follows primary shock. The programs are supported by documentation and worksheets, and in MECC programs have been constructed with such peripheral aims as widening the student's vocabulary and installing innate understanding of geometry and allied sciences.

Much geography teaching is now concerned with the people who inhabit the world's countries. Many programs now exist which help pupils to chart population movements and such social and economic changes as industrial development. With high quality graphic displays, pupils are able to display various parts of Africa, for example, and introduce colour shadings according to their opinion about rainfall, crop occurrence, population density, etc. The computer is available to provide help at all times and the pupil can flip from the map display to an information display which helps them arrive at correct opinions about a region. It will be realised that such powerful programs will contain the ability to cross over the boundaries which education has artificially created between subjects, and whilst examining the topography of a region of Zimbabwe the pupil may, if he or she so chooses, also add shadings which indicate industrial output, average incomes, health statistics and geological information.

The power of the computer is so immense that it seems likely to break down some of the barriers between parallel subjects such as geography, botany, geology and anthropology and also between even more discrete subjects such as sociology and political history.

**Maths and the computer**

In mathematics pupils are for the first time able to create models of problems under consideration. Maths is perhaps one of the most abstract disciplines, and the ability to provide both graphic and formula models is very powerful. In an arithmetical role the 'what if?' power of the computer is extremely useful in illustrating the interaction of various mathematical occurrences. Using a popular commercial program such as 'Visicalc' pupils can create an imaginary business complete with all the overheads and production costs and then add all the sales figures and related expenses. Because this powerful program is fully interactive, the pupil has only to alter one factor – the number of goods sold per month for example – to see the effect that such a change in business would have on profitability and on more subtle elements such as the percentage of overhead which is ascribed to vehicle depreciation. It is possible to build such models manually; but each one would take many hours, and one change would mean that all other calculations would be incorrect. With the computer program the pupil is able to 'play' endlessly with the model of the business, and the result is that he or she gains a very thorough understanding of the vital elements which combine to produce a profit – or a loss. The sort of instinctive feel for business this produces after a few weeks of playing is often very much better than the instinct which supports many professional business people who have not had the chance to study computer-based models.

Computer studies as a separate subject is now quite clearly defined in most schools and covers such areas as electronic appreciation, programming and applications. Very few schools (as distinct from colleges of further education) study the impact of computers upon society.

In the other sciences – chemistry and physics for example – computers are well established, and a considerable amount of proven software is available. Outside the sciences it is a different story.

The British organisation MUSE (Microcomputer Users in Secondary Education) currently has a list of 120 programs available for schools, but more than 100 of them are maths or science oriented. There are many arts programs for children of primary school age, but few for children between 11 and 18. English is particularly poorly served. Nouns and adjectives are easy meat for computers during the early years of education, but the programs capable of handling languages are more complex and require more powerful computers.

The word-processor for Britain's BBC Microcomputer, described in the previous chapter, is one of the first text-editing programs to become available specifically for educational use. Its powers are somewhat limited and would prove of use only to the younger pupils in a secondary school. There are many commercial word-processing systems available, but despite the enormous advantages word-processing brings to creative writing (discussed in the last chapter) very few schools offer word-processing as part of the English syllabus. Some schools which have computers with word-processing programs consider them 'office oriented' and only offer training in these programs to those studying commerce (usually girls).

Music and art are subjects in which the micro has such an

important and distinct role to play that I have discussed it in a separate chapter, but despite the many benefits currently available few schools are yet making use of the computer in these subject areas.

### Imaginative computer projects

Outdoor occupations can all benefit from computer control: each year Commodore demonstrates how its Pet microcomputers can monitor an arduous hike over the treacherous Yorkshire moors in Northern England. With a little supervision the boys involved in the hike input all of the necessary data – the route, conditions, number and names of entrants, etc. – and the computer allows the command post to keep a very watchful eye on the progress of the hike. The computers are also able to record the time and progress of each team in the hike and automatically supply results. This is an ideal type of application to illustrate that the computer's role is not confined to a corner of the science laboratory.

A secondary school in San Diego, California, annually plots the migration course of the whale on micros. Although this could be described as a purely scientific use, 150 students become involved and, after a great deal of work, take to the boats to travel out into the Pacific, to San Diego's Point Loma. Here they discover whether their computer simulation of the world's longest mammalian migration makes whale finding easier. It is a pity more schools can't provide this

```
LIST
10 CALL CLEAR
20 FOR A=1 TO 95
30 X=INT(24*RND)+1
40 Y=INT(32*RND)+1
50 CALL COLOR(2,5,5)
60 CALL HCHAR(Y,X,42)
70 NEXT A
80 GO TO 80
```

type of imagination when applying computer power to problem solving.

But computing is moving quickly and, although the situation is a far from happy one at the moment, within a couple of years may well have changed so that the boy or girl studying woodwork will consider it natural to turn to the woodwork shop's computer to program a robot arm for a repetitious piece of machining.

What of children about to leave school, however? Some may have learned a bit of BASIC, others may have pursued the subject in more detail whilst still more may have been pushed into the 'also ran' group which had to listen to verbal explanations and make do with a few minutes per week practical experience.

For the school-leaver with a profound interest in computers, a college course on the subject or direct career entry to computing would seem an obvious choice. Many colleges and universities offer degree courses with a computer qualification at the end, and successful students are likely to find themselves able to select from a variety of job offers. There has been some newspaper discussion in recent years about unemployment hitting even the computing industry (often seen as the cause of unemployment in the first place); but this has been limited to lower-level computer staff – such as programmers and operators – and the hot demand for engineers, systems analysts and designers continues (and is likely to continue) unabated.

*Although BASIC is still taught in many schools, its value to any child considering a career in computing is questionable.*

128

An interesting option, just becoming available, is for the computing student to consider going back to school to teach computing. Until now computing as a proper subject has been the preserve of universities and colleges. One problem is that teachers need to have a far broader view of computing than the limited view developed in a computing industry career. It is clear that education is desperately short of trained computer personnel, and such a career would undoubtedly be very rewarding.

### Jobs in computing

In the computing industry proper there are several levels of hierarchy, and, although it is possible to step up through the system, those entering at a high level from a university or similar institution are bound to find career progress more rapid.

There are six main levels of hierarchy in the computer industry. The lowest grade may be described as 'skilled user'. This category would include workers who have learned to operate computers to do particular tasks such as word-processing or accountancy. Often these skills are picked up as a sub-set of skills to other occupations – e.g. secretarial or office administration – but they also include functions particular to the computer industry such as terminal operator, card-punch (data) operator and similar. Starting in these jobs requires a basic set of school or college qualifications and the ability to think clearly. Skills such as keyboard operation are normally taught on the job.

Next step up is the computer operator. Operators control work as it goes through the computer, whether on tapes or on magnetic disks. Operators have to understand the basics of how computers work, and this type of job often involves shift work as many of the large computer centres work 24 hours a day. Employers look for a good general standard of education and consider some knowledge of computer operation to be a definite advantage. Becoming a computer operator is a good springboard to becoming a programmer.

A computer programmer enters instructions to the computer in a language it understands, such as COBOL or FORTRAN. The qualifications needed to become a programmer include a clear methodical mind and an ability to concentrate on minute detail. It is a very special type of person who becomes a skilled programmer, and although normal entry qualifications are a degree or senior school-leaving exam passes, natural ability to work with machine logic often counts for more. Many programmers enter the industry without formal qualifications.

Programming is split into two groups: applications programmers and systems programmers. Applications programmers write programs to carry out a specific task. Systems programs write programs to keep the computer system in order – e.g. writing a program to detect computer faults. The applications programmer is likely to meet people outside the computer room – clients using the computer for example – and is likely to work with a team of programmers developing programs for a specific task. The systems programmers are more specialist and tend to work alone. They are talking directly to the machine intelligence and probably come closest to direct communication with it.

After programming, the computer industry draws an artificial dividing line, beyond which it denies access to all but the brightest programmers and the best-qualified university graduates. This is the realm of the systems analysts and designers.

### Systems analysis and design

Systems analysts consider a problem and then decide how a computer can help to solve it. For example, an oil company discovers a new deposit under the sea bed. They have measured the extent of the deposit and found that the quality of oil varies, with some parts of the field yielding crude good enough to make petrol, other parts producing oils only useful for the manufacture of plastic. The oil company has to decide whether or not to invest the millions of pounds necessary to exploit the oil field. This decision will be based on projections about the state of the international oil market for the life of the field (say 20 years), and the company must decide which part of the field to drill first. Because the investment is so vast, the oil company considers it a wise investment to take the problem to a computer consultancy and hand the problem to them for analysis.

The analyst considers the problem. Information about the past performances of the oil market has to be gathered, information about the demand for various types of crude oil is found out and the leading economic pundits consulted about their predictions for the future of different markets in different parts of the world. All available measurements from the oil field are gathered together to form a computer model which will allow the consultancy to simulate the various options for drilling and exploring the field. The analyst, along with economists and program designers, designs the necessary computer programs. The end result is likely to consist of a large suite of programs (perhaps including a graphic representation of the field's structure) which by careful design and deduction can offer logical conclusions about the potential for the field's exploitation. The oil company executives will be able to play 'what if?' with this model, discovering how various decisions about price, refining techniques and market approaches would affect overall performance, and are

130

provided with all the information they need to make their final decisions about how best to exploit their field.

These are oversimplified examples, and a real project could well take several years, involve a large computing team, and be based on detailed computer projections of the field's output and the prospects for the world's economies. But from this example it can be seen that the role of the analyst and program designer is vital, as computers are only able to work in the method prescribed and on the information provided. The analyst is the deciding factor on how well the computer is used, and the computer effectively becomes an adjunct and extension of the analyst's brain.

There are several other important roles in the computer industry, although few are as highly regarded as the systems analyst. Perhaps the exception is hardware design. There are openings for electronics engineers at all levels from high street repair centres to research departments, but the areas of product development and pure research are only open to those with the highest electronic engineering qualifications.

Many analysts and designers of both machines and software move on to managerial and consultancy positions, but these titles often indicate only that the individual is working in a more powerful role, very often self-employed. The work content of the job often remains the same.

But if the computer industry is booming, many other industries are suffering recession, and a grim OECD report published at the end of 1982 suggests that this malaise will hang over most Western countries for some years to come – with the significant exceptions of America and Japan.

**Microcomputing centres**

Several governments, Britain's in particular, consider that microelectronics may provide an answer to some of the short-term unemployment problems. The Youth Opportunities Scheme, established by the British government to provide some work experience for the large number of unemployed youngsters (before they become unemployable), now offer places at 40 microcomputing centres in Britain. At these centres young school leavers can take a course in various aspects of microcomputing while receiving a small wage. This scheme has the double benefit of offering some computer familiarisation to those who slipped through the net at school (either because they left school before the computer arrived, or because they weren't 'selected' to use it) and of improving their prospects of finding a job.

You may be forgiven if you wonder how the training of one school leaver to take on a computer-based job (which is probably designed to replace several manual jobs) assists the unemployment problem. Ambiguity over the role of computers in employment is prompted by reports which predict mass unemployment as a direct result of computer automation. One recent report suggests that automation-induced unemployment will reach 16% in Western Europe. For those who leave school without any computer familiarity or literacy, employment prospects seem grim. Many experts consider that microtechnology increases the gap between the 'haves' and the 'have-nots', rather than producing greater equality as some futurists predict. It would certainly seem that young black Americans, who currently face an appalling 50% unemployment rate, will have yet another barrier to overcome if their education fails to equip them for the computer age.

Whatever their abilities and interests, children approaching school leaving age deserve our sympathies. In education, essentially an information-passing process, they are caught up in the midst of an information revolution to which they are proving far more able to adapt than their teachers. After education, they face a world that during the transition between the pre- and post-computer ages finds itself in turmoil. They must be fit to survive in this world, and one of the essential qualifications of fitness is the ability to command and apply computer intelligence.

# COMPUTERS AND THE SPECIAL CHILD

No matter how significant the contribution made by the microcomputer to the development of the normal child, it is dwarfed by the benefit the microprocessor is now bringing to the handicapped child (and adult). The help it offers special children is little short of miraculous.

'Special children' or 'exceptional children' are phrases which encompass all children whose needs are outside normal educational practices, and the British Special Education Act (1981) identifies 20% of all pupils as having special educational needs at some stage during their school careers. (At the time of writing only 3% of British school children receive special education.)

Special children include the slow learners, the backward children, autistic children, children with dyslexia and the mentally and physically handicapped including the sensorially deprived such as the blind and the deaf. The category also includes gifted children and children who suffer learning problems through social maladjustment.

I will not resist the urge to describe the benefits offered to these children by computer technology as 'God-like', for in some instances the blind are helped to 'see', the deaf to 'hear' and in the future probably the lame to walk. In some cases of severe or multiple handicap communication, and therefore education, would be impossible without the microprocessor.

At the furthest frontiers of medical research computer scientists are now working with doctors to provide the physically handicapped with microprocessor control over functions normally undertaken by the brain. The aim is to replicate part of the brain's control over the body.

The American physiologist Dr Jerrold Petrofsky has been experimenting with the connection of microprocessors to the animate nervous system. This work has been carried out at the Wright State University in Dayton, Ohio, where Dr Petrofsky is head of biomedical engineering. When I started writing this book in the summer of 1982 he had succeeded in linking a microprocessor to a surgically paralysed cat and controlling the activation of one of the animal's leg muscles. His team – consisting of other consultants and 23 graduate students –

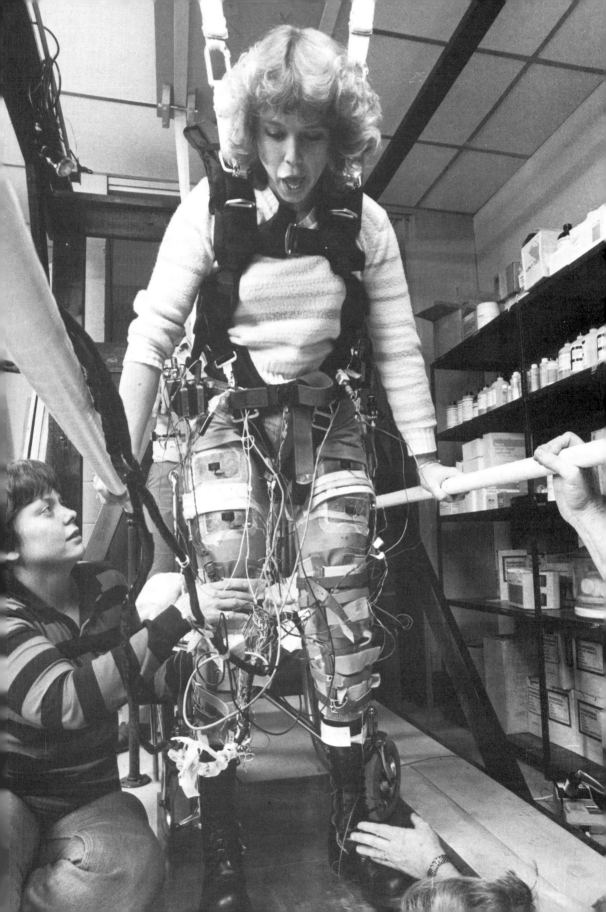

*Nan Davis walking with the aid of computer control.*

was then working on the development of a mathematical model which would project how muscles react to various electrical charges. It was hoped that this would allow microprocessors to be programmed to control muscles in the same way as the brain. Although microprocessors are easily able to undertake the necessary calculations to control a limb, problems still existed in creating the right program and in interfacing the output to the muscles concerned. It has long been established that electrical charges can stimulate muscles, and although much work had already been done it was expected that the first experiments with humans would not take place for a few years. Shortly before I finished the final draft of this book, the *Sunday Times* carried a report that Dr Petrofsky had successfully helped a paraplegic woman to walk by using a microcomputer to control her otherwise paralysed leg muscles.

**Computer-aided walking**

The patient was Nan Davis, a 22-year-old Ohio student teacher who was paralysed from the waist down following a car accident. Supported by a parachute-type harness, 30 electrodes were externally attached to her leg muscles which, under the control of the computer, were successfully stimulated to operate in the correct order to make her legs walk. Nan became the first paraplegic ever to walk using her own muscle power, although her body weight still required support. It is important to comment that the muscle instruction currently comes from the computer program, not from a microprocessor interpretation of her brain's commands – but she, Dr Petrofsky and the microcomputer have made history. The difficulties that stand between direct connection of the microprocessor to the neurons of the human nervous system (to link brain and limb) remain immense. It must be stressed that this work is experimental, and no commercial microprocessor limb-control systems yet exist, or are likely to for some considerable time.

Now that science has developed a machine capable of reproducing some brain functions, it seems certain that in the future we will learn how to connect the microprocessor to the brain, the nervous system and then to the outside world. Blind people who have suffered damage either to the eye or to the optic nerve may be able to see through a camera system in which the microprocessor creates the interface (making a matching connection) between the output from the camera and the input to the brain. Equally, deaf people are likely to be able to hear by the connection of a microphone to a microprocessor which in turn translates the signals into a form acceptable to the human brain. People handicapped by severe motor impairment – spastics for example – may find that, even if their limbs do not come under

135

microprocessor control, their intelligence will be released from its awful prison, and they will find themselves able to communicate via artificial devices interfaced with their brain – a system which will bypass their uncontrollable body. Only those with the most severe mental handicaps may remain beyond the help of the computer. It is impossible to say when all of these miracles will come about. It is tempting to think that medical advances will move as quickly as computer development, but it is unlikely that this will be the case. I would hazard a guess that such 'miracles' will have become commonplace inside the normal lifespan of today's handicapped, but otherwise healthy child.

In the meantime the computer is already bringing previously undreamed of help to the handicapped, and coincidentally society is at last beginning to reconsider its attitude towards the handicapped. Describing a child as needing 'special help' is one step towards redefining this group, and the USA's 1975 Education for All Handicapped Children Act began the movement to integrate handicapped children into normal schools (rather than consigning them to a special institution and tidying them away out of sight!), an important step in re-educating society to accept the handicapped as people rather than objects.

### Handicapped in normal education

Teachers working with special children are as confused about the arrival of the computer in their classrooms as are their counterparts in normal education; but resource levels are generally higher where special children are concerned, and teachers also have in general a greater level of commitment in response to a far greater need. Consequently the microcomputer is already being put to far more effective use in special education than in normal classrooms.

While conventional education is struggling to make the micro conform to traditional educational practices, teachers in special education have greeted the arrival with more open minds. Schools are often said to be expert at the containment of innovation, and (as I have suggested in earlier chapters) microcomputers are being bent to the will of teachers who are unwilling, and often unable, to adapt their teaching techniques to its arrival. As a result the computer is often being used in a 'teacher-centred' way in conventional education, and the alternative, a 'child-centred' approach (such as the philosophy behind the Logo language), stands little chance.

In special education, however, the child-centred approach has been flourishing. This is partly because the need for individual tuition is well established in special education and partly because considerable experimentation has taken place in introducing special children to

Logo and other child-motivating computer programs. The results are extremely encouraging. The USA has a lead on the rest of the world in special education. There are over four million children requiring special help in the USA, and relatively high funding levels have been available for special education for years.

Before considering the computer benefits now available for special children, we need to identify each group's needs. The groups can be identified as: (a) slow learners and those with language difficulties such as autistic children, (b) those with identifiable mental handicaps, the educationally subnormal children, (c) those children who are sensorially handicapped, the deaf and the blind, and (d) those with motor impairments and with severe multiple or total handicap.

The final category (e) concerns gifted children, who are often put in the special child category, although the American expression 'exceptional child' seems more suitable. Gifted children, who often rapidly outstrip the ability of normal teachers to teach them, are discovering greater opportunities to learn with computer assistance and are now far more likely to achieve their full potential.

A large group of children find learning difficult for a variety of reasons – social, mental or physical – but do not suffer any obvious sensory or physical disability. Many of these children have already found the computer to be a great friend.

### Special education

In special education there is a need for a high pupil-equipment ratio, and all schools which have special children need to be able to offer each slow-learning child a significant amount of individual access to a microcomputer. The drill and practice programs, which elsewhere in this book I have criticised, take on an important role with children slow to grasp concepts or techniques. No human teacher has limitless patience, but a computer will repeat an explanation endlessly, freeing the human teacher to add additional illumination where necessary. The drill and practice of an arithmetic or reading program can be tailored to an individual pupil's needs so that he or she can work at whatever speed is most suitable. This has been found to have very beneficial effects, and children who have become used to public failure – e.g. always being shown up as having misunderstood a concept in class – began to regain confidence as they work in impersonal privacy with a computer.

Impersonal privacy is an important quality of artificial intelligence, and the medical profession has discovered that in many instances this factor has made computers better at making initial illness diagnoses than humans. Left in privacy with an intelligent computer, humans feel no shame at telling the computer about venereal disease or admitting their true level of alcohol or nicotine intake, and thus quicker, more accurate diagnoses can be made. In the same way the child who is normal except for being slower than most other children at learning is prepared to go on making mistakes in front of a computer long after he or she would have stopped risking public failure in a classroom. This leads on to another important use of computers in special education: they are extremely useful diagnostic aids.

Children become very adept at disguising their inabilities and often present confusing signals to human interrogators. Although teachers in special education are trained to recognise such behaviour, the correct diagnosis of a child's learning problem hangs as much on the child's response as on the teacher's ability to assess it, and the computer can often highlight a condition that otherwise might be overlooked. Once again, the child is prepared to be totally honest with the non-intimidating computer, and a well written program can quickly produce responses from the child that will allow teachers to assess the child's learning strengths and weaknesses accurately.

In addition to patient and graphically attractive drill and practice programs, which are able to repeat endlessly an explanation for a slow learner, the child-centred programs such as Logo produce astonishing results with some under-achieving students.

**Logo and dyslexia**

Many reports about the results of the use of Logo with slow learners have been published, but typical is a report by Sylvia Wier MD which appeared in the American magazine *Microcomputing*. In the report she cited the example of 'Keith' a dyslexic 11-year-old she introduced to Logo on an Apple II microcomputer:

> Keith had been a pupil at a special school for the learning disabled for four years and had come to the clinic at Children's Hospital for assessment. He spent 40 minutes interacting with the Logo computer system that I was demonstrating to the clinic personnel. His performance was excellent – way beyond what one would expect from a child of his age, or from a beginner of any age, for that matter. In the first half-hour he wrote a program which drew a snowman, effortlessly mastering the set of Logo primitives needed and centering the hat on the circular head without hesitation or error. He had been labelled as having a 'low motivation and a poor attention span'. We saw no evidence of that. All through the session his attention was totally engaged by the programming he was doing, and he had to be practically dragged away from the machine, long before he was ready to go (Copyright 1981 by *Microcomputing*,

138

Dr Weir goes on to identify the aspects of the computer and the Logo program which she considers motivated Keith. She believes that the fact that he was in control of progress (rather than controlled by it) was very important. She identifies Keith as being 'spatially gifted' (although language handicapped) and gives the opinion that there are a great many children who share this gift – many of them those who excel at games and athletics, but are very poor in academic subjects. She points out that as much of the present school curriculum is language-based, these children are at a disadvantage, and their gift of spatial understanding is not allowed to develop in a formal academic sense.

Autistic children seem to benefit particularly from contact with child-centred computer programs. Autism is still only partly understood, but what seems clear is that the autistic child, who in all pathological respects has a normal brain, fails to develop external personal relationships and very often prefers objects and machines to people. The autistic child often fails to speak (although he or she usually has the ability) and is normally severely retarded as a result of an inability to learn in normal teaching situations. The child is considered withdrawn and (when speaking) appears to utter meaningless phrases. When sufficient help is given, the child can passively participate in formal learning and may well be able to learn 'parrot fashion'. True comprehension in this state is rare. The root of autism seems to lie in the failure of the child to relate to situations and people, and thus any real learning that takes place in the child's mind must be self-taught. The floor turtle, controlled by the Logo program described in Chapter 4, provides a physical method by which the autistic child can explore the concepts of 'cause and effect' and externalise the self-taught lessons.

**Logo and autism**

There have been many individual experiments in which autistic children have been exposed to Logo on computers (and some in which they have used other computer languages), but it must be pointed out that there has not been any long-term investigation of the effect of computer-based learning on autism (or other special needs). It will be some years before such long-term results can be available. All early indications are, however, extremely promising. A research report, published by the Artificial Intelligence Department at Edinburgh University, holds out considerable hope for the parents and teachers of autistic children. The Edinburgh faculty has been experimenting with Logo in different applications for some years, but in this experiment they held six sessions with a seven-year-old autistic boy to discover whether interaction with the floor turtle would have any noticeable effect of his behaviour. The results were remarkable.

The Edinburgh team modified the turtle controls, mounting them as 16 buttons on a handheld box. This was considered preferable to the conventional system which controls the turtle from a typewriter-style keyboard. The buttons represent the various turtle functions – forwards, backwards, left, right, pen up, pen down, etc. – and, in addition to moving around the floor, the turtle 'hoots' and lights up as it executes a command.

'David' was slow to accept the instructions on how to control the turtle, which were given by the researchers. As usual, he avoided eye contact and, only when heavily prompted, passively and disinterestedly responded to an instruction. After discovering that manipulation of the buttons allowed him to take control of the turtle's activities David started to learn rapidly. He acted out the turtle's movements with his own body (a vital part of Logo pedagogy) and then, because he was so involved with the activity *he* was creating, started to talk about his success to the adults who were with him. After a few sessions David was explaining his actions to the researchers and offered sustained eye contact during his conversations. His 'passive' monotone voice was noted to have changed to a more natural excited tone, and David was ready to share his turtle experiences with the adults in the room.

The research team are quick to point out that this is the case history of only one child, but it is also fair to say that the child-centred motivation contained in Logo is closely allied to current thinking about childhood autism. The autistic child is not prepared to be taught (being unable to make sufficient commitment to the child-teacher or child-parent relationship), but will learn quickly when given tools with which to teach himself or herself and will then gain the confidence and desire to cross other bridges – such as communication.

Since clear definition of the condition was published in the 1940s, various methods of inducing response in autistic children have been tried, but computer control over external objects promises to be of great assistance in the treatment of autism and the education of autistic children.

An alternative form of child-centred learning based on the microprocessor is the programmable toy. I have mentioned the Big-trak programmable truck elsewhere in this book, but it has a particular use with special children. Up to 15 commands can be programmed into this toy, and children can immediately see the effect the commands have on the behaviour of the toy. Many children who have shown a reluctance to learn under instruction reveal that they do not lack ability when offered child-centred activities with which to learn. Many educators are being forced to revise their expectations about the performance limits of some groups of special children following the arrival of the microcomputer.


### Computer stars

Another surprising development that has followed the introduction of microcomputing in special education has been the emergence of 'computing stars' from the ranks of those previously considered to be backward. Longfield School in Kent prides itself on being Europe's foremost computer school, and, whether or not that label is justified, the work which has been done in the school's astonishingly well equipped computer room has produced some unexpected finds. The school reports that a surprisingly large number of illiterate and innumerate children, who get the opportunity to use the school's equipment, turn out to have a remarkable ability to work with computers. One child, 'Brian', was brain damaged at birth and, suffering from a speech defect, remained a persistent non-achiever until he discovered computer intelligence at Longfield. Today he is creating programs far beyond the comprehension of his teachers and is likely to go straight into the computer industry on leaving school. It seems that computers can open doors in the human mind which otherwise would remain firmly closed.

Remedial teaching is often necessary for children who have normal learning abilities, but who have fallen behind their age group for various reasons, lengthy stays in hospital being the most common. On returning to school such children are likely to develop the 'habit of failure' unless they can rapidly catch up with their contemporaries. The microcomputer is particularly useful in this work. Computers are also helping to nip this problem in the bud.

Children under 16 do receive some education whilst in hospital, but the arrival of the microcomputer is adding extra capacity to this service. Because of the wide range of age, needs and abilities found among the constantly changing population of child patients, human teachers find it difficult, if not impossible, to develop a successful teaching curriculum for children in hospital. Much hospital teaching is therefore therapeutic rather than instructional. The computer allows the hospital teacher to provide individual children (even those in weak physical condition) with tuition appropriate to their needs. Principals of hospital teaching units are discovering that an inexpensive microcomputer is the next best thing to acquiring an additional member of staff.

## Computers and maladjusted children

The children who are socially maladjusted usually need specialist treatment before they are willing to accept anything that smacks of formal education, but 'play' with a microcomputer (even PacMan or Space Invaders) will often find acceptance. Many children who are not prepared to give enough of themselves to another human being in order that teaching may take place will allow such a process to take place with a machine. There is no loss of face with a computer, and the children can present the activity to themselves any way they choose. But all computer use of this type must be carried out under professional supervision, and supplying a disturbed adolescent with a computer and PacMan program is unlikely on its own to solve any underlying behavioural problems.

The integration of children with special learning needs into ordinary classrooms is a change which is causing problems in many Western countries. Introducing a child with visual impairment into a class of normal pupils means either additional teaching staff or some other method of individual help for the pupil to be able to keep up with the rest of the class. This help could take the form of additional extra-mural tuition and general peripatetic support. In understaffed schools microcomputer assistance may play a major role in providing teaching support and making such integration possible. One limiting factor is money; another is the present clumsiness of microcomputers.

The latter problem, magnified when a child already classified as 'slow' has to learn to control such items as a cassette tape recorder and the attendant computer connections, is rapidly being solved by the arrival of the 'single unit' microcomputer which houses screen, keyboard, printer and storage system (perhaps a ROM chip or micro-drive disk) in one unit. When handicapped children can take a 'next to normal' place in school classrooms (with the backup of human and computer support to keep them there) we may have completed the first step towards the reintegration of the handicapped into general society since the large family group disintegrated.

A major problem besetting those who wish to use microcomputers in special education is a severe shortage of suitable programs. Teachers in normal education are also complaining of this shortage, but my earlier comment about their complaints (I suggest that many are seeking programs that teach the way they do, rather than being prepared to adapt their approach to the arrival of the microcomputer) does not apply to the genuine cry that is heard for software for special education.

Special education is a much smaller market than general education, and most profit-oriented companies are not motivated to invest the considerable research and production time necessary to produce programs for this small minority of children. For children with slight disabilities programs intended for normal children can be very useful, but major problems can occur if a slow learner is given a program outside his or her achievement range. One example of the sort of irritating problem that can be encountered when using microcomputers in special education is 'finger bounce'. This phenomenon occurs when a child is either hesitant or overenthusiastic in his or her use of a computer keyboard. The result is that the key 'bounces', and the intended letter is entered into the computer twice. This can result in an 'incorrect' response from the computer when actually the child's answer was correct, or it may frustrate the pupil as he or she is impeded in progress by having to discover how to get over the resultant 'error' message. Finger-bounce is caused by poor keyboard design, and on some computers the problem can be offset by writing a keyboard modification into the program.

Research projects are under way to develop programs suitable for slow learners and the educationally subnormal. By December 1983 a master program which will allow teachers to develop their own programs to suit individual children should become available as a result of work done by the Huddersfield Polytechnic in England, but at the moment there are no suitable programs available for a large proportion of special children, and in many parts of the world teachers and child psychologists are rapidly having to turn themselves into computer programmers in order to fill this need.

### Interactive reading program

Martin Long, a schools psychologist in the Yorkshire town of Rotherham, is typical of this new breed of programmer. He has created a program which links a stereo tape recorder with a microcomputer to produce an interactive reading program for remedial departments in primary schools. Pupils are presented with a written story on the screen, and a voice from the tape recorder reads the words in synchronisation. Where this system differs from earlier mechanised reading tutors is that the program constantly asks the pupil for input. The story stops at various points, and the child has to type in the ending to a sentence or choose an appropriate word or phrase.

It is this interaction that makes the system so much more successful than earlier mechanised reading machines. Children of all intelligences get bored reading automated screen texts, but a program which constantly demands their input before it continues (and no doubt in later versions will allow them decision-making power over the plot) holds them glued to their seats. The program is also able to assess the pupil's response to the various problems posed during the interaction and provide the teacher with a reliable scoring base by which to judge the pupil's reading progress.

Microcomputers are also allowing education for many slow learners to be continued outside school hours as well as for those children who for one reason or another are unable to attend school. Before the arrival of the inexpensive microcomputer the idea of providing computer terminals for these children (of secondary school age) had been tried, but the difficulty of telephone connection between the child's home and a central computer proved to be an obstacle. Microcomputers have provided an excellent answer, but programs have to be specially developed, almost for individual children. The results of some pilot experiments indicate that providing an unwell or socially maladjusted teenager with a microcomputer at home offers the greatest promise in the fight to provide these children with a reasonable level of education.

## Teenage blocks

Just as it has been observed that many 'slower' children do better with computer logic than more eager able children, who tend to become exasperated by the step-by-step approach demanded by many computer programs and languages, it has also emerged that special programs, such as word-processing and number 'games', can break down blocks in teenagers which threaten to deny them any ability in these subjects. Teenage children who are unable to create even one neat page of handwritten text often seem to discover that the labour-saving facility of word-processing programs is the key they have been looking for. Many of these children show that they are for the first time prepared to consider written language in its basic terms of sentence and paragraph construction once the laborious part of the process is automated. The same observation has been made when number games are provided to pupils who have previously refused all types of conventional arithmetical explanation.

My earlier comment that companies are not motivated sufficiently to produce programs designed for special education should not be taken to mean that all companies ignore the problem. Just as the Lamplighter School in Dallas (Chapter 4) benefits from being a stone's throw from the Texas Instruments headquarters, so schools in Walsall have benefited by being close to the UK head office of Tandy, the corporation which manufactures the Tandy Radio Shack TRS-80 microcomputers.

With the advice and cooperation of Tandy, the local education authority in Walsall has set up a microelectronics development team which has pioneered much work with microcomputers in both normal and special education and now boasts an extensive catalogue of tried and tested software, much of it suitable for special children, which it offers to all other educational institutions. These programs are naturally tailored for TRS-80 machines, but the microcomputer facilities that the Walsall group have had at their disposal have allowed them to assess the various types of programming approaches that work well with different groups of children. The Walsall group reports enthusiastically about the benefits that special children derive from contact with microcomputers, and their work has led them into hardware development designed to make the power of the microcomputer even more accessible to special children.

Although the Walsall team noted that excellent results were obtained when slow learners, either in ordinary schools or in schools for the educationally subnormal, were given the chance to use drill and practice programs, they considered that far more could be achieved if children could respond via a simplified keyboard which would display the symbol or words in a way more appropriate to a child's learning development rather than by the usual, rather complex array of keys on a typewriter-style keyboard. The team have developed two keyboards intended to replace the standard microcomputer keyboard, and these have considerably extended the ability of the microcomputer to help special children.

### New keyboards

The first keyboard developed has 12 large keys and is designed to be used with overlays on which pictures, symbols, letters or numbers are printed. The predominant use of symbols or pictures (rather than words or letters) allows children with language difficulties, or children who have not yet gained any literacy, to use computer programs. This considerably extends the relevance of microcomputers in special education – especially with the educationally subnormal. The Walsall team managed to find a local plastics company to produce their 'Primary' keyboard which is now commercially available, accompanied by full software and instructions.

The second keyboard the team developed is called an 'Adventure Keyboard' and is rather more ambitious than the first device. The Adventure Keyboard has a particularly useful application for the teaching of deaf and partially deaf children as well as for more general teaching in special education. The original Adventure Keyboard consists of a large board on a wooden base on which a three-dimensional model scene is built. The first model made was of a village, and as the child moves a marker (e.g. a model car) through the streets of the village, along a track rather like that found in electric slot-car racing sets, microswitches in the keyboard cause the computer to deliver the appropriate word and graphic symbol on the screen, e.g.

house, shop, church, etc.

The vocabulary used by the computer is under the control of the teacher and has the particular advantage of always being relevant to the position of the child's marker. With the addition of speech synthesis (now available quite cheaply) the appropriate word could also be spoken by the computer, and the electrical output is well suited to the hearing amplifier of a partially deaf child. Programs of various complexity are available for children of different ages and at different levels of learning ability, and it will be realised that in producing an externalised representation of the computer program (which appears like a model of the real world) the activity has become firmly child-centred rather than teacher-centred. The child can play with the marker in the 'model world' in any way he or she chooses, and thus self-remediation becomes not only possible, but likely as the child realises that he or she has the power to discover the way in which the word for an object looks (and, once speech synthesis is added, sounds).

The Walsall team have also made commercial versions of their Adventure Keyboard available, and these take the form of two-dimensional plastic overlays which are used on a multipurpose board. Other overlays for the Adventure Keyboard include a castle, a haunted house and a space station.

There are many teams and individuals all over the world busily

*The prototype 'Adventure Control Board' from Britain's Walsall team offers children with learning difficulties the opportunity to play in a model world. As the child moves a 'marker' along a slot-track, the TRS-80 computer provides either a written description of the activity (left) or a graphic representation (right).*

146

producing peripheral aids to adapt microcomputers to the special needs of the handicapped: the Walsall developments are merely a good example of what can be achieved. One disappointment is that many teams in separate locations are duplicating research and are effectively reinventing the wheel: microcomputing is so new that proper communication between such groups is not yet established.

Winners of 'Young Computer Brain of the Year Award' competitions frequently win by coming up with a device suitable for the handicapped. The last two annual competitions organised by the *Sunday Times* in London and Commodore Computers were won by programmers who had developed computer aids for the disabled. The 1982 award went to a gifted 14-year-old, Derek Reynolds, who built a keyboard input which consists only of two large keys and then created programs which would run with this very limited form of input. In 1981 the winner was Jennifer Penswick, a 14-year-old from Norwich, who devised a spelling program to assist deaf children to learn key words.

### Computing for ethnic minorities

Universities and polytechnics are also undertaking interesting social experiments with microcomputers. Because computer logic has shown itself to be unexpectedly accessible to pupils who in other areas show only low performance levels, some supporters of minority groups have persuaded colleges to allow teenage under-achievers access and training in the subject of computing. One interesting British experiment of this type is taking place at the Polytechnic of Central London. A local community relations officer persuaded the college to open a computing course for under-achieving school-leavers from ethnic minority groups. All normal college entry qualifications were waived for the experiment, and 15 students joined a course which started in September 1981. None of the students was considered capable of even intermediate literacy or numeracy examinations, and none had any school-leaving certificates. Of the 11 who finished the course five found permanent jobs in computing, and the remainder opted to go on to further education. They proved that their under-achievement at school was not because of any innate lack of ability. The experiment (still continuing) demands considerable support from the community relations organisation both in and out of college, and such experiments are now being repeated all over the developed world. It is the microcomputer which is the catalyst that makes it possible.

Many children suffer one or more sensory disabilities without suffering any other form of physical handicap. We have not yet arrived at the stage where the gifts of sight, hearing or speech can be automatically granted by computer, but the machines are having a quite remarkable impact on the rehabilitation of such children.

The special keyboards which offer large symbols as a form of microcomputer control have a special relevance to the partially sighted and to those who have not learned a language.

The Bliss representational symbols will be well known to anyone who has had contact with non-communicating children. Over 1,400 symbols exist in the Bliss vocabulary, although only a third of these might be regularly used by experienced users. The language was developed by Dr C.K. Bliss as an international language for communication and, although it failed to win the support of the United Nations and the EEC, it has proved extremely useful for those with speech-impairment.

The Bliss symbols are usually placed on a lap tray and the user will point in sequence at different symbols to form a message. In some models the symbol tray is electrically powered and the chosen symbols illuminated. For any lengthy communication to be achieved the recipient must wait patiently as the user points out each symbol (sometimes very slowly) and must remember the sequence of symbols in order to gather the sense of the message. Not all speech-impaired children are capable of pointing, and techniques for helping the severely disabled are discussed later in the chapter.

'Blissapple' is an inexpensive program for the Apple II microcomputer which allows symbols to be selected (from a set of symbols which the user has specified) on the screen. The program accumulates and remembers the symbols selected and, when the user has finished symbol selection, is capable of delivering the message quickly to a recipient via the screen or in written form on a printer. A variety of input devices may be used to control the program, and with a little knowledge of the system one may construct a control device that will be suitable for all but the most severely handicapped.


**Impetus from parents**

The requirement of a 'little knowledge' is, however, a stumbling block which is slowing down the introduction of such aids in many classrooms. All educational systems in the developed world are busily trying to train teachers in microcomputer technology and applications; but it takes time, and it does not always follow that because a certain facility exists a school will have the ability to implement it. Parents of special children are often highly motivated and instrumental in providing initial help and specialist knowledge.

An alternative to the Bliss language is offered by 'Splink' (speech/link), a microprocessor-controlled system which provides the handicapped user with a board containing 950 commonly used words. The user selects words from the board and builds sentences on the screen. A useful feature is that the board is connected to the screen by an infra-red link; there are no trailing wires to trip over. Speeds of up to 24 words per minute are claimed to be possible, and individual letters on the board allow unusual words to be composed.

A new symbolic language is being developed at Bristol University, England, for the severely deaf child. Deaf children have enormous problems in learning to read as the written language is a coded form of the spoken sounds rather than of the ideas contained in words. The Bristol project depends on a microcomputer to provide the graphic display and uses a special keyboard that allows very young children access to the system. The Bristol researchers believe that children should be exposed to the symbol vocabulary as soon as speech starts to develop.

The special keyboard developed from the program is flat and uses 'picture' overlays which represent action situations – a cat jumping, a person parking a car, etc. The screen symbols for verbs are animated – the graphic of a man walking shows his legs moving – and all symbols are matched to the nouns, verbs, adjectives, etc. which are used in written language. Traditional language pedagogy is followed with a child assimilating the building bricks of language before going on to the 'joining words'. A scoring system allows the teacher (and the older student) to evaluate progress. As the child becomes familiar with the symbolic language, conventional text begins to accompany the symbols and, it is hoped, the child is slowly but surely led to understand the complex relationship between the written word and the thought.

The Bristol team plan to produce a commercial version of the symbolic program and make it available to the teachers of language-impaired children and to the parents of pre-school deaf children.

### Improving speech in the deaf

The problems deaf children face in learning to read are exceeded only by the problems they encounter when they try to speak. Many profoundly deaf children fail to speak intelligibly because they cannot hear any sound against which to compare their efforts at speech. Microcomputers are now providing a visual form of speech comparison which is of great assistance in helping older deaf children and deaf adults to speak clearly.

Typical of the many microcomputer aids designed for this purpose is the 'Visispeech Speech Display Computer', a system based on the Apple II microcomputer and which is made by Jessop Acoustics in London. This system, which consists of a microphone and input device, the Apple and an appropriate program, enables the voice patterns of both therapist and pupil to be displayed on the computer screen. Any differences in the two patterns are clearly shown. The deaf child is able to repeat the word continually until the screen pattern matches that of the teacher. Thus the deaf have confirmation when their spoken words sound 'normal' to other people.

The computer's storage ability allows older children to use the Visispeech system unsupervised as a large number of words and their corresponding screen patterns may be stored in memory and recalled at will, allowing the user to practice matching the patterns of his or her speech against the stored 'correct' patterns. The computer program has the ability to display sound in several different ways, and in attempting to understand all the various aspects of sound the user may command the computer to display visual graphs of individual elements of speech – such as pitch, duration or volume pattern. Another extremely useful computer-based device is called 'The Synthetic Mouth'. This system, developed by the Royal National Institute for the Deaf, produces the picture of a mouth on an oscilloscope screen. The student is provided with a mouth shape to copy for particular words and sounds.

Less severe, but still unpleasant, disabilities such as stammering can also be helped by the micro. A device called the Edinburgh Masker was developed at that famous university and creates a noise which prevents the user from hearing the sound of his or her own voice. The noise, which is fed to the user by a hearing-aid type device, is triggered by the user's own speech. The pitch of the noise alters with the variation in the user's own voice, encouraging normal intonation. This device has proved extremely effective in helping stammerers to overcome the difficulty.

### Help with lip-reading

In terms of direct aid in overcoming the disability of deafness, the microprocessor has only just started to help. It will be used in many existing ways in the next few years. As speech recognition systems improve, telephones for the deaf will incorporate screens on which the caller's words will appear. Already recognition systems are in use which allow the elements of speech to be recognised. One US researcher has a prototype of a pair of spectacles which offer him forward projection of speech analysis which is of considerable help when lip-reading.

This system comprises a miniature microphone (worn on a lapel or tie) which is connected to a small pocket pack containing an amplifier, a microprocessor and batteries. The microprocessor is programmed to recognise the various elements of speech – vowels, consonants and dipthongs – and sends corresponding signals to three tiny light-emitting diodes (LEDs) housed in the hinge of the researcher's glasses.

The red, green or yellow diodes project their colours on to the inside of the spectacle lens and provide the user with a visual clue to the nature of the sound, reinforcing lip-reading techniques. The projected lights are low-level in intensity and strike the lens at an angle which makes them completely invisible to anyone but the user (rather as a newsreader's auto-prompt projected on to the television camera is totally transparent to the viewer). The entire system is minute, and the diodes in the spectacle frames are the size of pin heads. It must be emphasised that this system was not in commercial production at the time of writing, but the researcher reports the colour projections are of enormous value in the difficult task of lip-reading.

It will be some years before speech recognition systems are both foolproof and small enough to become part of such a system. When that happens, the deaf may be given a complete 'scrolling' read-out of conversations with the words projected invisibly on to spectacle lenses. Whether that will happen before doctors and computer engineers discover the means of connecting microphones to the auditory centres of the brain via microprocessor translation is impossible to predict.

Visual information is considered to contribute 75% to human communication, and its loss, or partial loss, produces considerable deprivation of information. Speech synthesis forms a major part of the microcomputer's contribution to special education for the visually impaired, and many programs exist which teach language through automated speech. The two main concerns of special education have been the cost of speech synthesis units and the intelligibility of the spoken word. Both problems have now been solved.

Several manufacturers are producing voice-synthesis chips which semiskilled programmers can incorporate into home computers at very little cost. These ROM chips make up speech from phonemes, the basic phonetic elements of speech, and combine them to form words. Any computer program can benefit from the addition of synthesised speech, and it requires very little modification to programs to add this vital facility. The quality of speech depends on two things: the quality of the voice chip and the thoroughness of the programming. As visually handicapped people will know, providing the synthesised speech is intelligible, the ear adapts to peculiarities of inflection and rhythm very quickly, although good programming should ensure that such elements mimic human delivery quite closely and prevent the voice from becoming boring. Several microcomputers have synthesised speech either built in or available as an inexpensive add-on (the USA's TI-99/4A and Britain's BBC 'B' spring to mind), although with a little ingenuity it is possible to add a speech synthesis peripheral unit to almost any microcomputer. Such a facility opens up the world of computing for the visually handicapped.

Computers have the ability to reproduce the sound of the human voice perfectly, with all the intonation and inflection accurately captured. The reason that 'voice quality' synthesisers are not yet generally available is that the procedure demands that a voice be digitally analysed before it can be available for computer reproduction. To be accurate, such analysis demands a large amount of random access memory, and in the majority of current generation home computers very little power would be left over to control the voice. As more powerful microcomputers become available, the metallic sound of today's synthesised voices will completely disappear, and all computers will talk in a natural male or female voice. This development is only a few years away.

**The talking typewriter**

Everyday uses of speech synthesis include simple programs such as keyboard confirmation routines. (These allow a visually handicapped person to learn to use the machine's keyboard, listening as the computer speaks a confirmation of the keys pressed.) Mathematical programs may be run with all the input confirmed by speech and the results announced aloud. Many microprocessor-based aids now exist which automatically produce braille read-outs, and these may be attached to a microcomputer for permanent record. The microprocessor is finding its way into aids which are not obviously computers. There are several 'talking typewriters' on the market, and although these have really been superseded by microcomputers (with speech ability and word-processing programs), as they are able to read back typewritten work these tools are of great help in their own right.

The microprocessor is rapidly outdating many of the reading aids which have been painstakingly developed for the visually impaired over the last ten years. The expensive and cumbersome suitcase aids which are capable of reading pages and converting the text into braille will disappear as handheld sensors with built-in microprocessor and loudspeaker appear. But the microprocessor is also making the development of powerful dedicated aids possible. There are many such aids now available for the visually disabled, but a few deserve special mention because of their relevance to children and education. The Viewscan unit is a compact self-contained aid which displays words in huge letters on its built-in screen. The aid is of help to the partially sighted, and the size of the letters on the screen can be altered at will. For adults and older children who wish to develop their computer skills a braille computer terminal has been developed. Called Brailink, the terminal has a standard qwerty keyboard and can be used off-line (on its own) or in direct communication with a mainframe computer. A 48-character braille line takes the place of the

TV screen. The keyboard also operates in the six-key Perkins mode enabling contracted Grade II braille to be used for faster reading. The system contains sufficient memory to allow programmers to store work for telephone transmission to a host computer.

There are some microprocessor-based aids which are of considerable, but indirect benefit to the visually impaired. 'BITS' is a system which allows a typist without special skills to produce documents in braille. The system uses a microprocessor to translate the typed text into braille, and this significantly reduces the time taken for the production of transcripts. It is hoped that a development of this system will allow automatic text-to-braille translation to take place from inputs such as Prestel – the viewdata information service.

Visual impairment does not always take the form of optical loss. Dyslexia (formerly called word-blindness) is often considered to be in this category even though the person's optical system functions normally, if not with complete binocularity. Diagnosis of dyslexia is often difficult, especially when the condition is mild, as most children jumble up letters whilst they are learning to read. Microcomputers are useful in assisting in diagnosis. A program's ability to keep careful and constant score of a child's attempts at word or letter recognition can often provide an overall view of performance which allows a considered diagnosis to be made. Computers are also useful in helping children overcome the problem.

Structured learning is the key to success in teaching dyslexic children, and the addition of a speech synthesis unit is vital in assisting a non-reading child to gather meaning from what may seem like a confusing jumble of letters.

### Reading machines

For blind, or partially blind children the greatest problem, apart from the loss of physical freedom, is the loss of reading ability. Several microprocessor-based aids exist which can translate the printed page into the spoken word, but most of these are expensive and are therefore likely to be found in the library rather than the home. Perhaps the best-known device is the Kursweil Reading Machine. This device scans a printed page with a camera and produces spoken words from printed text (the machine is able to decipher most forms of typeface). A smaller machine with similar potential is the Optacon. This device, still undergoing trials at the time of writing, is handheld and produces spoken translation from written text. It is anticipated that it will be cheap enough for many individuals to be able to afford for their homes.

Speech output permits many blind children to develop writing and programming skills, and microprocessor aids have also begun to help the blind in spatial navigation. Sonic aids operating under microprocessor control are capable of feeding the visually impaired person with 'radar' tones which indicate the presence of objects in the path. The microprocessor holds out a similar promise to the blind as it does to the deaf: experimental implants of microprocessors into the human optical system have *already* taken place, but no results have been published.

For many children and adults with multiple and severe disabilities, the computer has already revolutionised their lives, but the real impact of computer power is still to follow. Severely disabled children now have a real hope of both communication and independence.

Many university and college faculties have been devoting time and money researching how best to use microelectronics for the benefit of the severely handicapped. Brighton Polytechnic has been pioneering the use of computer-based cartoon animation for the handicapped. Under the name CAAT (the Computer-Aided Arts Theatre), the project aims to bring the creation of animated cartoon stories within the scope of special education. One special feature of the project is that input and output may be made via speech recognition and synthesis, and the severely disabled pupil can tell the computer how to create or move the cartoon figure enabling the computer to respond in completely understandable language. The cartoon programs are based on 'Superman' programs and researchers have discovered that children with a variety of handicaps have often been able to control the program (through its limited speech recognition facility) more effectively than the adult guineapigs who have been allowed to try it.

An important aspect of the Brighton approach is that the speech recognition system of the microcomputer can be programmed to understand specific sounds emitted by pupils. This allows many pupils who are severely paralysed and incapable of normal speech to bring the computer under their control. (Conversely, an adaption of the system may find wide use in motivating the aurally handicapped to speak clearly. Offering the pupils the 'carrot' of computer action encourages them to enunciate the necessary word clearly enough for the computer to understand. The system's programmability would allow teachers to modify the shape of sound acceptable to the computer as the pupil progressed.)

There are many automated aids for the severely disabled already in common use. These range from automated page turners (never very successful) to typewriters which are operated by breath tubes. One particularly useful device is the Cannon Communicator. The President of the Japanese Cannon company committed his organisation to the development of this aid, and it is now marketed on a non-profit basis. The unit is small enough to be strapped to the wrist and offers buttons with both numerals and the letters of the alphabet. A ribbon of paper tape prints out any message the user wishes to deliver. But many of these aids are merely mechanised 'one operation' systems, and it is only when aids with programmable intelligence are used that severely handicapped children and adults can begin to communicate easily.

One of the greatest losses for severely handicapped children is the loss of play. The ability to play, taken so much for granted by able children and their parents, provides material vital for childhood development. The child who cannot play loses both psychologically and intellectually and inevitably becomes retarded no matter how able his or her innate intelligence may be. The microcomputer now enables all but the most severely handicapped to experience some play.

### Systems for the severely disabled

Britain's National Physical Laboratory has spent years developing microprocessor-based systems for the severely disabled. Since it became clear that the computer offered significant liberation to the handicapped the project has soared, and the exciting discoveries at the NPL were some of the factors which led the then director of the laboratory, Dr Christopher Evans, to write the bestselling book I mentioned in Chapter 2, *The Mighty Micro*. Tragically Dr Evans died before he could see the result of his work on micros for the disabled.

The NPL project (which grew out of a plan first formulated at Loughborough University of Technology) resulted in the Mavis computer-based system for the severely disabled. The system is designed as a multipurpose machine which will assist the users to communicate, to learn, to play and to control the environment around them (turning on lights, answering the telephone, etc.).

The Mavis system is contained in a suitcase, uses an ordinary colour television and may be attached to a printer. Although a normal keyboard is supplied, the designers of the system have assumed that most users will be unable to use it, and a variety of alternative input devices can control the system. These devices often have to be tailor-made for individual children (or adults). Spastics may have control of only one small part of their body, such as a hand or head movement. Contact switches can be used in hand-cradles or head-cradles, and control can be achieved even for a child with very limited physical movement, for example eyelid control.

One successful control system has already been built for a girl who has voluntary control only of her eyelids. Painting her eyelids black allows a light-sensitive diode to detect a change in reflection. The signals from her two eyelids are more than enough to control a microcomputer, and she is now able to communicate through the system and use it to control her environment and undertake many other tasks. In some cases the only control available is the intake and

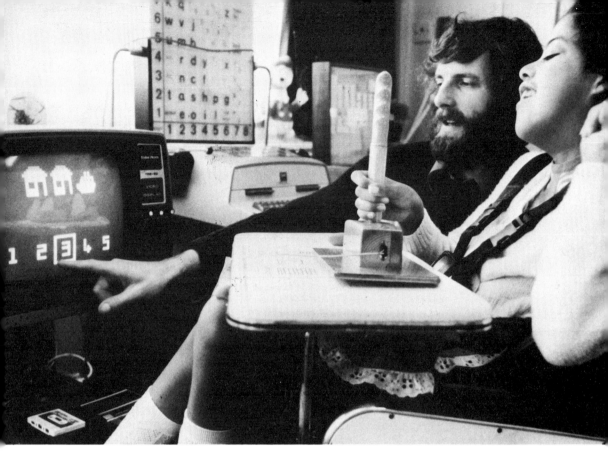

*For the severely handicapped, switches which provide computer input must be large and easy to use. This large 'joystick' system was developed by Tim Kitchen and the Walsall team.*

exhalation of breath, but input devices can be made easily which bring the Mavis system under the control of this function. The breath tube, originally developed for the Possum typewriter, can be used to control the Mavis system with 'suck' and 'blow' providing all necessary information. Each switching and control system is likely to require setting for the individual's characteristics, but the technical problems are not difficult to overcome. Once the handicapped child has control over the system, every computer control option is displayed on the screen and the user moves a cursor (position indicator) to cause the computer to carry out a task.

As well as playing games on the screen, the Mavis system can control robot toys (e.g. a turtle) which the child can move around the floor in play – still using only a couple of movements from hand, head or eye, for example.

With this system of control communication becomes possible. The child can select words from the 'menu' at the bottom of the screen by moving the cursor to the word desired. The word then appears in large letters in the main portion of the screen, and the child may select a word to follow it or choose to see a new range of word options. Children may draw on the screen using the cursor. Drawing is a vital part of childhood play as it is the means by which children mentally evaluate the size, shape and relationship of physical objects and finally produce a mental model of the real world on which they will base their future

156

life. Musicmaking is also possible with Mavis, and children can experiment with tones and sounds and create their own musical compositions.

The Mavis system is of course capable of two-way communication, and the child can write on the screen and equally well read messages typed in on the conventional keyboard.

### Flexible system for advanced learning

For older users, the Mavis system has all the computer power needed for letter writing, file keeping and mathematical work, and all these functions may be controlled from the few movements of the controllable part of the user's body. The system is flexible enough to allow mature users to create their own option menus on the screen, and the system allows advanced learning techniques – such as foreign language tuition – to come under simple control. Many examination authorities are now quite prepared to accept word-processor prepared papers from disabled candidates, and the challenge and opportunities of formal education become available to people with severe physical disabilities.

Special design features of the Mavis system ensure that many *Robotic devices are now* programs are contained in ROM chips, avoiding the need to load *relatively inexpensive.* programs from cassette or disk. An extra large RAM storage section is

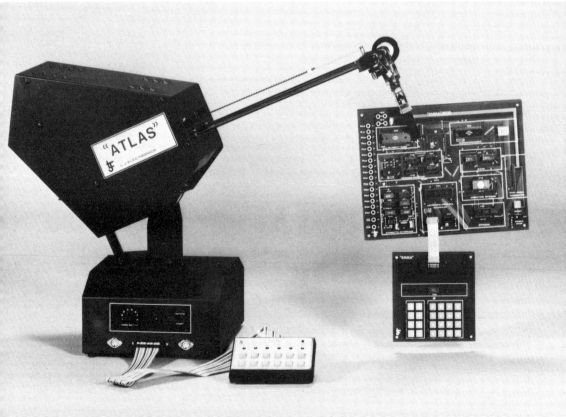

provided to facilitate the manipulation of programs, and the system's output facilities include several input-output ports for the connection to systems that will control telephones, robot arms, lights and even doors and windows as well as printers and other, more normal items.

Robotic arms are now relatively inexpensive, and the ability to lift a cup to the lips is one which many quadraplegics would like to have. Simple arms that are nevertheless equally capable of handling a book or holding an egg may be attached to the output port of Mavis – or to the output ports of many home computers. Current examples can typically lift up to 10 ounces and have an accuracy of plus or minus 0.1in. (2.5mm).

Another version of a computer communicator has been developed at King's College, London. Based on a Nascom 2 microcomputer, the system allows a severely handicapped person to operate the system with microswitches from any part of his or her body which is under voluntary control. Ordinary educational programs may be run on the machine, and recreational programs – such as Etcha-Sketcha for drawing – may be controlled, but unlike the Mavis system no built-in facilities are yet provided for interfacing with robotic control.

Some ready-made commercial microcomputers are of value to children and adults who suffer from a single disability, but severely disabled people usually require specially designed systems.

The computer has already improved the employment prospects for many severely handicapped school-leavers. In America an organisation called ARPDP (the Association of Rehabilitation Programmes in Data Processing – it seems acronyms are the language of the future) has been training severely handicapped people to be productive members of the computing industry since 1973.

This organisation restricts itself to training handicapped people to become computer programmers and is as concerned about adults as about older children. Reports received from employers who have taken on programmers trained by ARPDP indicate that the investment required – the necessary widening of doorways and the special toilet and canteen facilities – is more than offset by the dedication, enthusiasm and skill shown by the handicapped employees.

### Programming training

Training in computer programming for the physically disabled is now offered across 16 states in the US. The project was originally sponsored by IBM, and care has been taken to involve potential employers in the development of a curriculum which is tailored to ensure that students achieve skills relevant to the company they are likely to join. The courses take 38 weeks, and most are held in centres which also offer residential and medical facilities. Over 400 severely handicapped people have become financially independent as a result of the ARPDP project.

The British Computer Society's Committee for the Disabled is instigating similar opportunities for the severely disabled in the UK. Computer Based Training (CBT) allows many handicapped people the chance to train for a particular role at home, and the Employment Rehabilitation Centres within the Manpower Services Commission are now using microcomputers for vocational assessment and for training the handicapped in such roles as programming and office practice.

For the severely disabled the micro will offer increasing assistance and control over such things as synthetic speech, motorised wheelchairs and environmental controls, and only those disabled by severe mental incapacity will remain beyond the reach of help.

Gifted children qualify as special children, and many are already avidly using microcomputer power in their ascent to intellectual stardom. Special individual attention for gifted children offends some people's sense of justice; but every country needs its leaders and intellectuals, and the fine intellect needs guidance and training to fulfil its potential. Many older gifted children are concentrating on the abstract theories of artificial intelligence, but many more are using the model-building power of the computer to create simulations of real events in order to study the effect when various modifications are made.

The home computer is enabling the gifted child to learn from the greatest sources of knowledge, instead of being chained to those available locally. Any computer program is merely a mental extension of the programmer, but if a chess program is developed by a very skilled player the gifted child at home with his or her bedroom computer will actually be facing the intellect of that highly skilled player. Our concept of a 'gifted' child is being modified by the microcomputer. The demands of machine intelligence seem an irresistible challenge to some young minds: Londoner Daniel Isaaman is an example of this type of gifted child. Following his introduction to computing when he was 11, Daniel started working part-time for a computer company when he was 14. At the time of writing he is due to put in a full year's programming before going on to university. At 17 he had published two books of and about computer programs. He built his first computer from a kit and has long since graduated from high-level programming languages such as BASIC to machine code, the language of the microprocessors themselves.

In the past only gifted adults have had the capacity to teach gifted children, and in some situations the children have been held back by a lack of suitable teaching. The microcomputer has changed all this – as it is changing almost everything else – and with computer access to the finest teaching our gifted children may be able to realise their full potential for the first time.

# COMPUTERS IN THE ARTS

It has been some years since computers were regarded as pure 'number crunchers' capable only of spewing out statistics and forecasts. Today computers are undertaking tasks which would have been inconceivable even ten years ago.

Art is often considered to be the highest form of self-expression, but even this hallowed territory is under invasion from the microprocessor. To be fair to both man and micro, 'pure' art remains pure: the painting, the sculpture and the poem remain supreme examples of man's own expression, but other, slightly more mechanical art forms, like writing and musical composition, are receiving such tremendous help from the micro that it will not be long before the origin of the art itself is challenged.

The contribution which word-processing makes to the child writer has been discussed elsewhere, and although it remains true that all invention and imagination originates in the human and not the electronic brain, the effect which micro control has over the act of writing is affecting the act of writing itself and, some might say, contributing to it. As this power increases the micro will play a greater role in artistic endeavour.

Graphic art, applied art, commercial art and film animation are all areas in which the micro is working to its fullest extent. Very little of the micro's power in these areas has yet penetrated schools, although the graphics capabilities of machines such as the Atari 800 and the BBC 'B' Microcomputer offer older art students some exciting opportunities to experiment with computer aided design (CAD) and new approaches to graphic design. But freehand art remains freehand, and the computer can only be of marginal help (e.g. researching reference material or allowing sculptors to construct computer projections of models for consideration).

The art in which the microcomputer is making the greatest headway in both schools and professional applications is music. As all music is based on a mathematical division of pitch, the creation, composition and storage of music lends itself easily to computer power. The chromatic scale is an (almost) equal division of pitch ranging from the

160

Computers are revolutionising the teaching of music.

lowest audible sound to the highest (although very few musical instruments cover the entire range), and this information can easily be handled by a computer.

The computer can also create sound in several ways: it can vibrate a loudspeaker cone at a certain frequency to induce the loudspeaker to produce a tone of corresponding pitch. It can control an electronic circuit especially designed to make sounds (a synthesizer), or most excitingly it can analyse sound as it occurs in the natural environment and reproduce it. This last ability demands a powerful microcomputer with advanced programs, and such a system is unlikely to be found in any but the most exclusive schools for some years. This type of computer sound-production program 'listens' to every element of sound – a bird song, a piano or a jet plane – and expresses each element of the sound in numeric form. There are many elements in sound – pitch, volume, duration, decay, etc. – and some expensive com puter musical instruments have been commercially produced which are able to 'collect' any sound from the natural world and place it under the control of composers and musicians. It is this sort of power which is providing the exciting and previously unheard sounds which are now appearing on so many hit records.

But as well as helping the professional musician to compose and make new sounds, the microprocessor also has the remarkable ability of being able to remember information and then re-offer it for subsequent editing. This power is of enormous help to children

161

learning how to play a musical instrument, learning musical theory or studying composition.

### 'Real-time' and 'non real-time'

Musical composition is the part of musicmaking which is currently deriving most benefit from the microcomputer. The micro allows composers painstakingly to build up compositions step by step, working out of 'real-time', before finally pressing a button and 'playing' the music. 'Real-time' is an expression which means 'happening now' or 'live', and non real-time musicmaking refers to the process of building up a composition step by step at any pace chosen by the user and then playing it back to form a complete piece of music. Such music, increasingly common in the hit-record charts, is called 'non real-time' music. The contribution which the microprocessor and the microcomputer are making to composition is so profound that a major change of musical emphasis is occurring: control in pop music is shifting from the performer to the composer.

For the musical child the computer promises to make the tedious process of learning musical theory much easier. An instruction book for a music lesson based on a microprocessor instrument would be very different from conventional music books and might (if it was written in a conversational style) read as follows:

> Press any note on the keyboard: the note will sound and appear on a musical stave displayed on the screen, its name appearing over it. Hold the note for one beat, and the note will sound for one beat and appear as a crotchet (quarter note). If you hold it longer, it will become a minim (half note). Press another note and then a second and a third, and the music you have written on the stave will move over to let the new notes in. When you have finished, press 'Play', and the computer will play the notes you have selected back to you at any tempo you want. If you have made a mistake, delete the note that is wrong and then listen to the piece again. Continue this process until the piece is perfect.
>
> Try something else: order the piece to be played back in tuition mode. Now the first note will appear on the screen, and you will be asked to find the same note on your keyboard. The note will not sound until you have found the correct note and pressed it. Then the next note will appear and you will have to find the right note again, and so on.

Computers are revolutionising the teaching of music. With a system such as this, few children would fail to see the relationship between written notation and musical sounds.

## Musical instruments with micros

There are two methods of using a microprocessor to assist in the making and tuition of music: the first is to build the microprocessor into musical instruments, and the second is to run programs on standard microcomputers which will cause them to produce sound and offer musical tuition from the screen. Many manufacturers offer additional sound-making hardware which is fitted to microcomputers and is controlled by the program. Increasingly microcomputers are being designed with built-in musical capability – the BBC model 'B', the TI-99/4A and the Sharp MZ 80A, for example.

The microprocessor musical instruments suitable for children are usually portable and inexpensive. Although microcomputers aren't as portable as these smaller one-purpose musical instruments, they are more powerful and often take the student further along the path to musical proficiency.

The first example of this new breed of portable micro musical instrument appeared in 1981. The musical world was shocked when Casio, the Japanese company, previously best known for calculators and watches, launched a tiny computer-based musical instrument called the VL-Tone. It then sold for £35 ($70).

This little instrument, 11 x 5in (280 x 127mm), was the first inexpensive programmable musical instrument on the market. The battery-powered VL-Tone can record up to 100 notes and then play them back at the pitch, rhythm and tempo of the student's choice with an appropriate, automatically provided rhythm accompaniment. There is a choice of 10 types of rhythm, and the balance between the rhythm and the melody may be adjusted. Five voices allow the user to select sounds from piano, synthesiser, violin, flute or guitar or ADSR sounds. ADSR (an acronym for the stages of the amplitude of a sound: attack, decay, sustain, release) is a surprising feature to find on such an inexpensive instrument, and selection of this sound base allows users to create their own sound, whilst learning about the nature of sound itself.

In all fairness, it must be pointed out that this tiny plastic instrument can't produce high quality sounds from its minute internal speaker, but they are perfectly acceptable when heard over headphones or with a reasonable hi-fi system. In addition to offering considerable musical power, the instrument becomes a full-feature calculator at the touch of a switch.

The VL-Tone delighted many forward-thinking educationalists by its interactive encouragement. Children can take an unknown piece of written music, enter it as slowly as they choose into the VL-Tone's memory and then hear it played back at the correct tempo. This leads to an understanding of the relationship between actual music and its written language which would otherwise only develop over a long period of time.

In a sales pitch to a mass market of adults whom Casio perceive as being musically frustrated, the company describes the VL-Tone as its 'technological gift to the ungifted'. Perhaps they are right – but its role in stimulating gifted young minds may end up being its most important contribution.

Many school teachers have invested in instruments such as the Casio VL Tone and have used them in classrooms to demonstrate how music is created. But specialist music teachers tend to be ultra-conservative, and, with the exception of a few forward-thinking tutors, most still insist that all musical development takes place on the student's chosen instrument.

Other manufacturers, however, were not slow to follow Casio's lead, and today there is a variety of inexpensive instrument/toys on the market. Each has particular selling points, and some pay more attention to educational aspects than others.

**Electronic pianola**

Tools like this are immensely powerful for teaching the 6-13 age group – larger models offer eight-note polyphony (the ability to sound eight notes at the same time) and sounds similar to professional music synthesizers. Within a very short time the successful development of inexpensive speech simulators and input devices will produce instruments which 'sing' the right note names and which produce a tune from a sung input. Larger keyboards already contain telltale lights which guide the fingers into the right positions on the keyboard, and Casio have produced a range of keyboards that can 'read' music from specially produced barcharts. A lightpen is fitted to these instruments which reads a barcode – similar to product identification barcodes used on items in supermarkets – and loads this digital information into the microprocessor memory. When required, the instrument will reproduce the information as music (a modern version of the pianola or player-piano concept).

Within a few years we can expect to see a small keyboard with sufficient memory capacity to house a program which can take a beginner from zero to accomplished player with all the steps built in. Keyboards will instruct on technique, timing and expression, and human teachers will be freed to guide music development paths, choice of material and individual expression.

One aspect in this dramatic change in musical tuition that worries traditionalists is that some of the conventional instruments are likely to lose popularity with children. A keyboard, alphanumeric or musical, is an excellent input device for a computer, and the majority of computer-based musical instruments will use keyboards. Traditional instruments such as the violin, which require many months of practice before pleasing sounds may be produced, may stand little chance of holding a child's attention against the significant attraction of playing musical 'games' with a keyboard-controlled computer toy.

It is, perhaps, arguable that an understanding of musical theory should be arrived at before a young student starts developing technique on a particular instrument, but with the ability of the microchip to store the sound of a violin and reproduce it perfectly, what incentive is there to produce the recruits for the Suzuki violin method?

Obviously some parents will go on steering their children towards conventional instruments, but unless society reacts against the mechanisation of musicmaking (not of music itself) it seems likely that far fewer children will become accomplished on traditional instruments in the medium to long-term future. This leads to the conclusion either that classical and other music written for traditional instruments will be performed by fewer musicians – and therefore by fewer good players – or, more likely, that the musician's role will be partly taken over by the programmed music computer. The only area likely to remain inviolate is live performance: in all recording situations – broadcasts, recording sessions, etc. – arrangers and composers will program computers to create the music.

Using your home computer to run a music program is an excellent method for your children to learn about musical theory, and although the cheaper programs have little facility for teaching musical keyboard technique, their ability to teach musical theory is excellent. Interaction is the principal advantage of these non-dedicated systems and the power available is entirely dependent upon the memory capacity of your computer and the thoroughness of the program.

### 'The Musician' program

One of the friendliest musical programs for small computers is 'The Musician' which is manufactured by the Philips company for the G7000 Videopac Computer.

The Musician program arrives with a card printed to represent a 16-note piano keyboard. This card fits over the printed two-dimensional keyboard on the computer for the duration of the program's operation, effectively dedicating the computer to musical use. The touch-sensitive keyboard works perfectly for normal computer work, but when converted for musical use, the player must develop positive fingering to avoid mistakes. Designers of touch-sensitive keyboards have to ensure that the keys are not oversensitive, and this requires

that the user be accurate in his or her key strokes. To be fair Philips make no suggestion that The Musician is a serious musical instrument. It is a teaching tool and, as such, is excellent.

On inserting the Musician program pack, placing the keyboard card over the alphanumeric keyboard and switching on, the TV screen becomes green and two musical staves appear with treble and bass clefs. The keyboard has an octave transpose function which allows the musician the use of 32 notes, although the printed card represents only 16.

Two modes of music playing are possible: 'Real-time' and 'recorded'. If the player starts to press notes whilst the screen is green, he is playing the keyboard as he would any normal keyboard instrument. As each note is pressed, the corresponding note appears on the screen.

There are no frills to the sound production system. It is impossible to add vibrato or to alter the sustain of a note. When a C is pressed, a C sounds for as long as it is held. The two-dimensional 'card keyboard' accurately displays full-size piano-type notes, but normal keyboard technique is out of the question. The best playing method is to play with an index finger. Each note has its name printed on the key with sharps and flats designated as C+, E– and so on.

Pressing a control on the keyboard changes the screen to red, and the player enters the record mode. In this mode a musical time value

*The Philips Musician program pack converts the Philips G7000 Videopac Computer into a musical instrument.*

appears in the top right-hand corner of the screen, and a metronome click is heard. The time expression is in crotchets (quarter notes) per minute, and this may be infinitely varied so that the metronome speeds up or slows down as the player requires.

After setting the right rhythm, the player begins to play as if he were playing a normal instrument. In practice, the best method of playing is to use written music and to enter the notes from the music – quite a few pieces are provided in the instruction book. 'Speed Music', or other easy-play music written with the note names contained in the notes themselves, makes this an easy process for the student. With the built-in metronome click as a reference, the individual notes may be held for the correct number of beats, and the corresponding note value will appear on the stave. Thus a student who presses 'A' and holds it down for two and a half beats will see a dotted minim (half note) appear at the 'A' position on the stave. Whether it appears on the treble or bass stave depends on which octave has been selected by the transpose control (treble is the default choice). When the student plays the next note it appears in the corresponding position on the stave, and the notes begin to 'scroll' off to the left of the screen as the music progresses. Four or five notes may be seen on the screen at a time. When no note is played, a rest appears equivalent to the amount of time passed without a note being played.

Real-time playing is converted by the computer into notes, note lengths, rhythms and rests. There are no mathematical values attached to any part of the program. The student hears and sees what he or she plays. The student will make mistakes, and these can be corrected at will. The tempo of the piece can be altered, and various sub-programs exist to drill the student in musical theory. Although the Musician and some of the other games and educational programs for the Videopac computer are excellent, it should be pointed out that this inexpensive machine is difficult to program and doesn't offer any facilities for storage of programs on cassette or any other means.


**Digital synthesizers**

Within a few years it is likely that home computers will be able to do far more for aspiring musicians than just assist in the learning of musical theory. Software programs will turn microcomputers into fully digital synthesizers similar to the models now being used by professional musicians. In addition these systems will be able to take dictation from a sung melody and convert it into instant music and will provide interactive tuition to an incredible degree. In the meantime many home computers are offering considerable control over composition.

One of the world's most popular computers is the Apple. Only just replaced by a new model, the 'Apple II plus' version, is the computer which most music-oriented companies have chosen to use as a base for computer music systems. Several of the systems are designed for professional use, but several are also intended as tuition aids. The advanced (and excellent) alphaSyntauri music teaching system is discussed later, but 'Musicomp', a simpler inexpensive music program for Apples allows the owner of a 32K+ Apple computer to use the system to compose music. The program is best described as an intermediate tutor for students interested in composition.

The system necessary to run the Musicomp is an Apple with a minimum RAM of 32K, one disk drive storage system and an extra printed circuit (a language or integer card) added inside the computer. Each item is available separately from Apple dealers and is easily fitted by the user.

The Musicomp program is supplied on a $5\frac{1}{4}$in (132mm) floppy disk, and for the best sound the 'cassette out' mini-jack socket at the back of the Apple may be connected to the input of an audio amplifier, although the program will run on the Apple's tiny internal speaker.

The program is menu driven (allowing the user to select from a range of options), and students are prompted to enter their requirements from the Apple's typewriter-style keyboard. The Musicomp program is totally different in concept to lower-level programs such as the Musician. The program assumes that the student understands musical theory and knows how to work a computer. Some programming experience is necessary, and without a basic knowledge of how computer systems run it would be impossible to get this program up and running without assistance.

The program produces three 'voices' from the Apple without the aid of any special sound generation chips. As a result there is little tonal variation between the three square waves produced, but the voices offer the ability to change the basic sound into a hard attacking sound or a softer 'woodwind' sound. The large memory capacity of the Apple allows a store of up to 8,000 notes, making extended melody storage possible. The program is monophonic – it can create only one sound at one time, and must be regarded as a melody instrument: chords are not possible. The biggest lack in the program is a time base. The student is forced to use the tempo arbitrarily set by the program. All music is entered and edited from the alphanumeric keyboard, the keys being converted by the program to represent individual notes. There is no piano-type keyboard in the system.

In the Musicomp program the letters of the alphanumeric keyboard become notes. Middle C is W for example. The sharp above middle C is U. At first writing music with the Musicomp program is laborious, each note entered requiring several keystrokes, and the user must remember which key represents which note. After a while these details are remembered, and the input from the alphanumeric keyboard becomes quite rapid. After considerable use the student automatically identifies each note with its keyboard letter and can enter the notes at high speed.

For an existing Apple owner the small investment necessary to buy the Musicomp is a negligible investment, and the return, the ability to write music in the abstract and hear it replayed, is significant.

### 'Music Maker' program

Most other home computer manufacturers either distribute or recommend music programs to use with their computers. The giant Texas Instruments Corporation sells a program called 'Music Maker' for use with its TI-99/4A home computer. Much TI software for the 99/4A is cartridge-based, but unlike the cartridge-type computers such as the Philips Videopac, the TI has full interface facilities to allow connection with either cassette or disk storage systems.

Music Maker is an excellent program offering the student three voices controlled by menu driven software. As the TI 99/4A has full colour capability, considerable use is made of colour in guiding the novice. In the 'traditional mode' the student selects the note value from a range of notes shown at the side of the treble and bass clefs (semibreve to semiquaver, or whole note to sixteenth note) and then moves the cursor to the appropriate position on the stave. One bar at a time is completed with this program, and at the end of a bar the student may choose to go back and write a second and third voice in that bar before progressing to the next.

An important part of the Music Maker program is the 'Sound Graphs' sub-program. This is a method of music writing which abandons the traditional staves and allows novices to 'draw' their tunes on the screen, creating graphs which indicate the relative ascent and descent of the melody line. In the long term any serious student is likely to abandon this method of writing music, but the computer's graphics power is neatly harnessed to provide an interesting graphic representation of melodic progression which will undoubtedly assist many people who have no understanding of conventionally written music.

Unusually, the TI system allows for printed hard copy to be obtained from the screen display. Only TI's own thermal printer will work with the system, but several bars at a time may be printed if required.

The above programs are powerful teaching tools for children and adults; but the sounds produced are very limited, and serious teachers and musical education establishments will require far better sound production from computers before they consider this technology to be a useful aid for intermediate or advanced musical tuition.

Several specialist manufacturers have developed advanced packages for musical tuition based on the use of popular small computers, and these have found their way into music colleges and the music faculties of universities; but few have so far reached lower school music rooms.

Passport Designs of La Honda, California, have produced several different programs which will run with their Soundchaser musicmaking package. This package consists of a musical keyboard, printed circuit cards for sound production and software disks and is designed to work with an Apple II microcomputer.

Their Music Tutor program requires the student or tutor to possess the computer (48K) with a disk drive system. To this is added Passport's own musical keyboard which is connected to the Apple. One or two voice cards – providing an option of three or six voices – are also slotted into the Apple, and these give the computer 'voices' allowing acceptable music to be made. Apple actively encourage owners to dig about in the insides of the computer: indeed it is the only way many programs and packages may be connected.

Dr Charles Boody of the University of Minnesota wrote the Music Tutor system. It is designed for both the classroom and the home, and the four training units – Intervals, Matching & Tuning, Chords and Melodic Games – were designed to develop ear training as well as impart the basic principle of musical theory. The program incorporates drills which students can follow at their own pace. Each unit of the system has its own graphics display, and the program provides encouragement and learning incentives, scoring, etc., to help the student assimilate the information. The program even has sufficient power and range to be of use to accomplished musicians. For example, 'chord drill' questions students on the various inversions of chords, and complex counterpoints and harmonies are covered in the program.

### Printed music output

An additional program which is very useful for tuition is Passport's 'Notewriter'. This program drives a standard computer printer to deliver monophonic printed music directly from musical keyboard input. This program allows the student to play music directly into the computer from the musical keyboard. The music is converted to conventional notation on the screen – all time values automatically sensed – and if the student wishes this may be printed as hard copy by the printer.

In a classroom a system such as the Music Tutor frees a teacher from repetitive drilling of the basics of music and allows a far greater amount of individual assistance. The total package of the

■■■■■■■■■■■■■■■■■■■■■■■■■■■■■■■■

Soundchaser system and software is at present not much more than the price of one microcomputer system, and with many schools already owning an Apple computer such a program makes a useful contribution to a music syllabus.

Another Californian company, the Syntauri Corporation of Palo Alto, also markets a musicmaking package for use with the Apple. The software which is at the heart of the system was developed by Charles Kellner, one of Apple's own senior programmers, and Syntauri market his system which like the Passport has several software options.

Syntauri call their music tuition program MusicMaster, and it is capable of taking the student from basics through to orchestration. A major emphasis in the program is on ear-training. Techniques for the development of this gift include the sounding of random notes which the student is required to identify, and chord identification.

Three levels make up the MusicMaster program: beginner, intermediate and advanced. The beginner module comprises an introduction to major, natural and harmonic and melodic minor scales, and in pursuit of their ear training philosophy the authors of MusicMaster include recognition tests for scales which are played automatically. Alternatively students are required to play a scale as prompted by notation appearing on the video screen and to play scales from memory when the name of the scale appears. Interval tuition is developed similarly, and basic triad chords, major, minor, augmented and diminished, are presented for recognition in both aural and written form.

The intermediate and advanced modules cover such topics as rhythmic dictation, counterpoint and modulation.

Tutors may direct the program to concentrate on specific areas, and built-in software scoring allows tutors and students to assess progress.

As a bonus to educational establishments the program's designers, Dr Wolgand Kuhn (Stanford University) and Dr Paul Lorton (University of San Francisco), have incorporated administrative programs into the software which allow users to keep school, teacher and class files and which assist teachers in the preparation of reports. Facilities are embedded in the program to allow teachers to write their own sub-programs in order to analyse student performance.

Computers are taking the monotony out of both the theory of music and the practice of musical instrument technique. Contrary to the fears voiced by some anti-computer musicians, microcomputer music systems demand considerable appreciation of musical theory before full use of musical programs can be made, but students and teachers are rewarded by being given unprecedented control over musicmaking and composition.

# THE SOFTWARE

No matter how persuasive a computer salesperson might be about the merits of a particular microcomputer, do not buy it unless you are sure that there is a real variety of programs available for it. If you buy a machine and discover that the range of compatible programs is limited or is irrelevant to your needs, you will end up trading it in for another model within a year.

Rather than deciding on a particular microcomputer, I think it is a good idea to choose a range of software which will do what you want, and then to seek the machine on which to run it. If you can afford an expensive microcomputer system which incorporates disk drives, there is a strong case for choosing a machine which can use the CP/M operating system as this offers access to a vast range of software.

In choosing a less expensive microcomputer for your son or daughter, you should remember the value of choosing the same machine that your child uses at school. But if you do intend to make an alternative choice, it is worth examining the software catalogues and magazine ads very carefully to discover the range of software which is available.

More software is available for Apple microcomputers than for almost any other individual make of machine. This is because the Apple was one of the first microcomputers to become internationally popular, and software houses opt for the biggest market when they are investing in the development of new programs. The Apple II has now been replaced by the Apple II plus, but unless the company decide on a very eccentric policy, existing Apple programs will continue to run on all new models.

In Britain the Sinclair machines must give the Apple a close run for its money in terms of software available and may, in sheer number of programs, actually have more available than the Apple. Many of these are available for the Timex version of the Sinclair sold in the US. But the Apple is a more flexible system than any of the Sinclairs, and for that reason the range of programs and optional add-on hardware items for Apples is far greater.

In the USA, Radio Shack computers, made by the Tandy Corporation, must rank alongside Apple in terms of program variety,

*An enormous range of software is available for the Sinclair ZX81 computer.*

172

although be warned that some of the models in the Radio Shack range have incompatible software. The programs written for the most popular Radio Shack computers, the TRS Model I and Model III, will *not* run on their largest microcomputers, the Model II and the Model 16.

The Japanese microcomputers must seem an obvious omission from the above list, but despite many predictions from market observers, the invasion of the Japanese micro so far hasn't happened. Some Japanese microcomputers (the Sharp is a good example) have done reasonably well in the Western markets, but for one reason or another they have failed to find the sort of success in this market they have found in the field of hi-fi, video and musical instruments. I suspect that one reason is that Japanese machines simply do not have sufficient English-language software available.

When you have paid your money for a microcomputer, you can be sure that you will eventually spend far more on programs to run on it. Most computer owners will learn to do some programming, but writing lengthy and complex programs to create high quality educational, games or business programs is too costly in time and effort for the vast majority of home computer owners, and you will be forced to rely on commercially written software. This is why a wide range of compatible software is very important.

**The software gap**

Some of the new microcomputers described in the next chapter are more advanced and more exciting than some of the models which have been around for five years. But market enthusiasm for '16-bit' systems or for new computer languages – an excitement so often whipped-up by the computer press – must be tempered with the consideration of software availability. There is a 'software gap' between the time when a new machine is announced and the time when a decent supply of programs becomes available for it.

The example of the Tandy Radio Shack Model 16 illustrates this point: the Model 16 is a powerful new computer which uses an advanced 16-bit microprocessor and which Radio Shack developed at enormous cost. The 16-bit design means that the microprocessor circuit is wide enough to allow 16-bits, or two bytes of information, to travel through the circuit at the same time. It is analogous to widening the neck of a bottle: far more information can flow simultaneously, and thus the machine is far quicker and more powerful than its predecessor, the Model II (the circuit of which is 8 bits wide).

But, marvellous as the Model 16 is, at the time of writing there is very little software available for it, and in order to make the machine viable Tandy made sure that most of the programs written for the Model II would also work on the Model 16. What Tandy fail to publicise is that after spending 50% more to buy the Model 16 the purchaser will discover that Model II software actually runs *more slowly* on the Model 16 than it would on the old-fashioned Model II. In time, of course, a complete suite of very rapid programs for the Model 16 will arrive and make the Model II's performance seem positively antediluvian. But there will be a year or two's frustration before that happens. (This manuscript was prepared on a Model II.)

The IBM Personal Computer provides another example of the software problem. IBM have been the world leaders in the supply of mainframe computers since their pioneering efforts in computing, and today it is estimated that the company holds about 65% of the world market for the heavyweight machines. But, as so often happens, the David of the industry – Apple – proved that small is beautiful and created an entirely new industry under IBM's nose. It was six years before the Goliath responded, and when the IBM personal microcomputer was launched in 1982 very little software was available for it, despite the machine's advanced 16-bit design. Because IBM is a name to be reckoned with, software houses were immediately motivated to start producing material especially for the machine, but early owners of the machine (which bears the most prestigious trade name in computing) must have been stuck for things to do with it.

There are thousands, if not hundreds of thousands, of things to do with a personal microcomputer, and many of these applications are designed specifically for children. I have already discussed the games programs, and almost every manufacturer ensures that there are

*One of the thousands of computer games available for a TR80 colour computer.*

space-type games available for their microcomputers, even if they are not licensed to produce versions of the hit programs such as PacMan, Space Invaders or Asteroids. Some of these copycat games are better than others (some are even better than the originals), and the only way to discover which are best is to try them.


**Computer shows**

The cheapest and best way of trying the range of games software is to attend a computer show or exhibition. Staging public computer shows has become a bonanza business in its own right, and unless you live on a remote island you should be able to find a computer show in a local convention centre or town hall at which the exhibitors will be only too pleased to allow you to play with the various games and programs they will be running on various microcomputers.

Shows are not, however, good places to evaluate the computers themselves. Considering the relative merits of 'hardware' demands research in magazines, books and stores and among friends who are already computer owners, and exhibitions really don't offer anything other than the chance for a garrulous salesperson to give your ears a pounding.

If you can collect all of the free literature available at a computer show, you should soon be able to establish which microcomputers have a wide range of software available and those which belong to the 'software soon to be available' category.

Although I find it tempting to describe in detail some of the more exciting computer programs, such as master chess programs (so good now that only world champion players can beat them) or some of the simulations such as the Scott Adams 'Adventure' games (originally designed for mainframes and only recently scaled down for a variety of microcomputers), only you know for what use you want a home computer, and I will restrict myself to offering a list (necessarily incomplete) of some of the things microcomputers can be persuaded to do by well written programs.


**Fun games**

The most popular fun games are of the war or space type in which the user pits his or her wits against the computer. Usually shootings and explosions are involved, and the better programs and computers use full colour and sound. Race games in which the user tries to keep a racing car on a track are also popular. Games of dexterity in which you have to try to land a 'lunar module' gently on the surface of the Moon amuse some, and success in these programs hangs on your ability to

control the retro-rockets, avoiding crashing into the lunar surface while conserving fuel. A particularly popular game requires the player to 'eat dots' before being 'caught'.

### Games of skill

Games of skill include draughts (checkers), chess, backgammon, blackjack, craps, cribbage and many more. The more complex the game – chess being supreme – the more computer power is necessary for a good contest. Chess is one of the most popular skill games purchased for the computer, and many 'dedicated' chess computers have been marketed. The quality of the game depends primarily on the power of the computer and the skill of the programmer. If the program is well written, and the computer is fast enough, a high standard of play will be available, and the time the computer requires for consideration of a move will be minimised. I have a couple of chess games which operate on a powerful computer, but which nevertheless can take an hour between moves when an advanced skill level is selected. This is because a computer plays chess by analysing every move that is possible on the board and selecting the best move strictly according to logic. Very few humans have the ability to assess and *remember* the first (and developmental) consequences of every move, but computers, like elephants, never forget (so long as there's power in their circuits). Well written chess programs almost seem to take on a human quality as the computer will sometimes make a seemingly illogical and 'instinctive' move. This is of course part of the program which a skilled chess player and programmer have created (probably working together), and such a move should really sound a note of warning in the human opponent. (As an aside, larger computers have begun to act 'unpredictably'. Researchers into artificial intelligence in mainframe computers are now regularly reporting results and reactions that are not known to have a program origin.)

Powerful computers and well written chess programs are unbeatable except by the world's greatest players, and within the next couple of years even their genius is expected to succumb to the well written chess program which relies on the ultimate logic and memory capacity of the computer. From this it will be obvious that on lesser games, such as backgammon and checkers, a good computer program can beat you every time, if you select a high skill level of play.

### Other games

Believe it or not, you can now get 'adult' games for microcomputers. Whether or not the idea of responding to erotic suggestions made by a computer turns you on, some software houses have perceived a market for such programs (and good luck to them!).

### Education

This whole book is about computers and children, and educational programs of different sorts for different age groups are described in appropriate chapters. Later in this chapter there is a section on computer languages, and there you will find a further discussion on Logo, probably the most important computer language for children.

The best method of selecting drill and practice educational programs is to observe which machines have made special headway in the world's educational systems. These are: Apple, Commodore (Pets and Vics), Tandy Radio Shack, Acorn/BBC (but only in Britain), Sinclair and its US version, Timex/Sinclair, Atari, TI and Research Machines (Britain only). In some territories there are locally built machines used in education – the Piccolo in Denmark and Eire, the MicroBee in New Zealand for example – but the majority of educational programs have been written for the internationally accepted machines. (The exception to this rule is the BBC computer which, although not yet internationally accepted, has the incredible power of the BBC behind it and as a result already has a range of programs that seems likely to become one of the best and most comprehensive available for any machine in the world.)

These programs range from the home-written program on cassette which is sold via mail order and arrives with no explanatory documentation to the elaborate colour program on disk or ROM cartridge which is accompanied by a lavishly produced book. The difference between the various types of educational programs – computer aided instruction, computer aided learning, computer managed learning and child-centred programs – has been discussed elsewhere, and you will have to choose the right sort of program for the computer application you have in mind. Most people end up with a variety of programs.

Copying computer programs from cassette to cassette or disk to disk is widespread and is often in contravention of program copyright. The situation regarding computer programs is analogous to the problems of audio cassette copying of record albums, and although most proprietary programs are accompanied by warnings about the possible consequences of illegally copying programs, it contradicts human nature to expect that friends won't copy cassette programs for each other. This illegal copying (and the accompanying photocopying of the documentation) occurs a great deal with the simpler programs designed to be run on the cheaper microcomputers. Once a program reaches any size and complexity, the documentation also grows, and

the task of photocopying three or four hundred pages of documentation takes the fun out of getting a 'free' program. There is nothing program makers can really do to prevent this illegal traffic, even though some attempt is being made to create programs that cannot be copied: any knowledgeable programmer can defeat anti-copy measures, and companies are now marketing devices designed to defeat protection systems and facilitate 'illegal' copying.

If you have children under eight, it is well worth considering purchasing a microcomputer which allows you to buy software in cartridge form. As mentioned in Chapter 5, this form of program storage allows very young children to use the computer years before they would be capable of loading a program from audio cassette.

For older children, there are some very useful 'revision' programs arriving on the market which are designed to help students get through particular exams – college entrance, for example. These can prove extremely effective, but before selecting one it is wise to consult with your child's school to ensure that the programs are approved by the relevant examination board (or at least follow an appropriate syllabus).

### Household management

Household management programs often have initial family appeal. There are programs that keep diaries, store recipes, keep an index of books or magazines, keep telephone numbers, check your health, check your pet's health, plan your diet, plan your exercise, monitor your smoking, plan your household budget, work out your motoring expenses and undertake hundreds of other similar tasks. Most of these programs aren't worth the time it takes to load them into the computer. The idea of keeping a personal chequebook record on computer is nonsense: cheque stub records are quicker and easier to keep, and if you're bad at keeping those (like me) the computer will only make you more efficient so long as it is a novelty for you to use the computer. Soon it becomes far more of a nuisance to turn the machine on to check the bank statement than it is to go through it with a paper and pencil.

Despite my earlier aside about my inability to keep close track of my chequebook account, one definite result which has come out of my years of work with microcomputers has been a more methodical approach to such subjects – even to unpleasant items such as my bank account. Work carried out on a microcomputer can easily be lost, unless copies of it are made regularly and are carefully filed. A few losses soon teach even the most careless user the need for painstaking file-keeping, and I have found that this 'backup' discipline has also spilled over into my private life – I've never been better at filing and

A computer at home will be able to provide the possible diagnoses and recommend the action that needs to be taken.

finance checking than I am now, and I owe it to the discipline the computer has demanded.

An exception to these 'novelty' programs are the new generation of 'health check' programs just emerging in the USA. I have mentioned in an earlier chapter how useful computers are at diagnosing illness (patients are much more ready to talk to an impersonal computer than to a potentially censorious GP), and 'home doctor' programs are beginning to appear which will in years to come completely change the GP's role in society.

The community doctor is a storehouse of medical knowledge (excluding, of course, the doctor's vital social role – formerly filled in many communities by the religious 'head man'). When a patient visits a doctor, the GP will collect information by questioning and by physical examination. This information will provide the doctor with clues which will either point to a diagnosis of a common ailment or to the possibility of an unusual or serious condition existing, or will leave the GP perplexed. The doctor's ability to diagnose depends strictly on the amount of information the doctor has about the patient, how familiar the symptoms appear and how good the doctor's memory (data base) of ailments and symptoms is.

The amount of medical information required for the diagnosis of all but the most common disorders is vast, and the present method by which the medical profession copes with this complexity is to divide the health system up into specialised compartments. If you visit your doctor with an ear problem which he or she can't diagnose and treat, you will be referred to an ear, nose and throat specialist. This is the

person who holds the 'data base' of all of the specialised information about that particular type of problem. It is the secure GP who will admit to being beaten by your symptoms and who will rise from behind the desk and start searching through the volumes of medical information on the shelves. In other words, medical diagnosis depends on a vast data base which at present is held in the combined brains and books of the many separate branches of the medical professional.

### Home medical data bases

Slowly but surely, and despite resistance from many doctors, this information is being transferred to computer data bases, and programs already exist which will assist in home diagnoses of common complaints. Before long these home medical data bases will be extremely powerful, and it is likely that on feeling unwell the computer owner will load the 'health check' program and then attach the various peripherals such as blood pressure gauge, stethoscope, pulse strap, etc., to his or her own body which will provide the program with physical information. The patient will then answer a long set of questions designed to discover the symptoms. The patient's answers will provide the program with the necessary information to provide a further set of questions.

Having recorded information from physical examination, and having taken a description of symptoms together with a medical history, the program will extract from the data base all ailments which might be causing the symptoms and provide a print-out of the possible diagnoses. The print-out will contain all the questions and responses which led to the computer's diagnostical suggestions and will also recommend any X-rays, scans and other physiological tests necessary. This information will be made available to a human doctor who, as the next link in the chain, will consider the computer's suggested diagnoses and procedures for investigation. Patients who don't want to know what might be wrong with them need not apply.

Of course, only a fool would consider that today's computers are capable of dealing with illness more effectively than a human doctor, but equally only a fool would deny the computer's power to examine all the possibilities faster and more accurately than any human physician. For some years the two will work hand in hand, and patients will first respond to computer questioning when visiting a physician's surgery (it will be especially necessary for doctors to guard against over-reliance on computer diagnosis).

The early mistakes which will inevitably be thrown up by the system – a sprained ankle being diagnosed as a cobra bite – are bound to provide the cynics and Luddites with all of the humorous fuel which will help them delay this much needed medical assistance. Despite this there is little doubt that medicine will benefit from microcomputer assistance to an extraordinary degree. The time saved by rapid and accurate diagnostic suggestions may perhaps allow GPs to start working on the prevention of illness and on improving general community health rather than following their present role as referral agencies and placebo prescribers.

### Computer control

Once a computer is hooked up to external systems many things become possible. If you are considering building your own house in the near future, I would advise wiring every room with a cable-carrying conduit as before long many normal household functions will come under the control of the microcomputer. At the moment it all sounds a little futuristic, and only the do-it-yourself computer enthusiast is likely to start soldering all the bits and pieces together to bring environmental control under the computer. But we'll all be using it before long. (UK readers can get a glimpse of the future in a electronic showhouse in the new city of Milton Keynes, 50 miles north of London. It is signposted 'IT House' from junction 14 from the M1 motorway.)

Our present houses are rather like our cars: they are wasteful of energy and function with only the loosest sort of control – human control (e.g. when we remember to turn off the lights or turn down the heating). Cars are first in line for microprocessor control, and models which use on-board computers to govern fuel supply, mixture control,

With the computer screen located on the dashboard the driver follows the instructions to his destination.

ignition timing, exhaust emission and other mechanical factors are now rolling off the assembly lines.

There's a prototype Honda navigational system in which a VDU screen is mounted on the car dashboard. Drivers tell the computer which town they are in and then enter both their current street location and heading and their destination. The computer calculates the most *efficient* route for the urban journey, planning one which optimises both fuel consumption and speed. The computer displays the relevant section of road map on the screen, and the driver follows the instructions (spoken as well as visual) to find his or her destination. The system will in time be hooked into local traffic control computer systems so that the dashboard computer is constantly updating its information about traffic jams, road works and other obstructions and allowing it to revise the route options constantly as the journey proceeds. This type of automatic control is also arriving in the home.

All functions of the house will come under the control of the central house command computer. Because microprocessor capacity will be so vast in a few years, this one computer will be able to undertake house management at the same time as providing us with amusement or educational facilities. How much computer control is needed naturally depends on where you live. A one-room apartment will need far less control than a country estate, but the type of control the computer offers will allow everybody to achieve significant savings in their living costs.

The 'home control' program will take care of heating and air conditioning, and after a 'default' setting has been established (the system set to maintain the normal room temperatures you require) the computer will monitor the various temperatures in the rooms and will adjust the radiator valves, vent apertures and boiler or air conditioning units accordingly. For this to be possible the computer has to be connected to various external devices – motors to turn valves, switches to control lights, etc. These devices are coupled to a microcomputer via interface boxes known as 'digital to analog converters' (DACs) and 'analog to digital converters' (ADCs), which interpret the computer commands into normal electrical signals. All information on the computer is digital, and these converters translate the information necessary for the motorised control of heating valves or electrical switches.

Once thermometers have been installed in every room and wired to the computer, the computer can check the input against the levels determined in the program. If more heat is needed in a particular room, the computer can send a signal to a small motor which will open the heating valve or vent for that room. Many other household systems such as hot water, security surveillance systems, swimming pool water maintenance and telephone, mail and teletext links can come under computer control. This science fiction age has not yet arrived for most of us, but there are quite a few homes around the world in which enthusiasts have built all the necessary connections, and within a very few years these programs and control systems will seem commonplace. Far from being luxuries, the savings they will offer on energy consumption will make them almost necessary purchases.

### Business programs

Microcomputers were first marketed for the business community, and there is a vast range of business programs available. Almost every specialist business has a program tailored to make life easier. Newsvendors, dentists, real estate agents, writers, accountants, doctors, builders, designers, architects, TV rental managers, vehicle fleet controllers, garage owners, road hauliers, farmers, publicans and people in a hundred other occupations will find that there is a program written especially to help control their business. These programs are additional to the general management programs such as accounting, stock control and payroll organisation. There is no business too small to benefit from the installation of a microcomputer, and many of the specialist programs are able to run on very small inexpensive microcomputers. If a family has any business connections whatsoever, a computer has ceased to be a luxury and has become a necessity.

The above categories all concern 'ready-made' programs. Before leaving the subject it is worth mentioning 'operating systems'. Larger microcomputers often use disk drives for storage, and the method by which the microcomputer organises that storage governs the variety of programs which can be used. The most common is called CP/M (Control Program for Microprocessors), and because of its popularity there is a wealth of software available to run on the system.

Although I commented in Chapter 5 that the necessity for writing programs is diminishing as 'program writers' such as 'The Last One' appear, almost every family which decides to purchase a home computer will attempt to write their own programs for it – if only in an effort to understand the beast. There are many programming languages available that are suitable for home programming, and your choice of language may ultimately decide your choice of microcomputer.

There are 'high level' languages and 'low level' languages. The high level languages allow the user to command the computer in English words, although the syntax must follow the language's formula. The microcomputer then translates the high level language in the 1s and 0s that the microprocessor understands and then carries out the task. The time taken for translation (although it seems very rapid) means

that high level languages are considered 'slow' by the professional computing fraternity. 'Low level' languages are the languages that the microprocessors themselves understand. These languages may be the actual 1s and 0s or may be a 'compiler', a language only one step removed from the 'machine code' language, as the microprocessor language is called.

The disadvantage of low level languages is that they are incomprehensible to non-trained users and are also slow to write. The advantage is that the program, once created in a low level language, will run faster, and probably better, than one written in a high level language. Low level language writing requires considerable training. I will restrict my descriptions to high level languages. Because this book is about children and computers, I will also restrict my descriptions of computer languages to those that children are likely to use, either at school or at home.

The whole of Chapter 4 was devoted to a discussion about the Logo computer language for children, but the description of the language only covered the part of the program which controlled a robot – the turtle – and its screen-based cousin.

### Logo's 'sprites'

After a child has become used to the idea that simple commands can cause direct action in a computer, the Logo program offers the child the chance to play with 'sprites', shapes created within the program. The child can ask to 'call Sprite 1' and, after a few more details about the colour and position of the sprite have been entered on the screen, the graphic representation of a rocket (for example) appears. That rocket can then be set in motion, at any speed and in any direction the child chooses and will remain in that orbit until stopped. The child may then 'call Sprite 2' and, with similar details provided, the graphic representation of a plane will appear. Once given a heading (90 is horizontal, 180 is down) and a speed, this little plane will start flying around the screen quite independently of the rocket.

Implementations of Logo on different microcomputers vary slightly and this description is based on one of the earliest implementations of the language – made for the Texas TI-99/4A. There are three other ready-made sprites in the program and the child can call up a box, a truck or a ball and cause them to dance around the screen at will. Simple keystrokes allow the child to command the shapes individually or all together. Each shape exists in its own dimensional plane, and if the child places them all in the same spot on the screen they will line up behind each other in order of dimensional plane precedence.

There are actually 32 sprites which can be simultaneously called up on to the TI-Logo screen, but the program demands that the child create his or her own sprite shape after the five pre-shaped sprites have been called. To draw these, the child asks the computer for the 'makeshape' grid. This is a blank grid, and using only two directional keys even very young children (as young as three) can draw pictures creating cars, houses, ships, cats, dogs – in fact almost anything, although all representations are graphic with angular edges.

Having created his or her own sprite shape, the child can then return to the main sprite program and call it up ('call sprite 15', for example), and it will join the rocket, plane, ball, etc., dancing around the screen under the user's command. The child can go on drawing shapes and adding them to the animated scene taking place on the screen, and most importantly the shapes can each be 'taught' to do certain things. For example, the ball can be taught to bounce across the screen, the plane to land and take off, the truck to reverse into a garage that the child has drawn and so on. Each of these events will require a small program to be written, but the language used is plain English (e.g. 'Tell Sprite 1: Set Heading 45'), and a child can build a scene which has infinite variety and animated action. The colour of each sprite may be changed (there are 16 colours to choose from), and the colour of the background may also be independently changed. All programs (or procedures, as they are called in Logo) may be saved on to a cassette or a disk for reloading at a later date.

### Building a cartoon fantasy

From this description it will be seen that a child can build his or her own cartoon fantasy, and this is certainly the most appealing program for children under 13 that I have come across.

Other features within the TI-Logo program include 'Makechar' – a smaller grid on which children can create letters or numerals and 'tiles' which offer the user a huge grid and allow the creation of graphic shapes which fill the screen.

The Logo features I have described are creative and stimulating, but the mathematic content is limited to spatial and geometric concepts (which many, however, would argue are the most important). The TI-Logo program can also act as an advanced calculator which allows arithmetical problems to be written and solved in a conventional way. The TI implementation of Logo goes no further, but other versions offer a fully structured programming language with advanced mathematical features. The program is especially designed for children, and I have yet to see a more suitable method of introducing children to computing.

The most common language used on home computers is BASIC. This is a 'high level' language, as are many other common computer languages such as Pascal, Algol, APL, COBOL, COMAL, FORTRAN,

Pilot, LISP, Prolog and FORTH. There are others, and new ones are constantly being developed. Some of these languages are designed for a specific task – FORTRAN and Pascal, for example, are considered 'scientific' languages whilst COBOL is considered suitable for creating business programs. LISP is considered to be the most suitable language for pure research into artficial intelligence.

BASIC is the language most likely to be supplied with your home computer. BASIC was written in 1965, and the columns of the computing press are now filled with letters condemning the idea of a whole new generation of programmers growing up using such an archaic and, some say, poorly structured programming language.

For older children and adults BASIC is a very easy computer language to understand. Within an hour newcomers can write simple programs on a computer, and a few weeks of evening study will turn most into programmers capable of creating guessing games, simple educational programs or mathematics teasers. A major advantage of BASIC is that many of the less expensive pre-prepared computer programs are written in BASIC, and this provides a wide choice of programs for many machines. Although I am repeating an earlier warning, I must stress that BASIC written on one machine is unlikely to work on one of a different make. Programs written in BASIC on an Apple II will not run on a Pet, or on a Tandy Radio Shack, or on a BBC Microcomputer. There are a few standards: Microsoft BASIC, developed by a successful software house in the USA, is implemented on many machines, and new versions of BASIC are often built 'on the Microsoft principle' which will allow programs to match Microsoft systems. But as a general (insane) pattern all manufacturers have developed their own dialect of the language, and, except in a few fluke conditions, one machine's program is another machine's garbage.

Another advantage in gaining a familiarity with BASIC is that many magazines and books publish BASIC programs in print form. Games, quizzes and simple financial programs are the most popular for publication, and although it is possible for someone who does not understand BASIC slavishly to copy out such a program from a book, some understanding is necessary when the 'debugging' procedure has to take place. It is, of course, possible to start a computing career in one language and later switch to another, but experienced programmers point out that it is hard to break habits which are peculiar to a particular language.

The vast majority of people who learn to program a home computer have no intention of ever becoming professional computer programmers, and for them the argument about which is the best computer language is academic. They should use the one they find the easiest to learn and which will create the programs they want to write.

But teachers burdened with the responsibility of training tomorrow's computer programmers (or of teaching children how to

187

program for no other good reason than that this is education's current response to the arrival of computers in education) are very concerned with the choice of first language on the computer.

### Alternatives to BASIC

The main alternative to BASIC which is being used in European schools (excluding France, which prefers to use minicomputers in some schools) is COMAL, particularly COMAL 80. This language, developed in Denmark, was derived from BASIC, but it has a programming structure that is more in line with those used by more powerful professional programming languages, and significantly it has now become the 'official' school computer language of both Denmark and Eire. COMAL 80 is now rapidly gaining popularity all over Europe. The principal hindrance to its development is that few microcomputers offer it as a built-in feature.

All languages have their proponents: some scream for Algol (supposedly a very elegant computer language), some consider that children should be taught to use the very powerful Pascal language in secondary school, while others suggest their own particular favourites. FORTH is a language which is currently fashionable. It is very much faster in operation than BASIC, and at least one microcomputer has been specifically built round it (the Jupiter Ace). Without offering a detailed description of all these languages it is impossible to suggest one in preference to the other. For home computer use they are all minority languages beside the ubiquitous BASIC.

It is clear that BASIC is not an ideal choice for home computer programming; but like the qwerty keyboard it seems as though it is here to stay, and unless an educational system acts in a concerted effort to standardise on a language (as the French have done with LSE – Langage Symbolique d'Enseignement), it is perverse to ignore it in favour of another.

Programs which write programs, e.g. 'The Last One', demand that the user understands how they are created. The user works out the program he or she wishes to create and then answers a series of prompts from The Last One which causes it to create the necessary syntax automatically (in BASIC). This is very useful for people who write a lot of programs at home and who get fed up with all the meticulous typing necessary. But, with its competitors, The Last One should be seen as a program which automates program writing, rather than as a replacement for learning a computer language.

Computer languages are far easier to learn than spoken languages, and, once familiar with programming, most users can pick up the principles of any computer language in a few hours. Programming a computer is not difficult.

# BUYING A MICROCOMPUTER

In spite of all the well-meant advice handed out by the computer magazines, most people end up buying a microcomputer about which they know next to nothing. The main factors that influence choice seem to be price, local availability or the appeal of a mail-order advertisement. As there are a lot of microcomputers competing in the same price brackets, experienced and non-biased guidance can be useful (although hard to find), but which model you select must depend finally on what you want to do with the machine and, of course, on your budget. The notion of 'good' and 'bad' machines has disappeared as microtechnology has become increasingly reliable.

The list of microcomputers given here ranges from the cheapest to the most expensive models which are likely to be purchased for use in the home and, in particular, by children. There are many microcomputers outside this range (particularly the more expensive models) but, in compiling the list and in commenting on the various models, I have considered the suitability of various machines for the now famous hypothetical family of two adults with 2.7 children.

I have not mentioned prices as they will vary from month to month, from outlet to outlet and from country to country. But the list starts with the least expensive and in general works upwards. One point to remember when budgeting is that you are likely to want some add-on items, even if you don't buy them until later. If you are deciding between several similarly priced machines, ask about the cost of such peripherals as game paddles (joysticks), disk drives and printers. This may give you a clearer idea of the total cost of the system. A few manufacturers try to sneak up their profitability by overcharging for the extras.

The most important piece of advice to any family considering buying a microcomputer for their children is to buy a machine which is compatible with the microcomputer their children are using at school. The only exception to this general rule occurs if you discover that the school micro will not run programs which you particularly want your child to use: e.g. Logo or a specific business program which will help to justify the family's expenditure on a household computer.

189

### Guidelines

General points about microcomputer purchase have been made in earlier chapters, but let's recap.

The guidelines are:

1   It has to fit the budget – when considered with the add-ons you want
2   There has to be a large range of programs available for it
3   There have to be suitable educational programs for it
4   It is generally preferable to buy from a local store.

It is easier to solve any after-purchase problems locally, rather than by time-consuming post or expensive travel. Better-known makes of microcomputer usually have better after-sales back up.

Some manufacturers offer a guarantee as short as three months, others as much as a year. In many countries consumer laws exist which protect the purchaser against the supply of faulty goods. In these territories retailers or manufacturers have to offer extended service. But even if a manufacturer is forced to service a ten-month-old machine free of charge, you may be obliged to wait several weeks for the return of the machine. A relationship with a local retailer who has taken your money at the initial purchase and who has (probably) sold you programs and peripherals subsequently will be an easier target for your consumer wrath if the machine breaks down than a service department in a distant company.

A secondhand trade in microcomputers is beginning to open up, but the downwards spiral of micro costs is defeating the organisation of any secondhand market. If a fairly new microcomputer is on sale it is unlikely to be offered at a significant reduction on the retail price, but the purchaser may receive some valuable programs as a bonus. Beware that most secondhand computers offered at what seem like attractive prices are usually machines which are obsolete and are outperformed by machines with a lower new price than the 'bargain' secondhand deal. Because microcomputers are getting cheaper each year, secondhand purchasing is only a good idea if you know the market and know the machine in question. The inexpensive Timex/Sinclair ZX microcomputers are often offered secondhand as owners trade up to more powerful microcomputers, but the asking price would need to be considerably below retail prices (or the amount of 'thrown in' software considerable) to tempt me to ignore the shelter of a guarantee. Commercial computer service, although rarely needed, is quite expensive.

(Commodore have recently been offering Sinclair ZX81 owners the full retail price of the ZX81 as a trade-in deal against a Commodore Pet.)

### Buy now or wait?

As more powerful microcomputers are offered more cheaply each year, it must be valid to wonder if it is wise to wait before buying: on cost terms alone it could be, but if you decide to delay a purchase on these grounds you will have lost a year's experience and will have cost yourself (and your child) more than money. Another worry frequently stated is the concern over obsolescence: 'what if the machine I buy is obsolete in six months?' Most manufacturers are now anticipating this fear and are building expandable machines which allow the user to update the system as new technology becomes available.

If someone chained me in a darkened room until I was forced to decide which micro I would choose for my children, I would say it would have to depend on where I was living and the age of my children. In the USA my two choices (at different price levels) would be a TI-99/4A or a Tandy Radio Shack Model III. If I were in Britain it would be the Sinclair ZX Spectrum or the BBC Model 'B'. If I were elsewhere in the world the less expensive model would be the TI, and my choice of a more powerful unit would be between the Apple II (or its shortly arriving successor) or a Tandy Radio Shack Model III.

The reason that my choice would differ according to where I was living is that the choice depends strictly on the availability of software: for example, only a proportion of the thousands of the programs for TRS Radio Shack computers have found their way to Britain, and conversely the thousands of excellent programs developed for the BBC Microcomputer are not yet exported. If, at the time of asking, my children were under 11, I would ensure that the machine I purchased had the Logo program available. Many experts could argue that my choices are wrong for this or that reason, but whatever you (or I) choose microcomputing is a new phenomenon, and you can be sure that someone will always tell you why your choice was wrong.

I am limiting this guide to microcomputers which offer a full display on a domestic TV screen (or specially built VDU monitor) and excluding the pocket computers with single-line read-outs. This list will be incomplete for several additional reasons: some machines will not have been available at the time of writing, some machines will be on the brink of discontinuance (and obscurity), some I consider unsuitable for family use, and some machines are produced for only one small local market. For these reasons this buyer's guide must be seen as slightly idiosyncratic, but a perusal of the specialist computer magazines should supply information about any machines which I have not included.

### The jargon explained

Before listing the microcomputers suitable for family use, it is worthwhile providing a résumé of the jargon terms which are used to describe computer facilities.

RAM (Random Acess Memory) is the amount of 'live' memory the computer has at its disposal to carry out programs. Often expandable, microcomputer RAM ranges from 1K (1,024 bytes) to 900K. 48K is the maximum capacity required for most educational and domestic computing purposes.

Screen display: these measurements indicate how much information can appear on the TV screen (or monitor) at any one time: e.g. 32 characters (or columns) across the screen, by 24 lines down the screen.

Ports and sockets: there are cassette ports for linking the computer to a cassette tape recorder, ports or 'slots' for plugging in ROM program cartridges, ports for plugging in games paddles or joysticks (with which to control games such as PacMan), and special ports allow connection to the 'outside world' – usually called RS232, Centronics or IEEE ports. These multipin sockets are built to internationally agreed standards and allow various items from different manufacturers to interconnect. The devices which can be attached using such ports include printers, telephone line connectors, other computers and disk drive storage systems. There are several other sockets to be found on microcomputers: an 'expansion bus' is the connector to which the machine's own brand of peripherals are often attached, and you may also find a socket for a ROM chip as well as sockets for output to TV sets and the computer's power input.

*Keyboard:* these can range in type from the flat, printed-membrane keyboard to a full mechanical typewriter-style keyboard.

*CPU:* the central processing unit – the mighty microprocessor. The chip is the computer at the heart of the system and has its own machine code language. The type of chip used (there are remarkably few) is the final governing factor on compatability between languages and machines. Most microprocessors are '8-bit' and are slower than the newer '16-bit' processors which allow more information to travel through the computer at the same time.

*Languages:* most machines offer BASIC, but many offer other languages as options.

*Sound:* not all computers yet have the ability to make sound or music.

*Speech synthesis:* at present only a few microcomputer manufacturers offer this useful option, although specialist independent companies offer systems compatible with a variety of machines. If a major manufacturer produces a microcomputer without providing optional peripherals, small companies often go into business making items to fill this perceived need. Scanning the columns of the computer magazines is the only way of discovering such items. Almost every microcomputer can be given the power of speech with a little ingenuity.

This list of machines starts with the least expensive microcomputers and moves up. (In some countries you will find some of the market positions juxtaposed.)

### Sinclair ZX81 (Timex/Sinclair 1000)

Clive Sinclair brought computing to the masses in 1980 when he launched his ZX80 microcomputer. At that time it sold in Britain for £50. As a direct result of his design and marketing flair, Britain has more personal computers per head than any other country in the world.

The ZX80 was succeded in 1981 by the Sinclair ZX81/1000 – at the time of writing still ridiculously cheap, discounted in the US for $79.95 (as the Timex-Sinclair) and in Britain at £49.95. The difference between the ZX81 and the 1000 is that the 1000 has double the internal RAM capacity, 2K instead of 1K.

This machine (in either version) is the cheapest real computer you can buy. Over 750,000 units have been sold world-wide, and undoubtedly Clive Sinclair deserves some sort of recognition for his pioneering efforts in personal computing.

But I consider the ZX81/1000 to be the modern equivalent of the crystal set – it is fiddly and tiresome to use. You will find many exponents who claim miracles for it, but it demands a dedication from its users if it is to carry out more than the simplest computational functions.

The ZX81/1000 can actually be bought as a kit which people with minimal technical experience can put together and, unlike the ubiquitous non-flying model planes, will usually work after assembly. In kit form the machine is unbelievably cheap, and if you have a technically minded son or daughter who is keen on building things they'll get a great kick out of assembling this tiny machine (it is 6.3 x 6.8in, 160 x 172mm) and out of running programs. (I have excluded other kit computers from this list, not for any negative reasons, but simply because kit building isn't something every family would want to undertake.)

The big limitation of this machine is its tiny memory – 1 or 2K – although it has the potential capability of running far longer programs. If you decided to purchase the machine, it is likely that before long you'll be paying a similar price to the initial machine cost for an add-on 16K RAM package which will give the machine the power it needs for most educational programs. By that time you will have spent the sort of money which would have allowed you to consider a larger machine with a better keyboard.

The Keyboard on the ZX81/1000 is two-dimensional and the keys are 'printed' on to its surface. This requires very careful fingering, and the idea of 'typing' (and thus rapid program writing) is impossible.

Most people buy a ZX81/1000 to learn about computers and about programming. There really is no more cost-effective way of doing it. The machine arrives with its own dialect of BASIC and excellent training and instruction manuals. Be prepared, however, to trade the machine in fairly rapidly for a more powerful microcomputer if the computing bug bites. There is a plethora of inexpensive peripherals for the ZX81/1000 ranging from a tiny printer to a 'real typewriter-style' keyboard, and ZX81/1000 enthusiasts have managed to persuade these little beauties to undertake seemingly impossible tasks: everything from controlling Christmas tree lights to coastal navigation. It is possible to keep spending on a ZX81/1000 set-up, adding extra memory (up to 64K using items from independent manufacturers!), printers, sound, robotics control, communications ports, etc., until a powerful microcomputer centre exists, but in my view this is the computing equivalent of making a silk purse from a sow's ear.

Because of its extraordinarily low price, many adventurous (but underpaid) teachers have purchased their own ZX80 or ZX81/1000 (the software is compatible) and have taken them into the classrooms. The small size of the keyboard presents no problems for little fingers, but the keyboard is sometimes less than positive. Sinclair market a tray which will hold the computer and peripherals firmly in place – a useful extra for school or home. As a result of teacher interest, there are masses of educational programs available – although the system is not powerful enough to support the all-important Logo – and many of these programs are inexpensive.

Following the success of the ZX81/1000, there are many 'user groups' and clubs in existence and these organisations provide invaluable help and very good sources for programs. There are thousands of ready-made programs available for the machine including versions of all the usual space and arcade games.

My 'crystal set' categorisation of the ZX81/1000 mainly refers to its fiddly keyboard. To minimise the number of keys most of them have several functions, and some users find it is easy to get confused by them: others swear that Sinclair's BASIC, with many predefined program words, makes programming easier for the novice. The computer is also temperamental about accepting programs from certain cassette recorders, and the image on the TV screen is a bit fuzzy. Despite these criticisms, the machine is a real computer and serves as a great introduction to the subject of computing (Sinclair are reported to have sold 220,000 of these units in 1982 alone).

### Jupiter Ace

The Jupiter Ace is a 'Sinclair-type' portable microcomputer (9 x 7½in, 230 x 190mm), and similarities are probably due to the fact that two of Sinclair's leading designers left the Sinclair operation to produce the Ace. Unlike the ZX81/1000, the keyboard is semi-mechanical, but is not truly like a typewriter keyboard. The keys are more like calculator buttons than proper mechanical keys. One important advantage that the Ace has over the ZX81 is that the screen characters may be either upper or lower-case (an important educational consideration), but the main sales claim made for the machine is that it runs the FORTH computer language instead of BASIC. Whether this is perceived as a virtue or a disadvantage depends on how much, or how little, you know about computers. Those who understand a great deal about computing will realise that this is one of the earliest implementations of FORTH as a built-in language on a microcomputer and will know just how powerful the language is. It is very close to assembler and machine code and operates five to 20 times faster than an equivalent BASIC program. (The computer controlling the radio telescope at Jodrell Bank runs on FORTH.) This means that complex programs will operate faster and that games written in FORTH will be considerably more exciting than games written in BASIC. Almost certainly the programmer who makes real use of the FORTH's speed will want to add an additional RAM memory pack to the machine's limited 3K of built-in RAM.

If you know next to nothing about computers you may well be impressed by the sales talk about the wonders of FORTH: how simple it is to program, how fast it is in operation and how superior it is to BASIC. But beginners should be warned; there is little commercial software available written in FORTH, and you'll have to write every program yourself. Further you will be learning an uncommon programming language which is likely to remain uncommon for some years to come. Every specification points to the very inexpensive plastic-cased Ace as being an exciting machine, but it is one for experienced programmers who want to explore new languages, or schools which want to illustrate alternative methods of programming, not one on which 13-year-olds should start their computing careers (even if they might be able to learn FORTH more easily than BASIC).

*The Sinclair ZX81.*

*The Jupiter Ace.*

*The Sinclair ZX Spectrum running a geography program.*

### Sinclair ZX Spectrum

In a slightly higher price bracket is the very successfull Sinclair ZX Spectrum. This microcomputer was hailed as the second milestone in 'people's computing' when it was announced early in 1982 (the first milestone being the ZX80) and it won the distinction of official approval by Britain's Department of Trade and Industry which, by some extraordinary twist of government logic, carries the responsibility for deciding which microcomputers are eligible for subsidised introduction into British schools.

The excitement which surrounded the announcement of the Spectrum was matched only by the inability of the Sinclair organisation to supply the tiny machines (9 x $5\frac{1}{2}$ x $1\frac{1}{4}$in, 230 x 140 x 32mm). It is a testimony either to the brilliance of the product or to the patience of the British public that the product didn't fade away when mail order customers were kept waiting six months. By the end of 1982, over 75,000 Spectrums had been sold.

Having described its turbulent launch, it is fair to say that the Spectrum is a masterpiece of microengineering and is undoubtedly one of the two best British micros of both 1982 and 1983. For the first time, a full feature colour computer with a 40-key semi-mechanical keyboard (which appears to be the least-liked feature of the machine) came within the reach of millions at a very low price: indeed inflation meant that the Spectrum was being offered to the British public for about the same 'real' price as the ZX80 was offered in 1980.

There are two versions of the Spectrum, one with 16K of internal RAM, the other with 48K. The secret of the Spectrum is a new 16K ROM chip which controls all internal functions, provides the eight colours and stores Sinclair's version of BASIC.

Sinclair BASIC uses a lot of shorthand commands that some experts consider may lead users into sloppy programming habits. Many of the commands (List, Print, Load, etc.) which on most microcomputers would have to be spelled out in full are available as one-button functions on the ZX81/1000 and Spectrum: time saving, but hard to do without. It may be great for novices, but the multifunction buttons of the keyboard (some of them have up to eight different functions) will demand a complete reorientation when the user progresses to a computer which can accommodate a larger keyboard. Some primary school teachers, however, claim that the 'whole word' command feature allows young children, who would otherwise be quite likely to misspell programming commands, to write programs with a greater likelihood of success.

At the time of writing, the Spectrum was due to be provided with a new data storage system which Sinclair are calling 'Microdrive' and which will be a quasi disk drive system. Observers suggest that this system falls somewhere between the economy of a cassette system and the speed of a disk system. If the Microdrive is as good as previous Sinclair products, the system should kill off the accursed audio cassette storage system which slows down so much home computing.

Many Sinclair users swear an allegiance to the brand which seems disproportionate to the capabilities of the machines – cost-effective though they are. I am convinced that one of the reasons that the world is filled with so many Sinclair fanatics is that they simply haven't been lucky enough to own a large-scale microcomputer with disk drives. Once it is realised how fast and user-friendly a bigger microcomputer with disk drive system can be, I am sure that much of the hysterical loyalty to micro-cost Sinclairs will vaporise. Worthily, Sinclair seem determined to bring such facilities to their little machines before the fans trade up to more powerful systems.

Having praised Sinclair, it is only fair to point out that the UK launch of the Spectrum was also dogged by problems other than late delivery. Colours were bad on many machines, and many units worked well for the first ten minutes – after which all colour definition disappeared, and the screen became a mess. Keyboard problems developed, and many computers simply didn't work when they came out of the box. 'Oversubscription' was the cause, and as I write I believe that all these problems have been sorted out. I know many Spectrum owners who are delighted with the machine.

The Spectrum is an excellent choice for a home computer for several reasons: it has a version of Logo available, it is approved by many schools, it is inexpensive, it will run the multitude of programs created for the ZX80 and ZX81/1000 machines (although it uses a different format for tape storage of programs) and it will hook up to any TV. (Be warned, however, that although the ZX printer will work with the Spectrum, the other ZX peripherals – such as add-on RAM – will not. The screen graphics on the Spectrum are excellent, although the memory map is confusing (if you are knowledgeable enough to want to Poke around in it).

Against the Sinclair Spectrum is the fact that the keyboard is only semi-mechanical, there is no proper space bar (which is necessary for writing text at any speed) and so there's still no chance for any keyboard technique, other than single-finger prodding. I also consider the constant plugging and unplugging of cassette leads (the leads can't be left in place permanently) to be a real nuisance.

Early Spectrum models utilised red and green lettering to distinguish key functions, until someone pointed out that one in 12 children suffer a colour blindness in distinguishing between these two colours. The colour coding was swiftly changed.

There is a mass of software available for the Spectrum including Logo and simple word-processing, although only the simplest business programs will run on the system. One exciting Spectrum feature promised for 1983 is an adaption that will enable the machine to receive telesoftware – the pioneering experiment of broadcasting software which the BBC and Prestel (viewdata) are mounting in Britain.

Above the Spectrum 16K price range, the market is crowded with competing machines which have 'proper' keyboards, all of which have separate claims to be the best.

Discount structures in various countries make true cost comparison impossible, so the next half-a-dozen machines should really be judged according to the price currently available in your area.

### TI-99/4A

One amazing offer which was being made in both the US and the UK at the time of writing was for the Texas TI-99/4A colour microcomputer. This machine has had an astonishing marketing history in both countries. Throughout this guide I have avoided quoting too many prices because they vary from country to country (and they date quickly), but the financial history of the TI-99/4A machine illustrates a piece of marketing madness which will keep the advertising executives laughing into their martinis for years to come. It also illustrates the incredible downwards spiral of microcomputer prices and the fact that even the best of them – Texas are one of the biggest microelectronics companies and they claim to have invented the microcomputer – can get it wrong.

In the US the machine was first marketed at \$1,100 and became as *Time* magazine put it, 'a market failure of historic proportions'.

When the machine first arrived in Britain (in 1979) it was in its first TI-99/4 version and was the only computer in the world to be based on a 16-bit microprocessor (TI 9900) and which also offered a 'plug-in' slot for program cartridges. The majority of micros are still using 8-bit architecture and, if you recall the explanation from an earlier chapter, you'll know that 16-bit systems have a far greater potential than 8-bit systems. To say the least, the TI machine was way ahead of its time.

The TI-99/4's original British price was over £1,000! This put it in a 'super-micro' class and although it had its 16-bit claim going for it, the modest 16K of internal RAM and a rather poor keyboard didn't really stand up against the Pets and Apples which could provide an entire system plus screen for that sort of money. Two additional factors militated against the success of the machine: it would only work on American standard TV sets, not on British PAL sets, and laughably the TI BASIC on the 16-bit TI machine actually ran more slowly than the BASIC on competitive 8-bit computers. The natural result was that the Texas TI-99/4 became a joke in the British microcomputer industry.

But the 16-bit architecture was important enough for Texas to sustain the system in manufacture. The company produced an implementation of Seymour Papert's Logo computer language, and although the machine required an additional RAM pack to bring RAM up to 48K to run the program, the 16-bit processor allowed the program to work well and fast. That got the TI-99/4 and 99/4A into many US schools.

Realising that the impoverished Britains weren't about to mortgage their homes for a £1,000 TI machine (and in addition buy an American-standard TV), TI persuaded the machine's circuitry to interface with the European TV system, the unit (in its world-wide version) was updated to the 99/4A version and the price was cut, cut and cut still further. At the time of writing, the third version of the same machine (more rather than less powerful) is being sold in Britain for £150! The deal is curious; purchasers pay £200 and claim £50 back when they register their guarantee card. Nevertheless this price drop is the most startling in microcomputer history and indicates how ferociously competitive the microcomputer market is.

In the USA Texas hired Bill Cosby to do the commercials and slashed the US price of the unit. In 1982 Texas sold 530,000 TI-99/4As and at the time of writing were selling nearly 150,000 a month.

I consider the TI-99/4A to be a superlative microcomputer (especially for the current price). The keyboard is fully mechanical and is now a delight to use. The computer accepts programs from audio cassettes (although it's fussy about which cassette machine it works with), from ROM cartridge (excellent for young children) and from floppy disk – if you have purchased a disk drive system.

The TI-99/4A is part of a complete system including add-on RAM, printer, disk drive and RS232 interface which allows the machine to communicate with the outside world (telephone lines, general printers or other computers).

One special feature of the TI system is the add-on speech synthesizer. Texas were one of the first companies to produce a speech synthesis chip (it first appeared in their 'Speak and Spell' game in 1978 – which later helped out E.T.) and the inexpensive speech unit plugs straight into the side slot on the computer – no wire connections or fiddles.

Having commented that TI BASIC runs slowly despite the 16-bit architecture, it is fair to say that the TI version of BASIC is very good. An enhanced and extended version of TI BASIC is available as an optional extra and allows serious programming to be undertaken. The machine will also run the Pascal programming language which means the system will grow with the family if you have an older child who gets serious about programming.

The 16-bit power of the machine becomes evident when some of the commercially written educational programs (mostly cartridge-based) are run on the machine. These programs are written in machine code, and the power of the system allows the fullest use of colour graphics, upper and lower-case characters, music, sound and speech. With the exception of Logo (the TI implementation of which uses neither sound nor speech), nearly all the TI educational programs fall into the drill and practice CAL category. Despite this, they are stunning: children are mesmerised by the fast-moving visuals, and teachers are reluctant to return to the agonisingly slow, and comparatively boring, graphics presented on most inexpensive micros. The TI-99/4A is worthy of serious consideration for parents in areas where schools have adopted the machine, and even if that is not the case in your area a demonstration of some of the machine's educational programs may be enough to persuade you to fly in the face of the school's choice of micro (especially as the Logo option is available).

The disadvantage about making a TI choice is that there is at the moment a relatively limited amount of independently produced software available for the machine. Texas have produced a considerable range of programs, and one or two commercial houses have developed programs; but compared to the thousands of programs available for Apples or Spectrums the TI is not well served. This is because the machine has until recently been prohibitively priced: software houses will only write for machines that are selling well. Now that TIs are selling as fast as Texas can make them, several major software houses are rethinking their response to the machine, and I think it likely that the software shortage will be a thing of the past by the time these words are in print.

### Commodore Vic 20

Commodore is a famous name in personal computing, and the company claim that their Pet systems are the most widely used educational microcomputers in the world. In the last couple of years they have launched cheaper models designed to hook up to domestic TV sets as they saw the Sinclairs and Ataris threatening to create new brand loyalties.

The Commodore Vic 20 is a neat small colour microcomputer which has a proper mechanical keyboard and some very useful features. In line with all new generation micros, the Vic 20 is fully expandable (offering you the choice of adding a wide range of options). Its 5K of built-in RAM is capable of becoming 29K, and all connections for cassette, disk drives, game paddles, communications RS-232 port, printer and program cartridges are built in. I particularly like the light but positive keyboard, and the four 'special function' keys make programming and general use a lot easier than on some machines which have multiple-function keys. There are some really powerful

*The TI-99/4A.*

*The Dragon 32.*

*The Vic 20.*

musicmaking chips, but they need clever programming to make full use of the sound.

The screen display offered by the Vic 20 is 22 characters by 23 lines and for this (and other) reasons, the existing Pet programs – most 40 characters wide – won't automatically run on the Vic. They will load, but they will need adjustment by someone who knows a little about programming before they will run properly. Commodore themselves offer an upgrade kit which will convert the Vic 20 to what is effectively the Vic 40, but many specialist houses are now producing 'black boxes' that convert the Vic 20 into everything they think it should be: 32K, 80 character display, further RS-232 communications ports, etc. This turns the unit into a very powerful machine capable of undertaking tasks such as word-processing. Commodore clearly wanted to leave a capability gap between their 'cheap micro' and their home/business Pets, but the flexibility of the microprocessor is such that users and independent entrepreneurs are closing the gap for them.

The Vic 20 is a good, if not outstanding, buy, and there are lots of games and educational programs available for the machine. Be warned that the Vic 20 will only load programs from a Commodore cassette recorder, and the price of this purchase must be added to the budget. In 1982 UK sales of the Vic 20 were quoted as being around 100,000, and Commodore claim to have sold a million Vic 20s world-wide.

**Dragon 32**

The Dragon 32 is a new British microcomputer built by Mettoy, the toy manufacturer, and is unusual amongst inexpensive microcomputers in that it offers a basic built-in RAM of 32K. Having said that, there doesn't appear to be a lot going for the first version of the machine. The system is based on the 6809 central processing unit (the same chip used in the Tandy Radio Shack Colour Computer) and some of the Tandy software may turn out to be compatible. The Dragon is cheap for such a powerful computer, but it has several limitations including a reduced number of expansion and peripheral connectors. Because the machine is new, there is little ready-made software yet available for it, and this is probably the machine's main drawback. Recognising this, Mettoy (a company able to invest huge amounts in advertising and glossy brochures, so beware!) have already announced plans for an up-grade kit which will offer a 16-bit processor, disk drives, RAM expansion up to 256K and a host of other goodies which will, if they arrive, lift the machine way out of its present class. At the time of writing, however, its limitations seem to outweigh its advantages. UK sales of 25,000, however, suggest that many buyers either appreciate the 'power per pound' aspect of the

Dragon or have succumbed to the pressure of a powerful advertising campaign.

### Acorn Atom

The British manufacturer Acorn has rapidly expanded since they were awarded the contract to build the BBC Microcomputer. This unit is subsidised for use in British schools and is designed to accompany the popular BBC television series in microcomputing.

The company's Acorn Atom was popular in British schools even before the arrival of the Acorn/BBC microcomputer and is available in both kit and ready-built form. The system is expandable and can run a wide variety of programming languages. Acorn are offering up-grade kits to make the machine compatible with the BBC microcomputer, and with this option a wide range of software is available for the computer. The marketing policy of Acorn allows the user to buy an inexpensive basic system and gradually build up to a quite sophisticated machine. The keyboard is fully mechanical and a 'ROM socket' allows ROM-based software to be used. The Acorn brochure advises that kit constructors require 'reasonable skill' with a soldering iron.

### Atari 400

Atari have become a world-famous name since their arcade machines first brought us Space Invaders and PacMan (not created by them, but made under licence from the original Japanese author of the game program). The company quickly realised the potential for home versions of these compelling games, and two Atari home computers were produced. The Atari 400 is really a games-playing machine, but some successful attempts have been made by both Atari and independent manufacturers to build it into a complete computer system. It is unusual in its price range in having a printed-membrane keyboard with very few expandable options available, but what it lacks in 'serious' capabilities it makes up for in outstanding graphics and games-playing ability. This machine will provide you with the closest thing to the arcade game experience, and it is now possible to do some programming and semi-serious computing by adding peripheral units from independent suppliers.

### Lynx

The Lynx is a new British machine, announced at the end of 1982. This is a microcomputer which offers 48K RAM as standard (expandable to 192K!) and is based on a Z80 chip which allows CP/M compatability. Camputers, makers of the Lynx, have been careful not to opt for features which make the machine unique: the sales literature announces that the Lynx wants to make friends, not 'hostages'. Hostages are just what users of obscure operating systems or languages can become, and in ensuring that languages such as Pascal, COMAL and FORTH will run on the Lynx, Camputers have already begun to find a place in a crowded market. There is now a rash of such new machines produced by either small companies or companies new to computing – the Dragon, the Ace, etc. – and at the very least it will be interesting to see what effect their innovations have on the staid and well established manufacturers.

Tandy fall into this last category. Until a couple of years ago, the Tandy Corporation (which makes Radio Shack microcomputers), and the Apple Corporation, virtually had the personal computer market sewn up between them. Today, things have changed, and there are dozens of competitors each trying to effect one improvement or another over the computers made by these pioneers.

### TRS-80 Model I and Colour Computer

The Radio Shack TRS-80 Model I could be called a pioneering microcomputer as it was the first model available from Tandy. It is soon to be phased out of production because it does not meet some of the new standards laid down for personal computers in the USA, but there is such a wealth of software available for it that the TRS-80 Model I is likely to be used for many years to come. The TRS-80 Model I is in thousands of schools around the world, and in preparation for its demise there are some excellent bargains to be found on this particular microcomputer. In some territories Video Genie computers appear to be similar to TRS-80 Model I, and this is due to an 'own-brand' agreement between manufacturers. To all intents and purposes the machines are the same, and all software is interchangeable.

The TRS-80 Model I is a well proven inexpensive computer, and the huge program range available might be sufficient reason to consider the machine, if the price is right.

When Tandy launched the TRS-80 Colour Computer it was less than successful. It seemed overpriced in comparison to other machines, and because the company had opted to use a slightly

*The Acorn Atom.*

*The Lynx.*

*The NewBrain.*

unusual chip – the 6809E (the same used in the Dragon 32) – the range of software available was limited.

Today the machine is more competitively priced and, most importantly, has a version of Logo available. This implementation of the language is mainly centred around the turtle graphics part of the program, but with a wider range of software becoming available each month the TRS-80 Colour Computer is now worthy of serious consideration. One drawback, however, is that screen text is in upper case only, and this will limit the acceptance of the system by education authorities. The TRS-80 Colour Computer is the only Radio Shack computer available which will run a version of Logo.

### NewBrain

The NewBrain is another recently launched British microcomputer. Although this model is new, the designers offer the CP/M operating system as an option, and this brings a huge range of software (excluding Logo at present) into the machine's capability. Although the basic 32K machine is tiny (handheld in concept) and has a keyboard which is halfway between a full typewriter-style keyboard and a calculator pad, the machine has so many expansion possibilities that it is possible to build up a really powerful system able to compete with many of the biggest microcomputers. The RAM is expandable up to a staggering 512K, and a particularly useful option (which has to be decided on purchase) is the inclusion of a one-line liquid crystal display mounted in the computer keyboard itself. This display acts in tandem with the TV monitor during normal use, but when the NewBrain is removed from the home computer centre, it remains powered by an internal battery (which also protects the program currently in RAM) and allows the machine to be used as a real pocket computer.

The NewBrain was designed by a consortium of design houses including Sinclair, and if it fulfils its promise it seems set to be the first small/big computer. It is the sort of machine that can be carried in the school bag for class work and then brought home, hooked up to the disk drives and TV set to become a powerful word-processor or accounting machine.

The BASIC the machine uses as its built-in programming language is very close to Microsoft BASIC (one of the most popular BASIC dialects) – which means a number of BASIC programs will run on the machine with a minimum of alteration – but the addition of CP/M system disk drives places every sort of business program at the machine's command. An interesting additional feature is that the machine will run COMAL, the improved version of BASIC which so many European schools are now considering using as a main programming language.

The NewBrain – seen by many in its basic form as a strong competitor to the Spectrum – suffers by offering black and white display only, but gains by having a programming language which operates at twice the speed and a RAM capacity infinitely greater.

The NewBrain should be seen as a truncated version of a business microcomputer which the user may build up as he or she needs (or can afford) the extras.


## BBC Microcomputer

The BBC Microcomputer has caused an enormous stir in Britain, but has yet to gain world-wide acceptance. The microcomputer was built to specifications laid down jointly by the BBC (who wished to broadcast a computer education series with a standard machine available) and the British government's Department of Industry.

The specifications were chopped and changed during development, and after much acrimonious debate with the computer industry the contract for building the machine went to Acorn Computers (already well known for making microcomputers popular in education).

The BBC Microcomputer has been almost unanimously hailed by both the British and overseas computing press as the best microcomputer ever built, but the production of the machine was dogged by problems so severe that the whole project almost sunk.

Acorn's delivery problems with the BBC micro were occurring simultaneously with Sinclair's inability to deliver the Spectrum to the British market, and it seemed for a while as though the great British public would have to return to the slide rule and abacus. In both cases, an important contributing factor to the production problems was the massive, and previously underestimated, public response to the availability of inexpensive microcomputers.

The problems are now solved and the two models of the machine, the BBC 'A' and BBC 'B', are in plentiful supply, are working reliably and are served by masses of software (some programs better than others).

Because of the awesome world-wide power of 'Auntie' BBC, the computer literacy programs are being shown in many countries around the world, and consequently the BBC computers are following. UK sales in 1982 – it became generally available in the middle of the year – were around 40,000.

The principal language the BBC computer uses is a carefully developed version of BASIC which most experts agree is the best-ever implementation of the language. But many critics are furious that the BBC chose a 20-year-old language when it could have opted for a better-structured language, such as COMAL 80. Such is

*The BBC Microcomputer.*

*The Atari 800.*

*Research Machines' LINK 480Z with monitor.*

conservatism.

You can buy a BBC micro to suit your pocket: the 'A' version is a 16K machine, and the 32K 'B' version is a third more expensive. Thankfully, if you decided to buy an 'A' you can easily upgrade later to a 'B' by adding RAM chips. The 'B' machine would appear to be the most expandable microcomputer on the world market, with built-in facilities for interfacing with disk drives (CP/M if required), printers, speech synthesizers, teletext and networks. In addition, powerful 'ROM chip' programs (such as word-processing) may be plugged into the machine as well as the more usual ROM cartridges. The graphics and sound capabilities of the machine are outstanding. (At the time of writing there was a suggestion that BBC and Acorn were preparing to market an 'Electron' – a BBC compatible machine which would be cheap enough to compete with the Spectrum.)

## Atari 800

The Atari 800, the big brother of the 400 games machine, has proved to be a huge seller in the USA (200,000 units alone in 1982). Although it is still games orientated, the 800 has the advantage of a proper typewriter-style keyboard, and this allows games-crazy programmers to write games programs which make use of the astonishing graphics and colour capabilities of the machine. The computer is also powerful and flexible in its own right and has a massive amount of commercially produced, educational software available. Of particular importance is a recently produced colour version of logo.

The 800 has sockets for four joysticks (communal PacMan?), and many of the commercial programs are loaded via ROM cartridge. Despite its game-playing pedigree, the machine is a fully fledged computer with cassette or disk drive storage interfaces.

## Research Machines 380Z and 480Z

Two other machines which are popular in British schools – but are rarely found elsewhere – are the Research Machines 380Z and 480Z microcomputers. Both were designed exclusively for the educational market. The 380 is the larger version of the machine, and the 480 can be upgraded in both terms of RAM and software capability. The RML machines are often described as 'tank-like', and it is for this reason that they have found wide acceptability in schools where computers often come in for rough treatment. A version of Logo, complete with floor turtle, is available for the 380Z. Both machines are flexible with full interface facilities and with connections which allow experimental robotics and analog connections to be made in school science labs.

Outside the educational field, there is not a lot of RML-compatible software, but the machines are excellent for programming use. Once disk drives are added, however, the story changes as the machines are capable of running the CP/M system for which there is a massive amount of ready made software. If you decide to buy an RML system, you'll be spending quite a lot of money, but you can be sure that the machine will be reliable and will also be found in many British schools.

### Apple II

Apple was the company which really brought the computer into the home. Although the company have still to produce a really inexpensive home computer, the machines they have made have been so popular and so widely used that there is a wealth of Apple programs available, both educational and non-educational. Apple have sold over 450,000 units of the Apple II. In addition the Apple machines lend themselves so well to hardware modification that many peripheral manufacturers have chosen to base devices on the machine (there are at least four professional computer musical instruments based on the Apple II, for example), and the machine will remain a sensible purchase for a few more years.

The Apple II plus has recently been announced as well as a more expensive and very powerful machine, the Lisa. Apple IIs will go on for years (at the right price, they'd make a good secondhand buy) and as a percentage of the market they are one of the most widely used computers in educational establishments.

### Commodore Pet and Vic 64

Say 'Pet' to British teachers and most of them will complain that the British government's subsidy has not allowed them to increase their commitment to this excellent range of US-originated micros. Pet's makers, Commodore, have found far more success in Europe than in their native country, and the rugged and flexible 'all-in-one' Pets have found places in many schools.

The Commodore Pets are up-market microcomputers which comprise a computer, a screen and often built-in cassette units or disk drives. Teachers have found the machines to be extremely robust, testing them by carrying them from classroom to classroom (hopefully there will soon be sufficient micros in schools for this to be unnecessary), and there is a plethora of educational programs available for the three Pet versions currently available. The difference between the versions is screen display and memory size, and the 8032

*The Apple II e – the latest version of the Apple II microcomputer system.*

*The Sharp MZ 80A.*

*The Vic 64.*

with an 80-character wide display has considerable potential as a business microcomputer when fitted with disk drives and a printer.

Commodore are introducing the Vic 64, effectively a 64K version of the Vic 20, mentioned earlier. This machine is likely to have all of the necessary power to run the huge range of existing Pet programs; but as it is a stand-alone machine designed to hook up to a domestic TV it will be much less expensive than a Pet system and will allow home users to build the system as they need, or can afford, to. No technical specifications are available at press time.

### Sharp MZ 80A

Sharp are one of the few Japanese companies who have managed to make a breakthrough into the Western markets. The Sharp MZ 80A has proved to be a big seller and some schools have adopted the system. The interesting feature on this computer is that the cassette storage system is actually built in to the computer housing, and this does facilitate classroom use. The system has no built-in language: the user must load whichever programming language he or she wishes to use on a given day. Expansion is easy with the system, but several critics complain about the documentation which accompanies the system (perhaps the difficulty of writing good English manuals is one reason why the Japanese micros have been so slow to arrive in Western markets).

### TRS-80 Model III

Today's most popular Tandy microcomputer is the Radio Shack TRS-80 Model III. This is a relatively expensive microcomputer, but it is finding considerable acceptance in schools across the USA, Europe and Australasia. The reason is that the Model III is an 'all-in-one' package machine which offers keyboard, screen and disk drives in a single unit. The connections between all of these parts often cause problems, and to find a machine that automatically takes care of such worries is reassuring for novices. Apart from that advantage, the Model III is also a very good machine.

The Model III will run any of the multitudinous programs that have been written in either Tandy Level I or Level II BASIC, depending on which hardware option you choose for your Model III, and Tandy offer the Model III in a variety of options which allow the school or private user to build up the machines as and when necessary.

## Conclusion

In this guide to microcomputers I have left out many that have a valid claim to be suitable for children, and my only excuse is that I have tried to concentrate on those machines that either have found widespread educational acceptance or have features that make such acceptance likely in the future. I have also left out those machines which cost more than I consider most families would be prepared to pay for a home computer. By the time this guide is in print there will undoubtedly be even more exciting and flexible machines to choose from: at the moment the Western world is anxiously awaiting an invasion of Japanese-built microcomputers.

In the end the computer has to please the entire family. It will have to play a version of PacMan (and its successors) and it ought to be able to run Logo. It would be useful also if it could do some word-processing, and the widest possible range of software should be a decisive factor in choosing a machine. Enjoy your computing.

# APPENDIX

### TECHNICAL SPECIFICATIONS OF MACHINES DESCRIBED IN CHAPTER 10

#### The Sinclair ZX81 and Timex/Sinclair 1000

RAM: 1K (ZX81) or 2K (1000) built-in. Expandable to a maximum of 18K (up to 64K with peripherals from independent suppliers). Screen display: 32 characters by 24 lines, upper case, black and white. Interface ports: cassette loading port, game paddle sockets. Optional interfaces: disk drive ports, RS-232 sockets. Keyboard: printed-membrane, 40 keys. CPU: 8-bit Z80. Built-in languages: Sinclair BASIC. Optional languages: none. Built-in sound: no. Manufacturer's speech synthesis option: no.

#### The Jupiter Ace

RAM: 3K built-in. Expandable to a maximum of 19K. Screen display: 32 characters by 24 lines, upper and lower case, black and white. Interface ports: cassette loading port, game paddle sockets. Optional interfaces: disk drive ports, RS-232 sockets. Keyboard: calculator-style, 40 keys. CPU: 8-bit Z80. Built-in languages: FORTH. Optional languages: none. Built-in sound: no. Manufacturer's speed synthesis option: no. Special features: one of the few micros running FORTH.

#### The Sinclair ZX Spectrum

RAM: 16K or 48K built-in. Expandable to a maximum of 48K. Screen display: 32 characters by 24 lines, upper and lower case, colour. Interface ports: cassette loading port, printer port. Optional interfaces: micro-disk drive ports, RS-232 sockets. Keyboard: calculator-style mechanical, 40 keys. CPU: 8-bit Z80. Built-in languages: BASIC. Optional languages: Logo. Built-in sound: yes. Manufacturer's speech synthesis option: no. Special features: the Spectrum can be linked with other units to form a network.

#### The TI-99/4A

RAM: 16K built-in. Expandable to a maximum of 48K. Screen display: 32 characters by 24 lines, upper and lower case, colour. Interface ports: cassette loading port, game paddle sockets, cartridge program socket. Optional interfaces: disk drive ports, RS-232 sockets. Keyboard: typewriter-style mechanical, 48 keys. CPU: 16-bit 9900. Built-in languages: BASIC. Optional languages: Logo, Pascal, assembler, Extended BASIC. Built-in sound: yes. Manufacturer's speech synthesis option: yes. Special features: advanced 16-bit processor architecture allows advanced programming.

### The Commodore Vic 20

RAM: 5K built-in. Expandable to a maximum of 29K. Screen display: 22 characters by 23 lines, upper and lower case, colour. Interface ports: cassette loading port, game paddle sockets, cartridge program socket, printer port, disk drive, RS-232 port. Keyboard: typewriter-style mechanical, 66 keys. CPU: 8-bit 6602. Built-in language: BASIC. Optional languages: FORTH. Built-in sound: yes. Manufacturer's speech synthesis option: no. Special features: converter available to convert system to 40-column compatibility with Pets.

### The Dragon 32

RAM: 32K built-in. Expandable to a maximum of 64K. Screen display: 32 characters by 16 lines, upper case, colour. Interface ports: cassette loading port, game paddle sockets, program cartridge port, printer port. Keyboard: typewriter-style mechanical, 52 keys. CPU: 8-bit 6809E. Built-in languages: BASIC. Optional languages: none. Built-in sound: yes. Manufacturer's speech synthesis option: no.

### The Acorn Atom

RAM: 2K built-in. Expandable in 1K steps to a maximum of 12K. Screen display: 32 characters by 16 lines, upper and lower case, black and white, colour optional. Interface ports: Acorn 'bus' for disk drives, printer, cassette recorder. Special 'ROM' program chip slot. Keyboard: typewriter-style mechanical, 62 keys. CPU: 8-bit 6502. Built-in languages: BASIC, assembler. Optional languages: BBC BASIC, FORTH, LISP and Pascal. Built-in sound: yes. Manufacturer's speech synthesis option: no. Special features: available in kit form, can be used as part of a network with up to 255 units sharing a central floppy disk unit.

### The Atari 400

RAM: 16K built-in. Expandable to a maximum of 32K (from independent suppliers). Screen display: 40 characters by 24 lines (variable), upper and lower case, colour. Interface ports: cassette storage, game paddle sockets, cartridge program socket. Optional interfaces: disk drive ports, printer. Keyboard: printed membrane, 61 keys. CPU: 8-bit 6502. Built-in languages: none. Optional languages: (in cartridge form) FORTH, BASIC, Pascal, assembler. Built-in sound: yes. Manufacturer's speech synthesis option: no.

### The Lynx

RAM: 48K built-in. Expandable to a maximum of 192K. Screen display: 40 characters by 24 lines, upper and lower case, black and white. Interface ports: cassette loading port, game paddle sockets, RS-232 socket, parallel expansion bus, CP/M operating system. Keyboard: typewriter-style mechanical, 57 keys. CPU: 8-bit Z80A. Built-in languages: BASIC. Optional languages:

FORTH, Pascal, COMAL, all CP/M languages. Built-in sound: yes.
Manufacturer's speech synthesis option: no. Special features: large RAM
capacity.


### Tandy TRS-80 Model I

RAM: 16K built-in. Expandable to a maximum of 64K. Screen display: 64
characters by 16 lines, upper and lower case, black and white. Interface ports:
cassette loading port. Optional interfaces: disk drive ports, RS-232 sockets.
Keyboard: typewriter-style mechanical, 65 keys. CPU: 8-bit Z80. Built-in
languages: BASIC. Optional languages: COBOL, FORTH, FORTRAN,
COMAL, Pascal, assembler. Built-in sound: no. Manufacturer's speech
synthesis option: no. Special features: can be found at bargain prices.


### Tandy TRS-80 Colour Computer

RAM: 16K built-in. Expandable to a maximum of 32K. Screen display: 64
characters by 16 lines, upper case, colour. Interface ports: cassette loading
port, ROM cartridge slot, game paddle sockets, built-in RS-232 socket for
printer, disk drives, etc. Keyboard: typewriter-style mechanical, 52 keys.
CPU: 8-bit 6809E. Built-in languages: cartridge BASIC. Optional languages:
Logo, FORTH, assembler, Extended BASIC. Built-in sound: yes.
Manufacturer's speech synthesis option: no. Special features: capable of
forming part of a computer network.


### The NewBrain

RAM: 32K built-in. Expandable to a maximum of 512K. Screen display: 80
characters by 30 lines (variable), upper and lower case, black and white.
Interface ports: two cassette loading ports, disk drive sockets, two built-in RS-
232 sockets, teletext port, UHF and video output. Keyboard: calculator-style
mechanical, 62 keys. CPU: 8-bit Z80A. Built-in languages: BASIC. Optional
languages: using the CP/M disk operating system languages available
include COMAL, COBAL and Pascal. Built-in sound: no. Manufacturer's
speech synthesis option: no. Special features: a very expandable system.


### BBC Model 'B'

RAM: 32K built-in. Screen display: a wide variety of formats, 20 x 30 to 80 x
25, upper and lower case (definable teletext), colour. Interface ports: cassette
loading port, game paddle sockets, Centronics socket (for printer, etc.),
cartridge program socket, ROM board sockets, Prestel bus, disk drive sockets,
built-in RS-423 socket. Optional interfaces: 'tube' interface to allow addition
of other CPUs. Keyboard: typewriter-style mechanical, 72 keys. CPU: 8-bit
6502. Built-in languages: BBC BASIC, assembler. Optional languages: Logo,
LISP, FORTH, others to be announced. All CP/M based programs and
languages available. Built-in sound: yes. Manufacturer's speech synthesis
option: yes. Special features: network interface built in, telesoftware interface
built in (for broadcast computer programs).

### Atari 800

RAM: 16K built-in. Expandable to a maximum of 48K. Screen display: variable 40 x 24 to 20 x 13, upper and lower case, colour. Interface ports: cassette loading port, four game paddle sockets, cartridge program socket, disk drive sockets, printer socket. Optional interfaces: Centronics socket. Keyboard: typewriter-style mechanical, 61 Keys. CPU: 8-bit 6502. Built-in languages: BASIC. Optional languages: FORTH, Pascal, Logo, Pilot, Microsoft BASIC. Built-in sound: yes. Manufacturer's speech synthesis option: no. Special features: *the* games machine – but also a proper computer.

### RML 480Z

RAM: 32K built-in. Expandable to a maximum of 256K. Screen display: 80 characters by 24 lines, upper and lower case, black and white. Interface ports: cassette loading port, game paddle socket, disk drive sockets, built-in RS-232 socket. Keyboard: typewriter-style mechanical, 65 keys. CPU: 8-bit Z80A. Built-in languages: RML Extended BASIC. Optional languages: Logo, COBOL, FORTRAN, Pascal, Algol. Built-in sound: no. Manufacturer's speech synthesis option: yes. Special features: disk drive system CP/M compatible, network option available.

### Apple II

RAM: 48K built-in. Expandable to a maximum of 64K. Screen display: 40 characters by 24 lines, upper case, black and white, optional colour available. Interface ports: the Apple 'bus' slot system allows most interfaces except cartridge programs. Keyboard: typewriter-style mechanical, 52 keys. CPU: 8-bit 6502. Built-in languages: BASIC. Optional languages: Logo, COBOL, FORTH, FORTRAN, LISP, Pilot, Pascal. Built-in sounds: yes. Manufacturer's speech synthesis option: yes. Special features: very easy to expand with a host of peripherals available from independent manufacturers, but now obsolescent.

### Commodore Pet

RAM: 16K, 32K or 96K built-in, on Pet 4016, 8032 and 8096 respectively. 4016 expandable to a maximum of 32K. Screen display: 40 characters by 25 lines, upper and lower case, on 4016, 80 x 25 on 8032 and 8096. All black and white. Interface ports: cassette loading port, IEE 488 ports, disk drive sockets. Optional interfaces: vast range of add-on extras available. Keyboard: Typewriter-style mechanical, 73 keys. CPU: 8-bit 6502. Built-in languages: BASIC. Optional languages: COMAL, Pascal. Built-in sound: optional. Manufacturer's speech synthesis option: yes. Special features: disk drives may be made compatible with CP/M operating systems providing access to vast range of software.

### Sharp MZ 80A

RAM: 64K built-in. Screen display: 40 characters by 25 lines, upper and lower case, black and white. Integral cassette storage. Optional interfaces: disk drive ports, RS-232 sockets, IEEE port. Keyboard: typewriter-style mechanical, 68 keys. CPU: 8-bit Z80. Built-in languages: Sharp BASIC. Optional languages: Pascal and all CP/M languages. Built-in sound: yes. Manufacturer's speech synthesis option: no. Special features: optional CP/M disk system providing access to that vast range of software.

### Tandy TRS-80 Model III

RAM: 4K built-in. Expandable to a maximum of 48K. Screen display: 64 characters by 16 lines, upper and lower case, black and white. Interface ports: cassette loading port, game paddle sockets. Optional interfaces: disk drive ports, RS-232 sockets. Keyboard: typewriter-style mechanical, 65 keys. CPU: 8-bit Z80. Built-in languages: either Tandy Level I or Level II Basic. Optional languages: COBOL, COMAL, FORTH, FORTRAN, Pascal. Built-in sound: yes. Manufacturer's speech synthesis option: no. Special features: may be networked, CP/M compatability promised.

# LIST OF USEFUL ADDRESSES

**Magazines**
*Byte:* Byte Publications Inc., 70, Main St., Peterborough, NH 03458, USA.

*Personal Computer World:* Computing Publications Ltd., 62 Oxford Street, London W1A 2HG, Great Britain.

*Educational Computing:* Educational Computing Ltd., 8, Herbal Hill, London EC1R 5JB, Great Britain.

*Australian Personal Computer:* Howard Productions Ltd., 500 Clayton Road, Clayton, Victoria 3168, Australia.

**Organisations**
*CET (Council for Educational Technology):* 3, Devonshire Street, London W1N 2BA, Great Britain. This council offers advice and publications on computers in education.

*CEDAR:* CEDAR, Imperial College Computer Centre, Exhibition Road, London SW7, Great Britain. This organisation researches and coordinates computer-assisted learning.

*MUSE (Microcomputer Users in Secondary Schools):* MUSE Information Officer, c/o Ilmington School, Ilmington Road, Wesley Castle, Birmingham, Great Britain. A user group, primarily concerned with computers in secondary schools.

*MAPE (Micros and Primary Education):* Secretary, MAPE, Warren Close, Houghton, Cambridgeshire, Great Britain. A primary school equivalent of MUSE.

*AUCBE (Advisory Unit for Computer-Based Education):* 19, St. Alban's Road East, Hatfield, Hertfordshire AL10 0HU, Great Britain.

*MEP (Microelectronics Education Programme):* Cheviot House, Coach Lane Campus, Newcastle-upon-Tyne NE7 7XA, Great Britain. Government-run organising body for microelectronics education programme.

*GAPE (Geographical Association Package Exchange):* Department of Geography, University of Technology, Loughborough LE11 3TN, Great Britain.

*ITMA (Investigation into Teaching with Microprocessor Assistance):* College of St. Mark and St. John, Derriford Road, Plymouth, Devon PL6 8BH, Great Britain. A research project into the effect of microcomputers on education.

*SMDP (Scottish Microelectronics Development Programme):* 74, Victoria Crescent Road, Glasgow G12 9JN, Great Britain.

*MICE (Microcomputers in Computer Education):* Room 231C, County Hall, London SE1, Great Britain. Specifically concerned with the teaching of computer science.

# INDEX